THE FILM ACTOR:

ACTING
FOR MOTION PICTURES
AND TELEVISION

THE FILM ACTOR:

ACTING
FOR MOTION PICTURES
AND TELEVISION

BY MICHAEL PATE

SOUTH BRUNSWICK AND NEW YORK;
A. S. BARNES AND COMPANY
LONDON: THOMAS YOSELOFF LTD

© 1970 by A. S. Barnes and Co., Inc.
Library of Congress Catalogue Card Number: 69–15782

A. S. Barnes and Company, Inc.
Cranbury, New Jersey 08512

Thomas Yoseloff Ltd
108 New Bond Street
London W1Y OQX, England

SBN 498 06941 9
Printed in the United States of America

To my wife Felippa
and to my son Christopher.

CONTENTS

CONTENTS

FOREWORD

Acting is a very personal business, and I intend to be as personal as possible about it in the following pages for I know of no other way to tell you about that part of the craft of making motion pictures, the art of film-acting.

Many people in the arts and crafts contribute to the making of a motion picture. Each contribution, from the producer's to the laborer's on the set, is important. Some are more personal than others, but none are more personal than the actor's contribution to the completed motion picture.

When all is said and done, when the words and the images lock together to make the final print of the film, it is the actor who is the ultimate personal image with which an audience can identify. By the mere fact that he is a living, breathing human being, he is the one who moves all of us to laughter or to tears, for an actor is full of life, full of yearning, sometimes full of despair, always full of hope. He isn't an inanimate object. He feels, he thinks, he imagines, he idealizes, he aspires, he creates, he is the translator of man's dreams.

The task of the actor is to interpret life, as expressed in the written word, in his own image, ever extending his imagination to encompass new dimensions of creativity in his art. Let's see how to accomplish it in the medium of film.

M. P.

Sydney—Hollywood 1969

ACKNOWLEDGMENTS

This book might not have been written if Stacy Harris had not asked me in 1963 to join with him in establishing Screen Actors Studio in Hollywood.

Once we began teaching classes at the Studio, we were able to evolve, out of our experience as professional actors, a highly successful method of teaching those young actors who came to the Studio, how to perform for the camera.

At Screen Actors Studio, Stacy Harris and I were fortunate to have as associate teachers, two other fine actors, Eddie Firestone and Biff Elliott and the indefatigable help of another enthusiastic young actor, Ron Stokes. Much of the acting philosophy and the professional experience of all of us is included in this book.

I owe a great debt to the many actors with whom I have worked or observed over the years. They have all contributed to my knowledge of film acting. I should like to thank Cathy Lydon for her infinite patience in translating and typing up the many tapes upon which I recorded material for this book—for the words between these covers are spoken words, exactly as they were so often before uttered to our many students who gathered each week on the sound stage we used at Producers' Studio as a classroom.

I am especially grateful to Thomas Yoseloff for his encouragement to me to write this book.

Finally, I must record my gratitude to an understanding wife and an enthusiastic son. Both are professional performers and only they could truly understand and suffer gladly an actor trying to write a book about his own craft. For this, among many other reasons, I dedicate this book to them both.

INTRODUCTION

Acting, in any one of its many forms, is both a simple and a complex art. Simple, in that the actor need only reflect nature to be successful in his craft; complex, because the variety of human emotions that the actor must re-create within himself and express by his craft in playing a part is infinite.

In this book, I will not discuss the historical and interpretative aspects of acting. I will not urge or advise you to pursue any one method in order to portray a character. I will tell you simply how to go about becoming a thoroughly proficient and technically accomplished professional actor in the medium of motion pictures and television.

Acting for motion pictures is, as with all acting, both a profoundly simple and an extraordinarily complex art. *Simple*, because the essence of acting for motion pictures is in being able to be utterly natural and believable in front of a camera while playing a scene; *complex*, because of the many technical demands that the cinematic form of the script, the director, the camera, the lighting, the sets, the editor, and so on, place upon every actor and actress.

For the young actors who ask how they can become so proficient in the art of acting for motion pictures that they can go to Hollywood, New York, London, and Europe and work in films, the years of experience that can help them acquire this proficiency are likely to pass far too slowly. For an ambitious young actor, time is always of the essence. All young performers find out in their first few encounters with the world of film-making, that it's not enough just to act in an emotional way, to soar with the creation of a character. Acting for a camera is highly technical, and demands of them a skill that leaves them bewildered by their ignorance of it. All of their marvelously exciting, emotional "acting" goes down the drain because they don't know how to act for the camera.

The player in films, to achieve artistic perfection in his craft, must appear to be a real person on the screen. He must be honestly and fully creative or there will be only trickery and no validity to his performance, and he must be capable of being technically perfect in the way he carries out the playing of the part.

To put all of this on a more personal basis, let me tell you what happened when I first played a lead in a film. I had heard that a certain Charles Chauvel, a producer of some fine Australian films and a man I had worked for before, was about to make another film, an outdoor drama called *Sons of Matthew*, a film that was subsequently released in the United States of America under the title of *The Rugged O'Riordans*. I concentrated all my thoughts on getting the part of the eldest son, Shane O'Riordan, in Chauvel's film. The main problem was to get to Chauvel and convince him that I was the only one for the part.

I made myself known to Alec Kellaway, an old friend and, as it happened, Chauvel's Casting Director for the film, and in a day or so, through the efforts of Alec Kellaway, I was interviewed by Chauvel. He greeted me warmly when I walked into his office and he remembered me for one of four bit-parts I had played for him in a previous film of his, *Forty-Thousand Horsemen*. I was delighted when Chauvel, after talking to me for only a few minutes, asked me to test. I was given a scene to learn, and went home on a cloud to prepare the part for the screen test, which was to be in a day or two.

At home, I read the scene countless times, learned the lines, thought through the character of Shane O'Riordan—trying with an actor's usual desperation to find out all I could about this "Shane" that I would have to be in front of the camera in a few days' time. Eventually, I was able to decide how I wanted to play him.

On the day of the test I arrived at the studio very early, got into my wardrobe, was made up, went to the soundstage, met the girl I was to play the test-scene with, Noni Peifer, and then, suddenly, was panic-stricken. As I looked around the hurly-burly of the set, knowing that I had to act in the midst of this apparent confusion of a set still being dressed, lights being set, and the cold, black, unfriendly eye of the camera staring into the

set, I was appalled—physically sickened by my profound ignorance of how to perform under these circumstances. It was fine
to want the part, to feel I could play it, to be interviewed, to
be approved of, and asked to test, but now the moment of truth
was at hand. I faced the prospect of acting in a medium totally
alien to me. I didn't know what to do.

I wanted to run out of the studio and disappear into a friendly
hole, but instead, I took a walk around the soundstage. This
didn't help much at all, and so I went out into the street. It
was a cold, cheerless morning in late winter. I shivered a little;
I went back onto the soundstage again. I drank a cup of coffee;
I smoked a cigarette. I drank another cup of coffee and I smoked
several more cigarettes. I tried to think my way out of what
now appeared to me a disastrous artistic trap in which it seemed
that I was irrevocably enmeshed and in which I was about to
make an absolute fool of myself. Every actor since the beginning
of time has gone through that moment, often still goes through
it before the opening of a play or the first shot in a film, and
perhaps some dear-departed performer, seeing my youthful confusion, my anguish, my personal artistic agony, somehow got a
message through to me.

Suddenly, I was very clear-headed about the whole thing.
First, since I knew absolutely nothing of how to act for a camera, I knew I must ask questions of the director, of the cameraman, of *anyone* who could help me. Second, I knew because I
had watched so many great performers in so many fine films
over the years, that it was very important to appear, and to strive
to be completely "natural" on the screen.

When I was called onto the set that morning to begin rehearsing the test-scene with Noni Peifer, I felt that the only way
in which I could be secure in the scene, and so make her feel
secure along with me, was to revert back to my old training,
my tried-and-true method as an actor on the stage, and put a
Stanislavskian imaginary circle of concentration around myself
as the character Shane O'Riordan, and another imaginary circle
around Noni and myself for the scene, and then simply to proceed to play the scene as sincerely and honestly, as warmly and
compellingly as I knew how.

During the setting-up of the scene by the technicians and in
the time that Noni and I rehearsed it, I asked questions of Charles
Chauvel and Bert Nicolson, the cameraman, as to whether or not
I was "clear" to the camera—that is, seen in a proper framing by

the camera, or, conversely, not blocking the camera's view of Miss Peifer in any way. I listened intently and took notice immediately of every direction given to me that morning by Charles Chauvel, Bert Nicolson, and any other member of the crew who had to do with the setting-up of the scene.

Fortunately, because of this approach, which had somehow come to me out of the blue, I made a very good test, and a month or so later, Chauvel cast me in the part of Shane O'Riordan, the lead in his film.

Every moment I was on that film, I worked on my part. I not only thought about how it could be played, how I might discover more of the many nuances of the character itself, but I continually asked questions about everything to do with filmmaking.

After several months on location, I was told one day that Chauvel was going to screen some of the assembled footage of the film for his technical staff and some executives who had come up to location from the "front office." I asked Chauvel if I could see the film when he ran it for the others. Chauvel refused my request pointblank.

His main reason was that he felt that the inexperienced actors in the film could quite easily become self-conscious upon seeing themselves on the screen. This has often happened to actors because in seeing themselves on the screen in the rough rushes or even in the first assemblies of scenes, they are completely unable to judge their performances in the way that they should, and not having the ability to differentiate between what is truly good and right and what is truly bad and wrong in their performance, they start making changes in their basic approach to playing the part. This can be disastrous for the director who only wants them to be their natural selves, and for the film as a whole.

I discussed this with Chauvel, or tried to, saying that my performance wouldn't be affected by seeing the footage, and I believed what I said at the time. I told him that I needed to see what I was doing in the part so that I could correct any shortcomings in my characterization. I felt that as a professional actor I would be able to "see" myself quite clearly; I had "stepped back" and looked at many performances I had given on the stage; I had always been able to make any adjustments to my playing that were necessary. But I couldn't shift Chauvel. He was adamant. He wouldn't allow me to see the rushes, that night or any other night, and that was all there was to it, as far as he was concerned, but I knew I had to see what my work looked like on the screen.

That particular night when the footage was run by Chauvel, I crept into the back of the hall where the showing was to take place, and after the lights went out, found myself a seat and waited expectantly for the first glimpse of myself. As I sat there in that grim, bare, cold, little hall, watching the rushes run on a very small screen, I was *appalled* by my own performance. Although I thought everyone else in the film was good, as far as I was concerned, *I* was *terrible*. To me, I seemed stiff and self-conscious, awkward, ungainly, very inclined to "mug," not at all what I'd planned to be, or how I believed I was actually playing the part.

This, of course, was the natural reaction of any young and inexperienced performer to the first, gigantic numbing shock of seeing himself for the very first time on the screen in a big, demanding part. The bit-parts I had played before had been a snap. I had zipped in and out of a few scenes with hardly a word to say. No strain at all. Now it was all very different. I was in almost every scene of this film. The success of the film depended greatly on how good my performance would be.

The shock I suffered that night was physical, mental, and artistic. Every young actor must be prepared for it. No one can really hope to see himself as other people see him, even up on the silver screen. But in films, the performer *must* develop the ability to "see" himself on the screen as others see him. He must be able to judge the artistic entity of himself as a performer and view, quite dispassionately, his final image on the screen—as other people—the director, the audience—see him. A difficult task but one very necessary for proper self-criticism.

I do believe that it is good for all players to watch the "rushes" when they are permitted. If they can learn to watch them constructively, intelligently, and not egotistically or super-critically, they can learn a great deal about their craft. They can observe the mistakes they have made, look forward to correcting those sometimes minute errors of artistic judgment which they have committed in the practice of their craft. There are a thousand things to watch for when the rushes are run—camera angles, lighting, working within the frame, filling out the space that surrounds a performer whatever the shot may be, the adjustments that must be made in technique when working out-of-doors as opposed to working in an interior set, etc.—but the young performer should concern himself solely at first with the naturalness of his physical movements, his facial expressions, the modulation of his voice, the quality and depth of his characterization, the honesty of his playing. You will come to know, understand, appreciate, and take full advantage of camera angles, lighting, etc., but for the young performer, his primary consideration should be the final artistic quality of his performance, tuned and honed fine within the technical demands of the medium.

All young players should make a point of watching every film that they can, at every opportunity, if possible seeing a film two or three times. This is the only way a young performer can observe his craft in action. Many of the films and the television shows will be good and the young performer will learn a great deal, however, other films and TV segments will be bad. The young performer can learn just as much from these shows.

Now, once you've learned the fundamentals of the craft of film-acting—and this will not be an overnight achievement—you must begin practicing them. The young performer, in order to practice his craft, needs to go to work in a film, and, if jobs are few and far between, to go to a film workshop and work with other actors. Whether or not these opportunities present themselves, the beginner first and foremost must glue himself into a seat in a movie-house or in front of his television set and watch how the older, more experienced professionals do it. These are the men and the women who have been at this business of acting in films for a long time; they have been through the mill of learning their craft. Watch how they perform, watch how they devise a part, watch how simply they play it, how easily, presenting only the necessary essentials of the characterization in order to convince their audience that they are indeed the character they are playing. Then look even more closely at what they are doing, how they are managing to put all the tiny pieces of their part together—the movements, the facial expressions, the inflections of their voices in each line. You will find that by constant observation of these actors, you will fill to overflowing a notebook, both in your mind and on paper, which you can and will refer to countless times in the future. Every time you start preparing a part, every time you step into a set or onto a location site to play it, you can take a reference from this notebook, and depend on it to substantiate your judgment when a decision has to be made, artistically or technically.

This is the way this craft of film-acting is learned, not by rote in classes or out of books, but by observation, by a finely developed understanding of what makes a performer tick, by a kind of a "touch" in the mind that puts the performer who is actually there playing the scene "in touch" with all the skill, all the magic, that every great performer who has gone before him has possessed. Feel secure, when you're performing, in the knowledge that that magic and that skill is being passed down to every young performer in the course of every day's work by all those who have gone before and by all of us who are performing today. Look for it, watch the greats, watch how they performed, watch the fine actors of today—they offer you in their performances a classroom, a workshop no teacher could. Observe them diligently, and in due course you will acquire the ability to perform in the way you've always dreamed.

As an example of how much can be learned from watching the great performers of our day act, take the long list of superb films that Spencer Tracy and Katharine Hepburn made, select one from your TV Guide, and settle down to watch the film, to observe their techniques.

Tracy and Hepburn, in themselves, in the richness of their craft, are full, exciting chapters in an illustrious textbook on how to act for motion pictures. Observe how Tracy uses his eyes—a discerning look down at his hands or the desk, a look up again, always in control of the scene, subtly commanding attention to what he is doing and saying, thinking, in the scene. Analyze the pauses that he makes; every one has a purpose. Watch how he thinks in every pause, filling out the whole context of what he is saying. Observe how the two of them will play a long scene— perhaps three, four, or five minutes, sometimes longer—entering the scene in a loose longshot, settling into the set and composing themselves into two-shots and over-the-shoulder shots, then moving around the set again, the camera traveling with them, following their every move in concert, framing them perfectly. Once again, they settle into two-shots where they are sitting on a sofa, or into over-the-shoulder shots or open-twos where they move around each other within the set, in such rhythm and harmony with the camera, forever changing, for the best result possible, the image of themselves on the screen, so emphasizing, certain parts of the scene they are playing that we, the audience, are never aware of a camera moving around a set.

The movements of the scene have been so thoughtfully designed by the director and so superbly executed by the players, so exquisitely performed in concert with the camera, that the audience is swept along by the scene, not for a moment aware that they are simply watching shadows on a silver screen.

Actual classes on a soundstage or in a properly set-up workshop-studio are best, but since this is a book I thought it best to present the material as if I were teaching a class of young performers "off-the-floor" during the "filming" of a scene as I did when I taught at Screen Actors Studio in Hollywood. Since a certain amount of the material in this book is based upon the many sessions with which I was associated and taught at Screen Actors Studio, I think I should tell you something of the Screen Actors Studio itself.

In December of 1963, a colleague of mine, Stacy Harris, telephoned me and asked if I would consider starting a school with him to teach acting for motion pictures to a group of young beginning professionals. I told him that I was reluctant to enter into this area of teaching because I had never been involved in this kind of venture before, and because, up until that time, I had not evolved any method of teaching the craft of acting for motion pictures at all.

Admittedly, having been asked by talent agencies and friends in the past, I had, like many professional actors, occasionally coached, taught and/or directed beginners in scenes so that they could face up to auditions, cold-readings, screen tests, and assorted jobs in films. I had even been asked to lecture at various colleges, but I still did not feel that I had a clear idea in mind of the way to go about teaching a regularly instituted class. However, Stacy, telling me that the nucleus of the proposed group all had been at classes at another school where he and I had guest-directed and taught on various occasions, and that they were all young professionals who wanted a practical workshop in which to exercise their trade, eventually persuaded me to talk to them, adding that, if I would start the school with him, Fred Jordan at Producers Studio would give us stage-space and scenery for a minimal and very nominal charge.

I agreed to talk with the young people and met them one wet Saturday afternoon at the studio, and by their enthusiasm for the project they so persuaded me that, almost before I knew what was happening, I had agreed to teach one night a month. That seemed reasonable enough. After several more cups of coffee, I found I had agreed to teach one night a week; one night a week that, after a few weeks, found Stacy and me teaching three nights a week, and having to add two other fine actors to our teaching staff, Eddie Firestone and Biff Elliot. You will find a great deal of all our thoughts and teachings echoed in this book, for all four of us shared a very fine experience at Screen Actors Studio in our attempts, and I feel our very successful attempts, to teach an ever-changing group of young professionals how they could perform in the medium of motion pictures.

It is the knowledge that we offered to these young people that I offer you now in this book, a way of preparing yourself as a performer, so that you can go out fully equipped to make a living as a professional actor in the demanding, no-time-for-mistakes, instant-acting world of the motion picture and television industry.

At Screen Actors Studio, scenes to be played, and sometimes the whole script, if such scripts were available, were handed to the students a week to ten days before the date on which they would be performing in class. The people concerned learned the lines—we demanded that every student learn his lines perfectly—prepared the parts to the best of their ability, writing out character analyses if they were able to, and came to class as if they were actually going to work on a soundstage, reporting in to our Assistant, getting made-up and costumed if necessary, standing by for their call to come on the set at the proper time.

We tried to recreate on the set we had erected on Stage 6 at Producers Studio the conditions that existed on a working soundstage. We used red lights, bells, and buzzers to quiet the set before rehearsal or a "take"; a scriptgirl was ready to supply the players or the director with information regarding lines or business which needed to be "matched." There was a full camera crew and a sound crew, operating the dolly and the camera, the various cables for the camera, and the lights, and manipulating the sound boom. The scene was blocked-out and "shot" as it would be in any television show or feature picture that was being shot in Hollywood, or throughout the world, at that moment.

When we started the class at night, we would rehearse, block out, and "shoot" the scene, with emphasis on the "speed" methods of shooting, as apply on 99% of the soundstages all over the world today. It is, of course, always very pleasant, very comforting, very reassuring, to spend time with a director, discussing the scene, to sit down and leisurely find out everyone's ideas on

the scene—the director's, the cameraman's, the producer's, your
fellow performers'—but usually in making television segments,
where every second of time counts in terms of dollars, this is
seldom possible. There used to be a time when film-making was
generally so leisurely that days were spent discussing a scene and
rehearsing it before a single take of the film was achieved and
recorded on the production sheet for the day, but nowadays the
player must come to grasp immediately what the director wants
from the scene, what the director requires of him; in short, the
delivery of an "instant," complete character.

There are all kinds of directors—good and bad, articulate and
inarticulate. Regardless, the performer must be able to go to
work immediately in the scene and he must be able to keep on
working at the pace that the economy of the present television
industry, and in most instances, the feature motion picture industry demands. The performer must be so equipped, artistically
and technically, that there is never hesitation on his part. He
must be able to deliver an accomplished performance without
any "if's, and's, or but's!"

That way of working is what I would like to teach you in
this book. If you intend to make your living at acting for films,
then let's face the facts of life as they are spelled out for you
in Hollywood or anywhere else in the world today where they
are making films for the commercial market. Your talent is paid
for with money, and every producer wants his money's worth.
If you don't deliver, he isn't going to keep on buying. For every
job available today throughout the world in films, for every part
that needs to be cast, there are a hundred or more actors available, willing, and eager. Just be sure that when you get the job
and are cast in the part you've so desired, that you have the
know-all to deliver the performance you've been hired and will
be paid for. The amateur actor plays for fun and his own satisfaction; the professional plays for money, and his whole future
depends on how well he does in his work.

Today, whereas feature motion pictures of quality might take
from eighteen to twenty-four shooting days to six months or
longer, to make, only three days are usually required to make
a thirty-minute TV segment, and whereas at one time a minute
of finished, cut-together film completed in a day's shooting was
regarded as a major accomplishment, now eight minutes of film
is regarded as the norm for a day's shooting. According to those
figures, which I assure you are accurate, we are working eight

times faster today than we used to on the soundstages of the early Fifties.

A TV segment will occasionally go over schedule, but this is seldom the case. The script is thoroughly "broken-down" and scheduled to the minute by the production staff of the unit making the segment. The production unit manager and the assistants to the director, the first, second, and sometimes the third, assistant directors, see to it that the director and the actors keep on schedule. Barring bad weather on location, actors who become ill or are injured, "special effects" in certain shows which may take longer to achieve than anticipated, 99.9% of shows for television are finished on schedule.

That's only part of what the medium of film is. The part of the medium which mainly concerns the actor is the craft he must practice under the pressure of the economics of the business and the surroundings in which he must work, no longer the pampered domain of the super-stars of the old regime of movie-making but a go-go atmosphere of factory-orientated film-making, a battle-ground in which the young actor must be prepared to apply all the fire-power at his disposal. In other words, the young actor must come with all his artistic magazines fully loaded, his technique on automatic. He must walk onto the soundstage with all its paraphernalia, the outdoor location site with all its equipment, ready to do battle. He must be ready to accept and put to the best use the basic, material, artistic conditions under which he must work, where the emphasis today in TV, and generally also in feature film-making of modest budgets, the kind that are being made for the television two-hour shows, is on speed, on getting the picture shot on schedule.

In film-making, on location for a film or on a soundstage, conditions exist which make different, often very strange, demands on the performer. Whereas on the stage, the play, once rehearsed, is played through in a continuous stream of thought, speech, and action, a film is made in small scenes, composed of minuscule shots, all jumbled up as far as order of making goes, sometimes the last shot of the film being shot long before the first shot (as listed in the screenplay) is filmed. A kind of sophisticated Mad Hatter's Tea Party arrangement which only makes sense to those of us who are employed to participate in the charade.

Out of doors, the performer will be expected to walk lithe-somely on the most uneven and unfriendly, even treacherous, ground; climb mountains, ride horses, saddled or bareback, fight heroically with fist, club, or sword; swim, ride a runaway train, in short, perform an infinite and incredible variety of physical movements in the open air. Difficult as some of these motions may be to go through, the performer must be able to do them naturally and convincingly. Of course, if there is any element of danger involved in any of these actions, the actor will be "doubled" by a stuntman, but despite this concession to the actor's well-being, the actor will usually be asked to do the "close-ups" for such scenes and so therefore he must train himself to be as competent as possible in all forms of gymnastics and feats of athletics.

Other outdoor sets on which the actor might find himself working are the "backlots" of the various studios where all manners and kinds of streets have been laid down, and shop, house, and public-building fronts erected. Therein, he might have to drive an automobile or truck of any vintage, climb a fire-escape, push his way convincingly through a remonstrating crowd of extras, jump up on a soapbox and deliver an impassioned oration in a drenching, simulated rainstorm.

Another type of location in which he may work is the "actual" location, a real street which has been blocked-off by police permit for use by the film company. Here, the actor must be able to go through all the motions demanded of him by the script and the director with the same ease and grace as he would in everyday life, surrounded as he is with all kinds of equipment and usually viewed by an interested crowd of onlookers who have gathered to watch the film company shoot.

In contrast to working on location, the soundstage is usually limited to interior sets in the form of living rooms, kitchen, bedrooms, bathrooms, offices, conference rooms, hotel foyers, corridors, etc. He may have to take a bath or a shower, eat a meal, make love, fight, fence, talk on the telephone, go mad, perform an operation, plead a case in court, write a letter, fall down a flight of stairs, play dead, have a bitter argument, even a knock-down-drag-out battle with an estranged wife, mistress, or best friend, sink into a bog in the Okeefenokee Swamp or a reasonable facsimile thereof, react to the news that his wife just had a baby, be sad because his mother-in-law has been involved in a terrible traffic accident, be dunked in a huge tank of water where a storm is being simulated by technicians only intent on drowning the actor involved in the scene, or so it seems to the actor.

All these things and many others are demanded of the actor. At the same time, he is expected to say all of his lines in the scene while the director and fifty other members of the crew watch him, usually very unemotionally, being concerned with their own problems, providing no audience to him really except their mere physical presence, for the actor must "stay within" his character and the scene at all times, simply allowing the camera and the microphone to record his image and his voice, the end result of which concerted efforts, when both are later projected on screens, large and small, will bring him, the actor, his due public applause and appreciation.

Now, I'm sure, to all of you young beginning pros, much of the foregoing must sound very general. The semantics of any craft always do, until you learn the language—so let's get down to the body, the real core and spine of this book: the Terminology of film-making, of film-acting; the way a scene is prepared by an actor and shot by a director; the various exercises which an actor can practice and use to extend his craft, those exercises which are as necessary to the actor in films as setting-up exercises at the *barre d'appui* are to a ballet dancer, scales and *arpeggios* to a concert pianist, the "speed-ball" to a boxer who needs to sharpen his snap-punching ability, the practice range to a professional golfer.

Take this book slowly, read it thoroughly, digest it, go over and over it, especially the sections which follow. You won't grasp everything at one reading. There is no "instant" way to become a professional actor, either for the stage or for motion pictures. It takes time, continuous study, relentless application to learning the craft, infinite perseverance, and absolute dedication.

THE FILM ACTOR:

ACTING
FOR MOTION PICTURES
AND TELEVISION

1 THE TERMINOLOGY
OF THE FILM MEDIUM

The actor in motion pictures and television should have a complete knowledge of the terminology used in film-making, especially those terms which apply to him specifically as an actor. Every craft, every pursuit of mankind, has its terminology. The film business has its own esoteric one.

Just simply learning the various terms won't necessarily start you on your way to becoming a master at your craft, but it will certainly acquaint you with the working nomenclature of film-making and film-acting. There are literally hundreds of terms used in the film business by every department of this huge industry, however I intend to list and discuss only those terms which the performer will need to know and fully understand.

Usually such terms as the following are listed at the end of books on film-making and film techniques, gathered together in a Glossary—and rightly so in such highly technical books. However, I believe that it is important for the performer to have a working acquaintance with these very necessary, daily-usage terms right now, at the beginning of this book, so that he will be able to understand the terms when they are used in the sections which follow, even before he encounters them in the course of going to work in films. I will first name the term, define it, then go on to give you an explanation of what it is and its application in everyday work on a soundstage.

Some of the terms in the following list are general terms and not necessarily specifically for actor usage. They are sometimes terms to explain various pieces of equipment used in film-making and can be found, using very similar wordage, in a number of fine books written on the purely technical aspects of film-production and film-making. The rest of the terms, the bulk of them, are essentially terms used by actors, directors, and crew, and these are the terms to which you should pay particular attention. They are what might be called the "slang," the "shorthand," of the business—that personal kind of gibberish we talk with each other when we are working on a set or on location. The terms themselves are only important for the means of communication that they offer between director, actors, and crew, and that is the only reason why you should know about them before you get into the body of this book. When I get down to the many technicalities of acting in films, I must use the "shorthand" I know. You must fully understand the meaning of these terms in order to take full advantage of them as I talk about film-acting to you, and later, when you go out to work on a soundstage.

ACTION!: *The order given by a director when he wants the action of a shot to begin.*

When the scene has been fully rehearsed and it is ready to be shot, the set is turned over, momentarily, to the First Assistant Director who will ask for "Quiet!"—for the set to be *"put on a bell."*

The Sound Mixer will then press a button, on or attached to his console, which will cause a bell or a buzzer to sound inside and sometimes outside the stage (one long sound for scene beginning and two short ones for scene ended). At the same time, inside the studio if necessary but always outside, red lights come on alongside entrance doorways, revolving blinkers or wig-wagging flags are activated and keep in motion until the scene is ended.

After securing "Quiet!" and putting the set "on a bell," the First Assistant Director will call "Roll 'em!" The Sound Mixer will start both the Sound Recording Equipment (which is supervised by another member of the Sound Crew) and the camera electrically. When the film in the camera and the soundfilm in the Recorder are both synchronized, running at "speed," as it's called, i.e., 90 feet a minute—and this is usually achieved almost instantaneously—the Sound Mixer will call "Speed!" into a microphone on his console, the Mike-man will hear this on his head-set and repeat it aloud. A moment or two after this, the director will call "Action!"

Slates or clapperboards giving details of the scene, director's and cameraman's names, title of film, are always photographed after the camera is up to "speed." The black-and-white, diagonally-painted flap on the top of the clapperboard is banged down to give the editor who will cut the film a synchronized start for sound and image. With automatic slaters which are attached to the front of the camera—these are small, box-like counters containing on them the same information as on the manual slates—the procedure is much the same. Hinged as they are, they are lifted up to the lens and held there, lowered only after *"speed"* is called—"speed" in this instance being indicated by a beep from the automatic slater which has been directly activated from the console of the Sound Mixer after he has observed that camera and sound recorder are "in sync."

The actor must always discuss with the director how he personally will be *called into action.* Make sure of this—leave nothing to chance. Always talk to a director, know exactly what he intends, how he is going to call you—it saves time and nervous strain for everyone concerned. Decide, without any doubt, how he will call on you to begin a scene, and you will be able to prepare toward that moment no matter what happens before your actual entrance into a scene, whether it is a long-shot with hundreds of people involved, or a big close-up involving only yourself. Always "think" yourself into a scene well ahead of your beginning action in any case. That way you will always be "in motion," mentally and/or physically, and an immediate part of the scene being shot.

APPLEBOX: *A sturdy, wooden, rectangularly-shaped box, about 24" x 15" x 12", so named because it resembles a scaled-down, old-fashioned applebox. It always has some slits cut in the ends or on top, so that a hand can slide in, grasp it, and transport it easily.*

The applebox has many uses and comes in three sizes—apple, half-apple, and quarter-apple—roughly 10-12", 7-8", and 4-5" high. The applebox is also sometimes referred to as a "rise" or a "step." The performer may find himself sitting or standing on one or more of these appleboxes, even using them, laid flat on the ground, as a pathway to get out of a scene, especially if the performer is short in stature or a youngster and it has been necessary to raise his height in a scene with taller performers in order to accommodate a better framing of the scene for the camera.

ARC *or* ARC-LIGHT: *A large, powerful lamp, used both indoors and outdoors to illuminate the scene with an intense light.*

Indoors—and even at times outdoors when weather conditions are not the best—the arc serves the same purpose as the sun and becomes the "key-light" for the actor. There are two kinds of arcs—the carbon and the mercury. The various technicalities of their structure and operation does not concern the actor. Why they are used in a scene does.

These huge, powerful lamps, facing into a scene and directed at an actor, are brutal to look into while playing a scene, and because of this and their size, they are sometimes referred to as "brutes." Actually, the actor seldom looks directly into them—they are usually, though not always, directed on the actor from above head-height—but their light does shine into his eyes. This can cause the actor to squint badly, as can the glare from any white or sandy surface, even causing his eyes to close tight, especially if the irises of his eyes are light in coloration, blue, grey, green, or hazel. Even people with dark brown irises are sometimes troubled with this "glare" from lights and other reflecting surfaces—the standard reflector areas of sand, burnt-white grass, etc.

There is a way of mastering this discomfort caused by the lights, a method we all use, whether working out-of-doors or indoors. When working out-of-doors and the glare from the lights, etc., is such that it is difficult to keep your eyes *fully* open during the course of the scene being shot, when the scene is ready to be shot and you are in your starting position, close your eyes, not tightly, just comfortably, and "look" directly at the sun. If the sun is weak, as on an overcast day, use an arc in the same way. The sun, or the arc, will warm your eyes, causing them to adjust to the glare they will have to face in a few seconds. Every director understands this problem which the actor faces, but be sure yours doesn't simply think that you are staring off into space.

When the call of "speed" is heard, or the "beep" from the automatic slater sounds in the camera, open your eyes and blink them directly at the sun, once, twice, three times, for a "beat" each time. You will find that you can now make your way through the scene without too much discomfort from the glare and be able to concentrate solely on the playing of the scene rather than just on merely keeping your eyes open.

ARC OUT: *What happens when a performer, after determining the edge of the frame, i.e., the area framed by the particular lens of the camera, walks, turns away, rises out of, drops below, or leans out of the sides or top, bottom of the frame in the course of performing the scene.*

The actor must be sure to ask his director and the director of photography, but especially the operator of the camera, what his framing is in the shot, i.e., what the lens being used on the camera for that particular shot is framing, or "seeing," in its field of vision. The actor must determine not only the sidelines of the framing but the top and bottom lines. He must set these limits for himself, physically and mentally, whether they be *very tight* as in a close-up, or even *more confining* as in an extreme close-up, a big head, or *loose,* as in a longshot, and he must be sure that in the course of the scene's being filmed he never moves outside of these set limits. The limits can be determined in several ways —by knowing, for instance, that certain pieces of furniture on each side of the set are within the frame if the shot is a loose one. If the shot is a tight one, lay your hand across your chest, then vertically up from your shoulder, and then over the top of your head, and check with the operator the exact framing that he has set at the director's instruction for the shot. The actor must stay within the limits set to achieve a successful shot. He cannot stroll off the limits of the set in a loose shot if he feels the desire to do so while playing the scene, nor can he bob up and down or sideways in a tighter shot if his emotions get out of hand and override his ability to control his performance technically.

The camera operator usually cannot and most times *will not* follow the actor if his movements do not conform to what has been planned. Of course, certain small divergencies on the part of the actor(s) can be coped with, but as a rule the camera operator will just switch off his camera and point out that the actor has failed to do what has been asked of him. Framing limits are set by the director and the director of photography for each shot in order to achieve both what the director wants from an interpretative point-of-view and what the director of photography feels will be best visually. The operator's job is to get what he has been asked for; the actor's job is to determine the physical limitations of the set-up and act fully within those limits.

ASSISTANT DIRECTOR: *One of several assistants to the director of a film.*

Depending on the kind of film being made, there may be as many as three assistant directors on the set—the First, Second, and Third Assistant Directors. I have worked on films where five and six A.D.'s have been employed for certain, big, spectacular scenes. Each A.D. has his own particular function according to the construction of the unit itself and the film being shot.

As a rule, the First, as he is often abbreviatively called, runs the floor for the Director; the Second backs him up, handling all kinds of tasks with extras, etc.; the Third may be relegated to a desk on the floor and deal with the mass of paperwork which accrues during a day's shooting. In general, the duties of all Assistant Directors is to be responsible for seeing that every actor and extra is in the right place at the right time, that the members of the crew are doing their jobs efficiently, and that every wish of the Director of the film is carried out without any waste of time.

ATMOSPHERE (PEOPLE): *The various types of extras who fill out both the foreground and the background of many scenes in movies.*

The atmosphere people in any film are all members of Screen Extras Guild. Certain dispensations are offered the studios during holiday-periods to use college students if they are specifically needed in a film, but this is rare. Granted today there are quite a number of younger people, in their early twenties, girls mainly, who are members of the Guild, but most of the rank and file membership are mature people. Screen Extras Guild is a most difficult Guild to become a member of because of the conditions imposed on anyone who wishes to join. When any person applies for membership of the Guild, it must be the considered opinion of the Guild that there is a definite need for his or her type of person—age, national origin, etc.—or the applicant may not be granted admission.

Many people have been extras all their lives and are very competent at their work. Some old, no longer active, or retired actors have become extras. These old warhorses just can't keep away from the business. Atmosphere people earn a base salary per day for their work, and if they work more than the specified amount of hours, get adjustments for additional time on the set or on location. They also get what are called "whammies" (more money) for any special little bits of business they might do, costumes they might change into and wear after their first costumes for the day, beards they may have to put on, etc., in the various scenes.

There are a number of different types of atmosphere people, or extras. There are the "dress extras," those people who wear their own tuxedos or tails, cocktail or long evening dresses and furs for a scene; there are those extras who either wear their own clothes or are issued clothes by the wardrobe department and merely walk up and down the street in the background of a scene of *Gunsmoke* or a similar Western show; there are "riding extras" who work mostly in Westerns or action shows; there are other extras who dress up the background and foreground of modern-day shows, usually wearing their own street clothes. Often many of the men who work as "riding extras" are full or part-time stuntmen and usually belong also to that Guild. They may simply ride through one shot as Indians or Cavalrymen; the next scene they may be shot off a horse and take a fall. In these instances, if they take a fall off a horse or are shot down and fall while standing or running, they receive a pay adjustment for this stunt. These fees are worked out between the individual concerned and one of the assistants or a person on the production staff whose job it is to come to an agreement with the man involved as to what the stunt is worth in cold, hard cash. The amounts vary according to the stunts and the individual's ability to bargain.

Extras are not allowed to speak in a scene beyond a few, general, unintelligible "sounds," or in general response to an actor in a crowd scene, and again, the responses must be equally unintelligible. If an extra is instructed by the Director to reply to an actor in a scene, or if he does a special little bit of business on his own or with an actor, which is called a "silent-bit," the extra must be paid more than his base salary.

The actor must understand the function of an extra, how to use him in a scene and take advantage of his presence without going beyond the limits set by the production staff and the Guild. There are many wonderful people in the extra ranks. You can learn a lot from them, as I have over the years. Many of them have been around a long, long time, are very knowledgeable about the business and can prove very invaluable friends to the young performer.

BACKLOT: *The area situated within grounds of main studio or adjacent to the main studio lot where outdoor sets—house and building fronts, parks, town squares, lakes, wharves, western sets, and so on—have been erected or laid out.*

BARN-DOORS: *Hinged doors mounted on the front of any studio lamp.*

These *barn-doors* may be adjusted to direct or block off light from any area within the lighting pattern designed for the set in which the scene is to be shot. Barn doors come in many sizes, from the very smallest used on a lamp such as an *inky-dink*, which is a very small lamp that is directed into the performer's eyes to obtain the best results photographically of the expressions in his eyes while he is performing and which is usually mounted on a stand placed in front of the camera or upon the camera itself, below the lens, to the large type of barn doors, which are fitted on to the largest of the lamps used in a studio, an *arc*.

The actor need not concern himself with the function of barn-doors except that he should observe how they are directed on him or on the set, and be able to take advantage of that light placement which the barn-doors afford in order to look his very best in the scene. If, in a close-up, the barn-doors are so adjusted on the lamp as to create a certain pattern of light on the actor's face, then it is important that the actor disciplines himself in the shot, so as to maintain, photographically, the effect which has been created for him by the director of photography.

Primarily, in learning his craft, the actor should not concern himself with the various components of a camera or a light; these are the concern of the technicians involved in operating them. The actor should discover how these technical pieces of equipment have been used in the scene so as to show him to his best advantage, and learn to take full advantage of them.

BLEED: *To bleed is to ease oneself up, down, sideways, or diagonally, slowly into or out of position on the set.*

Sometimes an actor is requested to *bleed* himself *out* of a scene. He may be on the very edge of the frame, and as the camera moves in to a tighter shot of the other people in the scene, it is necessary that he be excluded from the scene. Therefore, as the camera moves into that closer shot, he should bleed or ease himself to the side of the frame on which he is working, as unobtrusively as possible, so that the camera movement into the other players is accomplished in a smooth and undistracting manner.

BLEND: *To blend is to stay in frame, i.e., on camera, as another performer and yourself move across the set, or up into the set diagonally.*

For example, if another performer crosses the set and the camera pans with him and you have been asked to stay close to that other performer in that movement, you must move or *blend* with that other performer in a manner that is calculated to keep you in the shot with him. The director will give you an indication of how this should be done, the camera operator will tell you the limitations of his framing, and as awkward as this maneuver is sometimes to accomplish, you must see that both you and the other performer stay in the frame. The camera operator will stay with the person who is leading the shot, and it is up to you if you are following, to stay in such proximity to the other performer that you can be properly framed by the camera.

There is a *secondary definition of blend* which is sometimes used in directing actors. I have sometimes directed one or more actors to blend with the other players in a scene. Occasionally, an actor's performance, right in itself, is, in its particular way, not right for the scene as a whole. It may be too dominant or it may not be strong enough, and in either instance, the actor must so modify his performance or bring it up that it blends with the performances of the other actors in the scene. It is the balance that actors must obtain between themselves in a scene so that the whole scene plays at a perfect pitch, both in voice, in movement; in characterization, in overall interpretation. If one or more actors have not blended their characterization into the scene as a whole, it can distort, or even destroy, the whole fabric of the scene, and the result is that the scene itself is not as entirely successful as the director would have wished.

BLIMP: *A general term for any soundproof housing which covers the magazine and body of a camera used to record dialogue.*

The blimp serves to prevent the noise of the camera from being superimposed on the recorded dialogue. However, most cameras which are used in scenes in which dialogue is to be recorded are termed "self-blimped," and thus this term is applied to those cameras in which the normal housing silences the noise of the mechanism of the camera itself, without the addition of an external blimp, such as the Barney.

BLOCK-OUT: *The movements of the actors in a scene, decided upon by the director beforehand, or worked out in conjunction with the actors during the rehearsals of the scene to be shot.*

Each director will work in his own distinct way. There are some directors who, in doing their "homework" for a scene, in their own minds, will have decided upon at least the general, often the exact, movements that each character should make within the scene to be filmed. This director will often draw diagrams, in this particular regard, to remind himself of what he has decided prior to coming onto the set to shoot the scene.

There are the directors who, having prepared a scene in their mind, and understanding it quite fully, sometimes, even though they have had a chance to look at the set in which the scene will be shot, have not specifically laid out in their minds or on paper, the movements that the actors will make during a scene. They prefer to begin the action in the set as indicated in the script, and then have the actors move their way through the scene, and between the director and the actors, decide finally on what the movements in the scene will be. This method of shooting is most ideal for a feature film in which there is more time allowed for rehearsal, but, on the other hand, with an intelligent director and actors who are thoroughly equipped to perform under these circumstances, even in television this method can be used to the utmost advantage.

However, whichever method is used, the actor must work quickly with the director, having done his own preparation beforehand as to how his character might react under certain circumstances; in every way, work fluidly and quickly to set down the movements of the scene as required by the director or indicated by the character or the scene itself, and put them into such a form that they can be performed for the camera. In addition to this, if there is any business involved in the scene, such as having a meal, lighting a cigarette, doing some gunplay, or the like, the actor must be sure in these particular instances that he so determines how that piece of business will be performed in the master shot, that should it need to be covered in a closer shot, he will be able to accurately, once again, do that piece of business exactly as he did it in the master shot. *This is a must as far as actors performing in America are concerned.*

There was one instance in which I was involved in a complicated master shot in which the difficulties of setting up the shot were such that the actors concerned in the scene, myself and an actress, *did not* really *have the time to settle exactly what we were going to do in the master shot.* However, the director, feeling that we could attempt the master and conclude it successfully, asked us whether we would like to attempt the shot. We both agreed, the cameras were rolled, and we were into Take One of the scene. We stayed as close as we could to all the movements that had been decided upon, and after some four or five minutes of acting, successfully completed the master shot. Now the director wanted to move in and get some closer shots, two shots over the shoulders and singles of the actress and myself, but we found that in the excitement of doing the first shot—that is, the *actor's excitement* of doing the first shot—we were not clearly able to recall precisely all of the many actions or movements, as far as personal business was concerned, that we had done in the master shot.

The script supervisor had done his best to note all our movements in the master shot, but he had only been able to cover some sixty percent of what we had done. Therefore, it was up to the actress and myself to sit down and quietly try to think our way through every single piece of business or movement that we had made or done during the scene, so that when we came to do the closer shots, we could accurately match the various little bits of business of turning to each other, lighting a cigarette, picking up a piece of correspondence from a desk, or taking out a gun that had happened in the scene. Write this in your notebook or *underline* the following: It is best to simplify all movements and all business in a scene unless there is plenty of time in which to rehearse them and to set them in your mind so that you, the other player(s), the director, and the script supervisor have all been able to make a careful note of them for the matching shots, which will be taken after the master shot is filmed.

BOOM (CAMERA): *A mobile camera mount consisting of a wheeled, motorized body, supporting a central column on which is suspended a boom, at one end of which is a frame which con-*

tains many slabs of lead, each with a handle attached to them
for easy handling, and at the other end, the long part of the
arm of the boom, a platform on which a camera can be mounted.

In this way, especially with a Chapman boom, the camera
may be projected out over the set, and/or raised above it, and/or
swung in a number of directions. The boom itself is driven as
a heavy duty truck might be, either independently over various
terrain, or along camera tracks by an operator, and there are
other operators who control the motion and placement of the arm
of the boom. The cameraman, sitting up behind the camera on
the mount, is able to control the camera by use of mechanical
control and by the Worrall (geared) head, which controls the
actual body of the camera and its attitude towards the subject
itself. The provisions made in the various booms for counter-
balancing, raising and lowering, rotating, or bodily moving the
boom, are such as either can be effected by the electric motors
or manually by hand by the members of the camera crew. The
wheels of certain camera booms are only designed to run on
wooden or aluminum tracks, but the wheels of the Chapman
boom have been designed to move in a number of directions,
and because of their similarity in width and tread to tractor tires,
this particular boom is able to move, given reasonable terrain,
into many positions where it would be extremely difficult to place
any other form of camera boom.

BOOM (MICROPHONE): *A simplified version of a basic camera*
boom, with an elevating pole which supports a telescopic arm,
from which a microphone is suspended, thereby enabling the
microphone to be placed over the set and twisted in any direc-
tion required to record the dialogue or sound effects in a scene
by the Sound Mixer.

There are a number of types of microphone booms, but they
all serve the same function, i.e., to place a microphone into or
over a set, and so record sound. Various types of microphones
with a variety of fabric coverings over them are used. The coverings are designed to eliminate the sound of wind against the
microphone itself. The men concerned with operating the microphone or recording and mixing the sound as the actor performs
are experts at their business and will make every adjustment possible to see that the actor is accommodated in the scene by the
microphone. The Mike Boy must also be sure that no shadows

of the microphone fall upon either the background of the set, or the actor.

BOOM (BOY): *The operator who controls the physical movement of the microphone (often referred to as mike man).*

BREAKDOWN: *The breaking down of a shooting script into various sequences, and then into the separate shots which make up those sequences.*

Each one of the sheets of a breakdown will contain necessary information regarding the scene itself. Subsequently, these breakdown sheets will be arranged in an order on what is called a *board,* and a *schedule* for the shooting of the film outlined. A typical breakdown sheet will contain the set, a description of the set in which the scene is to be shot, the scenes themselves, a description of the action in the scene, a note of the necessary equipment or horses, and such like, that will be needed in the scene. It will also contain a listing of the cast, and will indicate on what location, what stage within the studio or on the backlot, the scene will be shot. It will also indicate whether the scene is a day or a night scene and exactly the length of the scene in pages, i.e., one page, one and three-eighths pages, two-eighths of a page, one and five-eighths pages, etc.

BRUTE: *A brute is the largest of the arc lights used to illuminate a scene both indoors and out-of-doors.*

A brute is a large light standing on a triangular base which is raised to a certain height on a center column by a mechanism, usually an electric motor that can raise or lower this particular light at will. Often, because of the heat generated by this light, it is necessary to attach to the top of the light a cover and a funnel, which allows the heat generated by the light to escape at a greater height than the light itself, so that the heat waves generated will not in any way interfere with the light projected by the lamp onto the scene. The glass on the lamp itself, which, when the arc is struck through it, generates a pure, clear light, is often covered by a series of circular diffusers, which are called by different terms: *jellies* (gelatins) or silks, (single silks, double silks, half silks). In some instances, colored gelatin circular diffusers are used, which in color photography can cause certain effects on the subject on which the light is focused.

CALL SHEET: *A list of every performer, every technician, and every requirement for the next day's shooting.*

The call sheet, usually prepared by the unit production manager, contains all information pertinent to every person concerned with the next day's shooting. As far as the actor is concerned, when handed a call sheet for the next day, he should study it carefully, note his time of call, note the sets in which he will work, check off the scenes in which he will work, see that he is prepared for the work that is coming up the next day, and if he does this, he has fulfilled his function of accepting the call sheet and thus fully acknowledged his obligation for the next day's work. The call sheet, in essence but with reservations—and this means that the assistant working on the film may give him variations on the call—obligates the actor to observe the instructions to be at a studio at a certain time for makeup, to be on the set at a certain time, to have prepared the work listed for him, even though it may be changed overnight or in the course of the day. Having accepted the call sheet, the actor officially is notified of his obligations for the next day, both regarding time of reporting and the work that is expected of him.

CAMERA ANGLE: *The field of view which a camera sees when it is set up on a certain spot to shoot a shot.*

The term *camera angle* is also loosely used to indicate the various other shots which are used or indicated in film making: the over-the-shoulder, the two-shot, the close-up, the extreme close-up, etc., but essentially a camera angle can be defined in those basic three categories: high angle, low angle, or wide angle. There are an infinite variety of shots that can be called or nominated by a director or by a director of photography, and it is only essential that the actor understands that particular framing of the shot designated by the director, which will be achieved, hopefully, by the setting-up of the camera, and by the operator of the camera. The *name* of the shot is not important; that the actor is aware of the framing of the shot and what the actor does in the shot is all-important.

CAMERAS (MOTION PICTURE): *A camera is a precision instrument which enables a series of intermittent exposures to be made on a strip of sensitized film, so that, when these exposures are developed, they can be projected in such a way as to produce on a screen an illusion of movement.*

There are many types of cameras used in motion pictures, but, by-and-large, they fall into three large categories:

(1) *Studio Camera*: A large camera designed primarily for studio use, although it is often used outdoors. This type of camera is fully silenced, either within its own sound-deadening shell, or by the use of a *barney*. Its mechanism is highly complicated, with every possible refinement needed to accomplish such shooting as is required in a sound film.

(2) *Field Camera*: This type of camera is lighter in construction and is used primarily for outdoor shooting. It is a non-silenced camera and is used mainly for action sequences where the recording of actual sound is not important.

(3) *Hand Camera*: This type is a smaller version of a field camera which is light enough to be held in the hand, or mounted on a light chest-and-shoulder frame, so that it may be operated on batteries by an operator who, therefore, has the ability to move about in a scene and pick up shots as he sees fit. This camera is often used for covering action scenes close. A similar type of camera is used by television newsreel operators.

CAMERA TRACKS: *Planks or tracks of wood or metal laid down on the ground and levelled by wooden wedges, so that they can carry a crab or "western" dolly or a camera boom in a designated straight line, and thus, insure smoothness of camera movement in the scene.*

The primary purpose of laying tracks so that a camera dolly or boom could move along them was that the camera itself could precede the actors in a scene, and obtain a traveling shot. The reversal of this procedure is when the tracks themselves lead into the final settling point of the actors in the scene. This way the camera can move down the tracks and secure a closer angle of the actors in one smooth movement. The flat boards laid to insure the smooth movement of the crab dolly serve the same purpose: that the crab dolly can be pushed manually without the use of tracks into a tighter shot on the actors in the scene. However, today, with the advent of the zoom lens, this particular function of track and dolly has been negated to a degree, although the use of the zoom lens today in film-making is mainly confined to a silent shot. The zooming-in of both image and sound could possibly be achieved, but is not necessarily a desirable effect. Once the zoom-shot has settled in on the performer it is possible for sound to be recorded in synchronization with image.

CAMERA CREW: *Those persons who direct, manually operate, or contribute to the technical operation of a motion picture camera on a film set.*

The number of people in a camera crew varies according to the film being made, but they generally fall into the following categories:

(1) *First Cameraman:* This highly skilled technician is sometimes called director of photography or chief cameraman. He is the person who is responsible for deciding upon all movements and settings-up of the camera. He is also responsible for the lighting of the scene which is to be shot. The actual lighting of the scene itself is a combination of activities between the electrical crew, headed by the chief gaffer, and the construction crew, headed by the key grip. The first cameraman, except when working with very small units, does not, as a rule, manipulate the controls of the camera, either when making preliminary adjustments for the shot or during the actual shooting. He will, with a large unit, designate the shot, and the operator will frame it off. He will check the set-up making minor adjustments, indicating these to the operator, as well as getting the director's approval of the framing of the shot.

(2) *Second Cameraman:* This technician is often referred to as the assistant cameraman, or camera operator. He is a person who, having got his instructions from the first cameraman, sets up the shot, and then hands it over to the first cameraman to be checked out. Subsequently, during the actual shooting of the shot itself, he is behind the camera, monitoring the scene through a viewfinder, and making those necessary adjustments to the manual controls of the camera, so that the framing of the scene is always correct.

(3) *First Assistant Cameraman:* This technician is the chief assistant to the camera operator. His primary responsibility is usually in following focus, but if an automatic slater is used on the front of the camera, he may also handle this particular task. As far as following focus is concerned, he will have first measured the distances of the actor from the lens and made his particular decisions as to the split of the focus, and then

will either operate the knob that controls the focus of the camera by hand, or by the use of an aluminum rod. This telescoping rod enables this technician to position himself away from the camera to either side and control the focus of the camera at a distance of about four feet.

(4) *Second Assistant Camerman*: This second assistant to the camera operator is primarily concerned in supplying and changing the reels of film for the camera. He will thread the new magazines of film through the mechanism of the camera and check it out in that regard. He makes note of all footage shot which the operator will call to him after the completion of each take, and then either he himself, or his assistant, if there should be another man for this job, will then, when the reel of film is run through, i.e., used up, "shot," see that that film is immediately dispatched to the camera truck for temporary storage before it is sent off later that day to the laboratory for processing. This particular technician, too, may have the responsibility of changing and manipulating the manual slate, or clapperboard, for one or more cameras which might be in operation for the shooting of the scene.

(5) *Still Cameraman*: A specialist who is responsible for the taking of publicity and production still photographs. He will also be required by the wardrobe department, and by the makeup and hair departments, to take photographs of each actor in each of the wardrobes that the actor may wear, and in the makeup and hairpieces and wigs that the makeup and hairdressing people may have placed upon the actor.

CHEATING (LOOKS): *To cheat a look is to direct your look closer to camera, either left or right of camera, than the honest or actual look would be directed in the playing of the scene.*

The purpose of cheating is to reveal more of the performer's eyes, and the expression in them to the camera, than could be seen in an "honest" look. An "honest" look could be defined as one directed at a performer, or at a place, which is correct as far as the previous setup is concerned, but which, in the shot now being filmed, would be directed too far to the side of the lens to be effective cinematically.

CLAPPERBOARDS: *A pair of hinged, diagonally painted, black and white boards, attached to the top of the camera slate, which are clapped together in dialogue shooting before, and sometimes after each take.*

Before the commencement of a take—before action is called—the clapping of the boards together always takes place when the picture camera and the sound camera first start running at synchronized speeds. When the editor and his cutter come to assemble the developed film in the cutting room, the first frame of closure of the clapperboards on the picture is thus able to be synchronized with the modulations, resulting from the bang of the clapperboards itself, clearly evident on the sound track of the film, and in this way establishes the synchronization between the sound and the picture tracks for the purpose of cutting.

A clapperboard is sometimes simply referred to as a *slate*, or *slateboard*. As has been mentioned before, the clapperboard has been replaced, in many instances nowadays, by an automatic slater, which is hinged below the lens of the camera itself, and is then swung up into position just before the shot begins. However today, the clapperboard, in many instances, both in the very small size for 16mm shooting, and for the larger sizes for 35mm, and up shooting is always used as in the past, when the automatic slater is not available on the camera being used.

There is another type of board which the actor may encounter in the shooting of a color film. It is called a *lily*, a somewhat large board, often two feet square, on which are certain gradations of black through white. This board will be held alongside, or in front of, the actor or actors in the scene, and then removed while the camera is running for a short duration. In this way serving as a test on this small piece of film to the laboratory, and giving an indication of how the whole scene may be developed.

CLEAN ENTRANCE: *If the performer has been directed to make a clean entrance into a scene, he must make sure that no part of his body, or even the shadow of his body, is evident in the set or precedes him before his actual appearance in the shot.*

This will apply in every instance, whether or not the actor is making his entrance into the scene from without the set, or whether he is moving into a shot with another player or players in order to make a group shot, or a two-shot, or whether he is concerned with the rising into or sitting into a single, on his own. In essence, it is imperative that, the frame of the shot having been established, the actor stays outside of the frame until the precise moment he needs to come into the shot, not allowing any portion of his body, or his shadow, to fall into the shot before he actually makes his entrance inside the frame.

CLEAN SPEECH: *A clear and accurate delivery of the line or speech with which the actor is concerned at that moment in the scene.*

If the actor should bungle his line, the director may instruct him to start *From The Top* again. Not necessarily waiting for this direction, the actor can go back to the beginning of what he has to say, and say it again. The same procedure would apply in the instance of an *overlap*—one actor, either on or off camera, *overlapping* the other, where the actor on camera is in a single. (See: *Overlap.*)

CLEAR (YOURSELF): *To make sure no other actor, object, or piece of furniture, obscures the performer from being seen clearly by the lens of the camera.*

While blocking out the scene, the actor should be primarily concerned with the movements that he and the director have decided are necessary for the scene, but at each juncture where the movement might find him behind a piece of furniture, or behind another performer, he must make sure that he can, at all times in the playing of the scene, be seen by the lens of the camera. During the playing of the scene, the actor will develop a facility in his periphery vision to be sure, at all times, that he *can* be seen clearly by the lens, without actually looking at any time toward the lens itself.

COLD READING: *A reading given for a casting director, a producer, or director, by the performer, without any, or the very minimum of, preparation of the script, from which he must read portions of the part for which he is being considered.*

There are occasions when all performers, whether young or experienced, are asked to come to a studio for an interview, and because the producer and the director are not necessarily acquainted with the actor's ability to play a specific part, the performer may be asked to read for those people. Usually, he will be offered a script to read before he goes in for his interview; rarely, will he have more than a few minutes to gain some idea of what his character is all about, in the context of the script itself. Shortly thereafter, he must go in, and with someone else

—the casting director, the producer, or the director, reading back
to him—he must give a reading of the part for the people concerned. This is a typical cold reading.

The performer must, when he is handed the script in the
outer office, try as best as he can to understand what the scene
and the character is all about, but the primary thing that he must
keep in mind, when he reads inside, is to give a reading which
delineates the essence of the character. After some experience in
this kind of a venture, the average good actor will find that he
can immediately create an instant type of character, and so give
those people who are trying to judge his ability some idea of his
capabilities, and how he might, with due study and preparation,
make something of the part for which he is being considered.

It is very important to control one's nerves in this particular
situation. I find, in those certain circumstances where I've had
to read like this, that it is very important to take the reading at
a slower pace than one would normally. In this way, the brain
can operate on the material. You will find that if you do not rush
at the reading, then certain other values will occur, in other
words, come forth, from the reading, which, before that actual
moment, might not even have been considered. The main thing
in a reading like this is to have confidence in your ability to
create that *instant character,* and this confidence can be gained
by practicing at home on any kind of script or reading material
at every opportunity. It can be a play, it can be a film script, it
can be a novel, it can even be the telephone book. An actor
should be able to pick up any piece of material and read it
intelligently.

The people concerned in interviewing the actor do not expect
a finished, accomplished performance under these circumstances;
they merely want to see if the actor can read a line fluently and
make sense of it, to discover in meeting him and talking to him,
something of his personality. Under these circumstances, if the
actor gives a sensible, controlled, nerveless reading of the part,
more often than not, he will satisfy those people who are interviewing him. It does not necessarily mean that he will get the
part; he may not be right for it, but if he can develop the ability
to give a cold reading, he will find that many times on these
interviews, he will successfully gain the part for himself, in op-
position to other actors who simply are unable to train themselves to read for producers and directors in this manner.

The ability to cold read is never learned in the outside foyer of the producer's office; the performer must acquire this ability at home. Subsequently, when he is required to perform under these circumstances he will do so with the knowledge that he can handle this particular kind of a reading very well.

COLOR IT: *What a performer must do in playing his part to give a greater vitality and depth to his characterization.*

Sometimes, when playing a scene, a performer will not bring to his part those many necessary nuances of characterization, and, consequently, his playing of the part will be without any color. A director will often ask a performer to color his performance a little more, and the performer must then search for ways to bring more light and shade into the reading of the lines, more natural vitality and vivacity into the movements that he is expected to make, and a greater variety to the expressions that he may be using facially, or that are evidenced in his eyes. Also, the director may be seeking a more extraordinary character than the one that the actor is playing at the moment, and, in general, by saying "color it," the director is trying to give the actor a little more freedom to be more daring in the playing of his part. He may even ask the player to play it from another point of view; he may suggest certain pieces of business or reactions that the actor can use. If the actor feels that he cannot do what the director asked him to do, or that it is not entirely suitable to the playing of the character as he sees it, then he must sit down and discuss it with the director and come to an agreement with him.

CONSTRUCTION CREW: *A group of men, headed-up by a key grip, who do most of the physical labor necessary on a sound stage or a location site.*

On the back of your call sheet, you will find the construction crew listed in detail. Each one of these men has a specific task, which he attends to in the course of the day's work. Among these men, you will find one or more to whom you should pay special attention. These are the mechanical effects men. They are responsible for creating many of the special effects that take place on a set, such as explosions, rifle bullets hitting into certain parts of the set, etc. They will have to time many of their effects to your movements. In such shows, it is best that you have a clear understanding with them to exactly what you are going to do, so that they can best time their effects for your ultimate safety.

COOKIE: *A flat, irregularly shaped flag, usually constructed out of a piece of three-ply. The three-ply has been cut into and perforated with a pattern of leaves, branches, flowers, etc. The cookie is set so as to cast a shadow on an otherwise uniform and monotonous surface when a light striking that surface is set behind the cookie.*

Cookies are sometimes opaque in the instance of three-ply, and sometimes translucent, in the use of various plastics; they are of all sizes, small and large. Sometimes in placing them, both indoors and outdoors, an actual cluster of twigs and leaves from a tree, sometimes even a larger branch, is substituted for the cookie, and the shadow of such a collection of leaves, twigs, and/or branches, cast on a uniform or monotonous surface to break it up so that it is more attractive photographically.

COUNTER: *When an actor moves in the opposite direction to that of a camera in motion laterally.*

When a camera in position (C1) is viewing two performers, (A1 and B1) and then must move left (C2), and so still be able to see those two performers in perfect framing, it may be necessary for one of the performers to counter, that is, move in the

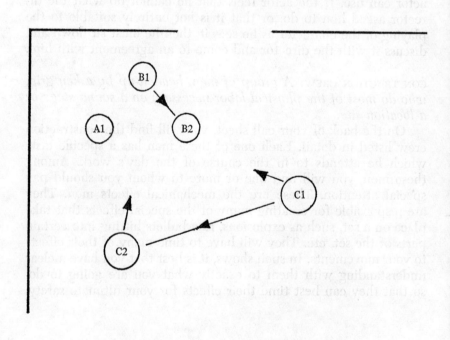

opposite direction of the camera movement itself, in order to accommodate the perfect framing of both actors at position (C2) of the camera.

COVER: *What a director does in obtaining all the shots of a scene which he considers necessary, in order that the editor may have sufficient film to cut—or put together—the scene as the director has envisioned it.*

Each director (and producer) has his own idea of the amount of coverage necessary for a scene. In feature films, he will generally apply himself to a scene by either shooting himself a complete master, or what may be termed a progressive master, i.e., breaking up a long scene into several master shots. He will then move in through the body of the scene, covering the players concerned in a variety of other shots, according to how he thinks that scene should be photographed.

In television, the director may, on analyzing an hour script, find that there are a certain number of major sequences—maybe 8, 10, 12—which he needs to cover, and sometimes, because of the exigencies of time, he may feel that one or two of these major scenes in the script can be covered in one master shot each, and thus not need breaking up. He will endeavor then to set up the action of the scenes, so that when the players move in concert with the camera, he will be able to have a variation of images on the screen, moving from a looser, longer shot into closer two-shots, into over-the-shoulder shots, into single heads, by so doing giving an automatic variety of images to the scene, despite the fact the scene plays from beginning to end without interruption. In this way he has a complete scene, or scenes—he does not need to break this up and shoot additional shots to be cut into the master, thus saving himself time which can be applied to more difficult, complex scenes.

COVER SET: *A set, usually on a soundstage, to which the unit shooting can move when, on location, the weather becomes too bad to permit continuous shooting.*

These are sets that would be used in the ordinary course of the film, in any case, but one or more are set aside and scheduled to be shot later on in the course of the shooting of the film, and are so designated cover sets so that they can be used if the location site is rained out or an accident on location prevents those actors continuing who were on the location site. Once having moved into the cover set, other actors can be used to sustain the continuity of production.

CRAB DOLLY: *A small, compact, highly mobile dolly which can be moved easily in many directions in order to place the camera in the correct position to photograph a shot.*

There are a number of crab dollies. You can find their various kinds and specifications listed in the American Cinematographer's Manual, a very fine book which I can recommend to all actors who are interested in the technical aspects of film-making, but it is not necessary for the actor to understand all the technical aspects of the various crab dollies which are made and used in film-making. It is, however, important that he should quickly learn what this particular crab dolly can do, and what its limitations are, as far as moving and positioning a camera is concerned.

The central column of the crab dolly, which supports the camera itself, can be lowered and raised by a pressure system. The four sets of wheels on which it runs can be turned in various directions, so that a variety of movements can be achieved with this dolly. Three men are concerned primarily with the operation of this dolly—a grip, who both pushes and pulls, guides, elevates and depresses the center supporting column of the dolly itself; the camera operator, who controls the camera mounted on this particular pedestal, being able to tilt it down, tilt it up, pan it to the right or to the left; and the first assistant cameraman who "follows focus."

It is important that the actor learn to move in concert with the planned movements of these men. They can achieve many complex patterns of camera movement between them, but the actor must endeavor to time his movements to theirs, as soon as possible in the blocking out of the scene, so that their job is made that much easier. If an actor hurries too much in the passage of a movement in the scene, it is not always possible for these men to place the camera in a continuous series of positions that will enable the camera to record the scene that is being acted. It is up to the actor to ascertain, during the blocking out of any scene, just how he can combine with these technicians in order to obtain the most perfect result. He will readily be told by the camera operator if he is not doing what he should be doing—hitting his marks, blending, etc.—and it is up to him, then, to modify his movements and so carry them out, that the shot is achieved without any undue delay.

CROP: *To frame an actor for a shot so that the top of his head and portion of his neck is excluded from the framing of the shot.*

In essence, this is what is called a "big head close-up," and the actor must be sure to ascertain from the camera operator just how much of his face is actually in the shot. After finding out that only from his forehead to his chin, and from cheekbone to cheekbone, is going to be exposed in the framing of the shot, the actor must compound both his physical action and his mental activity in the shot. He must match the structure of the shot itself photographically, powerful as it is under these circumstances, with the same controlled power in his acting. (See: *Give Him A Haircut!*)

CROSS IN-OUT: *The movement that an actor makes in entering into a scene from side of frame, or crossing out of a scene, and thereby exiting a frame.*

In a set shot, where the actor comes in one side of the frame, and exits on that same side, or on the opposite side of the frame, it is necessary always that the actor should make a perfectly clean entrance, and subsequently, a clean exit. It is important that the actor determine the side, or sides, of the frame in each case, so that in such a set shot, he can be quite sure that he has entered into and exited the frame cleanly.

"CUT!": *The order, command, or instruction given by the director of the film when the action in the shot has been completed to his satisfaction. This command indicates that the sound and/or the picture cameras are to be shut off.*

"Cut!" is an indication to the actor that the shot itself is over. Under ordinary circumstances, this is a mere courtesy, but if the actor has been playing dead in the scene, or is in uncomfortable circumstances, submerged in water, covered by mud, etc., then he knows that the shot is over, and he can extricate himself from the particular circumstances in which he finds himself.

It is important that the actor continues acting in the scene until the shot is cut by the director. It is very wrong for an actor to cut the scene himself just simply because he doesn't feel that it's going well for him. However, there will be occasions when an actor, with experience, must protect himself in a scene which has started badly for him, or which is not going well for him. He must manage to stop the scene in a thoroughly professional way, and be able then, because the actor's problems are understood by the director, to ask that same director if he may begin the scene again. This is the proper and courteous way of going about it, and with the gaining of experience, the professional actor usually can judge when the scene is playing well, and will then be able to work in concert with the director, as to continuing with it or cutting it, and asking that he be allowed to do it again. Under no circumstances should the beginning actor take it upon himself to cut a scene. This is up to the director to decide.

There is an additional expression, or order, that may be used or given by the director at the conclusion of the scene for specific reasons, and that is the directive "cut and hold," which means for the actor to stop the action but hold the position. So ordered, the actor must not move or change his particular physical attitude, as the director and the cameraman will wish to check the framing, the composition, or focus. Obey this command from the director explicitly. It is important that you should do so. It can save many another take.

CUT (FILM): *A means of making an instantaneous transition from any shot of a film to an immediate succeeding shot.*

To achieve this result, the two pieces of film are spliced together, by cementing them end to end at a designated frame. The discovery of the ability to cut film, to insert various other shots into the complete, continuous master shot, enabled filmmakers to construct a new framework of time and space as we know it today in films. This particular delineation of time and space that a film can make is also sometimes called filmic space.

CUE LIGHT: *A light bulb on a small stand, or affixed to the set, visible to the performer off-stage, often hung just outside a doorway to cue a performer's entrance into a scene.*

The cue light will go on, signalling the actor to enter, knock, or speak, etc. It will be operated, usually, in most places, by the director himself, and will take the place of a word cue or a signal from him to the actor, where such is not possible because of sound being recorded or because of the actor being outside of the set, and not visible to the director, or one of his assistants.

CUTTER (EDITOR): *The person who is responsible for assembling the many individual shots made during the course of the film, into a coherent whole, which matches, as a continuity, the screenplay itself.*

The editor first makes an assembly of the various scenes. Next, he puts those scenes together into sequences, and ultimately progresses until he has what is termed a rough cut of the film itself. When this has been reviewed, he can proceed to make himself a fine cut of the finished film. He will usually deputize the preparation of the music and sound effects tracks to a sound cutter. Finally, when all the tracks are assembled, they will be mixed in a session supervised by the head editor concerned with that particular film. It is usually considered that the terms cutter and editor are synonymous, although it usually is conceded that the designation editor is given to that person who has the final complete authority over the actual physical assembly of the film. It is usual in the cutting of the film, in many instances, that the director of the film has the right, and sometimes it is written into his contract, of the first cut of the film itself. This he will achieve in concert with the editor and the editor's various cutters who are working on the film. After that has been done, then it is up to the producer of the film to have the final say on how the film will be cut, and the editor, finally, is responsible to him, the producer, to see that his wishes are carried out.

CUTTER (FIXTURE): *A long, rectangular piece of three-ply, often two to three feet long, by some four to six inches wide, or a steel frame of similar dimensions covered with a black, opaque cloth.*

Such a cutter is equipped with a prong at one end that can be fixed into a stand, and the cutter, slanted across in front of a light, so that its shadow can be thrown on the performer or a portion of the set, thus achieves an effect desired by the director of photography. A cutter is sometimes used in other ways, either to eliminate glare from a certain portion of a wall, or a too conspicuous highlight on an actor's hair, according to the artistic desires of the director of photography.

DAILIES: *The prints of the negative film shot on the previous day, which are delivered daily, usually early in the morning, to the studio from the laboratory which has processed them. Dailies are also often called rushes.*

The dailies are usually viewed by the producer, the director, and his assistants, as well as the principals of the film, each day of shooting, at a convenient time, hence the name dailies.

In watching the dailies the producer can determine if there has been sufficient coverage of the previous day's work. They

can note if any of the shots have been unsuccessful as to interpretation, particular time of day in which they were shot, anything else that should have been in the scene and was omitted,
and subsequently, the production staff can list, if necessary, any
retakes or additional scenes that need to be shot to complete the
coverage of those scenes shown in the dailies that have been
viewed on that particular occasion.

I have discussed before, in Section One of this book, the importance to the actor of watching the dailies. With experience,
he can judge whether or not he is being completely successful in
the interpretation of his part, and with due course and discretion,
can make notes for himself of the various ways in which he can
improve his playing and characterization in the film. If the performer has developed the capacity to look at himself quite dispassionately, he will find, by viewing the rushes, that he can do
considerable homework on the rest of his part, which, up to that
date, is unfilmed. He can notice how he is being lighted, and be
absolutely sure that when he works again, the following day,
that he can take advantage of the lighting that has been created
for him by the director of photography. If the actor applies himself to watching the rushes in an intelligent way, he can learn
much from them that will be very helpful to him in the future,
immediate and otherwise.

In discussing the rushes at any time with the producer, the
director, or the other men concerned with them, the actor should,
out of pure professional courtesy, only discuss those aspects of
the rushes which concern himself, and not enter into any discussion with the other technicians. He must never voice an adverse
opinion of their work. They are all fully conscious of what they
have done, or what they have failed to do, and the actor should
simply only concern himself with his own performance on the
screen, and keep what other opinions he might have of his fellow
workers to himself.

DAY-FOR-NIGHT: *When a scene is shot during the daylight hours,
with a special filter, so that the scene looks as if it took place at
night.*
This is essentially a method of shooting often used on location. When it is too costly to light a complete outdoor set at
night, the day-for-night shooting procedure is often used. A
special filter is used in the camera, and adjustments made on the
exposure, so that the scene itself will appear to have been shot

at night. The problems involved here are for the director of photography to solve. He will try, in the setting up of the shot, to avoid shooting into a clear sky at all times, because this would vitiate the effectiveness of the shot. Ideally, he will hope to have clouds in whatever sky he frames in the shot.

In the making of big budget motion pictures, night shooting is still the usual custom, when called for in the script, but for television segments, within the economics of that particular part of the business, day-for-night shooting is often indulged in, to avoid the extra costs of night shooting which the lighting of the exterior sets entails.

DEPTH OF FIELD: *The depth of field of a lens is the range of acceptable sharpness before and behind the plane of focus obtained in the final screen image.*

This is the technical definition of depth of field, which all cameramen can quote you. The depth of field, which is the actor's concern, is very similar in its way, but is a reference, primarily, to the actor's movements within the scene, wherein he must conform with this depth of field. In it, the actor must not move back beyond the extreme of this depth of field, nor must he come forward in front of this depth of field, or it will be impossible for his image on the screen to be in focus.

DEPTH OF FOCUS: *The depth of focus is an infinitely small range behind the lens, at the focal plane, within which the film is positioned during exposure.*

The term depth of focus is often colloquially used when depth of field is meant. The depth of focus is most critical, particularly with short-focus lenses. However, the actor need not be concerned with the technicalities of both the terms depth of field and depth of focus. He must only concern himself with the area in which a lens confines him. He must ascertain that limitation and work fully within it.

DIALOGUE COACH: *A person who is sometimes employed, by the director of the film, to check with the actor to see that he knows his lines, and if not, to run them with him; to listen carefully while the scene is being played, and to be sure that the actor has said all of his lines satisfactorily; to act in the capacity of instructing the actor in the interpretation of his lines if he has been instructed to do so by the director of the film.*

A dialogue coach has many duties according to the desires of the director of the film. He might very simply just be there to see if the actor has learned his lines before going into a scene, and be available to run those lines with the actor to give the performer the assurity that he is "up" in his lines. His additional duty might be to listen very carefully to the dialogue, and see that the actor does not omit or change, in any way, drastically or otherwise, the lines that he has to say in the scene. This enables the director of the film to concentrate on the overall playing of the scene, and the expressions, etc., which the actor is using in each particular scene that he plays. On the other hand, it may be that the dialogue coach has been given the authority, by the director of the film, to check each one of the performers, certainly the supporting players, and the younger children, to see if their interpretation of the part measures up to what has been discussed previously with the director of the film.

There is another kind of dialogue coach, who is employed by professional actors privately, or by a studio to prepare certain of their contract players in their parts, before they step onto the soundstage. This is, in itself, specialized coaching, and is usually instituted, in the case of studios, to enable their contract players to prepare parts before actually filming them.

DIRECTOR: *A person who controls the action and dialogue of the film in front of the camera.*

The director is responsible for realizing the intentions and the desires of the producer, according to the script or the screenplay; in other words, the director is the person most responsible for the transforming of a shooting script into a completed film. Having obtained his authority from the producer of the film, the director is the absolute boss of the soundstage or the location site, and his word is law, both to all the technicians involved, and to the actors.

There are many kinds of directors, of course. It is up to the individual actor to approach each director as he would a fresh task, as in the preparing of a part. The performer will find, in almost every instance, that the director has come prepared, to the set or to the location site, to shoot a film according to how he sees it himself, prepared to work with his technicians and his actors to achieve the final and best result. It is therefore up to the actor, having done his preparation himself, to discuss how he wants to play the part with the director and find some accord with that man's wishes, preferably before the film starts, regarding the generalities of the part. There will be many times, during the course of filming of scenes, that the director and the actor must discuss various aspects of the scene being filmed. There will be many points for discussion. There will be points of agreement, and points of disagreement. The actor must know when to stick to his guns and make his point solidly, and so gain the right to play the scene in the way that he believes it should be played. The director will also have his points of view, and will request certain things of the actor. In this area, it is important for the director and for the actor not to be stubborn to an extreme. If their different points of view cannot be brought together, some compromise must be reached that will solve the problem immediately, and enable the scene to be played in a perfectly acceptable way. There is no cause for excessive temperament, either on the part of the actor or of the director, or for excessive stubbornness. They both must seek a solution that is satisfactory to all concerned. This is, in no way, a forfeiture of artistic integrity; it is merely a way of bringing two, perhaps divergent, points of view together, on a scene, so that the sensible compromise can be reached, and the filming can proceed without undue friction between any of the actors and the director concerned. In the final essence, the producer and the director can order the actor either to play the scene as they want it to be played, or not to continue with the film at all. This is a drastic extreme, and should be avoided at all costs.

DISSOLVE: *An optical effect between two superimposed shots on the screen, in which the second shot gradually begins to appear at the same time as the first shot is gradually disappearing.*
      This particular optical effect is also called a *lap dissolve*. Technically, it is of no concern to the actor but in the particular essence that the director may ask him to continue his look or to hold steady, or to walk away, out of the scene, at the conclusion of the shot, or any number of other things that the director may request, the actor must know that the director is seeking footage for a dissolve-out, that will then be lapped over onto the succeeding shot in the film. An actor may be asked to walk into a scene from a greater distance than would normally be required. The director may be using this preliminary footage in the scene to lap-over the footage of the preceding shot. If the actor is uncertain as to what he should do in the particular scene, or as to

how long he should sustain his look, or actions, it behooves him to discuss it thoroughly with the director, so that he has clearly in mind what the director desires from the shot that he has requested of the performer.

DOLLYING-CRABBING: *Movement of the camera dolly in the process of making a shot.*

Dollying is sometimes called trucking or tracking. It is called *crabbing* when all four wheels of the crab dolly are used to change its angle of movement in photographing the scene. A *crab dolly,* as has been explained earlier in this section, is a light and compact wheeled mount for a camera. There are four double wheels on a crab dolly, and they can be used in various positions, so that the camera can be moved easily from place to place on a set over a surface of hard boards, which have been laid down on the floor and adjusted for level. The *crab dolly* has been so called because of the ability of all four of its wheels to turn and move in the same direction, that is, they can be turned at right angles, or they can be moved to any degree towards the diagonal, so that the crab dolly is able to execute both forward, backward, sideways, and on the variance of the diagonal, an infinite number of movements to place it, and thus to position the camera in the most perfect position to photograph the progression of any scene.

DOUBLE (STUNT-PHOTOGRAPH): *A person who takes the performer's place in the scene, and is photographed in his stead.*

There are various kinds of doubles. The kind of double most often used is a "stunt" double. Where there is any possible danger to the actor in performing a certain action in a scene, such as falling off a horse, doing a fight, dropping off a cliff, swimming a river, etc., a stunt double will be employed to take the actor's place in the scene in the long, and often in the medium, shots. A stunt double is chosen for a number of reasons, primarily because he is able to do the stunt, and secondly, because he either in some way resembles the actor facially and physically, or can be made-up to resemble the actor. The actor will be required to observe the action of the stunt itself because he will usually be requested, later on, to do the close-ups, for that particular stunt. In this case, it will not usually entail any danger or hardship for the actor, out of the ordinary, and it is most important that the actor is photographed at close quarters to match into the stunt which his double has done for him at a longer distance. The actor should observe the whole of the stunt, memorize it, so that when he is called upon to act in the closer shot, he will be able, accurately to match the movements that the stunt double made at that particular point in the stunt.

The other form of double sometimes used for an actor is a *photo-double*. Often, when a unit has gone on location, to a distant part of the country, or out of the country, another man will be used in place of the actor himself, rather than taking the actor to that location for just that short period of time. If the actor has been engaged to play the part, he is well protected in this instance by the rules and regulations of Screen Actors Guild, and will be paid accordingly. Another use of a photo-double is where an actor might be playing two parts. A photo-double will be employed to sit into the scene with his back to the camera, while the actor is playing one of the two parts that he is interpreting in the film. A photo-double may also be used in a particular instance when an actor has been dismissed from the set, and has gone home, and it is necessary to get another shot of the actor in the scene, with other actors. In this case, there is no further compensation to the actor concerned, having been engaged for that day's work. It is wise to make yourself familiar with the man who is doubling you, whether it is as a stunt-double or as a photo-double. If you have done the work in the scene first, and he has then to double you, he can copy your mannerisms. If, on the other hand, he does the stunt or the doubling first, then it is very important for you to catch some of his mannerisms, if he has not been successful in imitating you and your physical mannerisms in the scene which is being shot. In other words, there must be a certain give-and-take between the stunt- or photo-double and the actor himself to obtain the very best results from any of the scenes in which both actors and doubles are involved.

DOWNSTAGE: *The forward area of any acting space, whether on the set of a soundstage, or on a location site.*

A director might instruct an actor to move downstage in the playing of the scene and arrive at a specific location in the set, there to continue the playing of the scene. On the other hand, a director might instruct an actor to move downstage and play slightly downstage of or to another actor. He might inhibit him further by suggesting that he does not in any way turn back, either with his head or with his body, to that upstage actor, and play to him thus, creating, in essence, instead of an open two-shot, a kind of raked two-shot.

If an actor is asked to play a scene in this specific way, with an actor back over his shoulder on either side, and further requested not to turn back to the other actor, either with a turn of his head or a turn of his body in any way, this creates a specific and difficult problem for the downstage actor. I have found it best, in these particular circumstances, to *think back through the side of my head.* I have found that by the merest inclination of my head to the side that the other actor is on upstage of me, by the lowering or raising of my eyes in the general direction of backwards, that I can fully imply to the camera photographing the scene that I am referring over my shoulder to the actor who is upstage of me.

D. P. (DAY PLAYER): *A performer who is engaged for a single day's work on a film.*

The term day player is also sometimes applied to a player who is engaged to do only two days' work on a film. He would not be engaged on the usual run of the picture or TV segment contract, but would be designated for each of the two days that he was engaged in performing as a day player, and would, each day, have to sign the particular form which day players sign at the beginning of the day's work.

Usually a day player is engaged for the minimum amount of money paid under the SAG contract. However, there are instances when a player of note is asked to do a single day's work, or just two day's work, in a film or in a TV segment, and because of his professional standing, is offered an amount of money often far in excess of the minimum daily rate for a day player. I have, myself, on occasions, accepted engagements for either one or two day's work in certain films or TV segments, where the producers of the films were willing to pay me an amount far in excess of what they would have necessarily had to pay another day player. It also so happens in certain films, or in certain TV segments, that the scenes of one player can be shot on the one day, and so therefore, if an actor is engaged for that part and he is an actor of merit, he can expect to demand a far greater salary for his work than the average player.

DRESS OFF: *To use another performer, an article of furniture, or an object, a doorway, an archway, or the like, to find and assume your position in the set.*

During the course of the blocking out of any scene in the filming of a motion picture or TV segment, as the players move from one position to another, they will be marked on the floor of the soundstage or on the location site, in a manner of ways. On a set on a soundstage, which is carpeted, it is customary to use small pieces of either black or white tape to mark the position of the actor's feet. Often, on a concrete floor or on boards, the marks will be put down with chalk. On location, other means are used. Small black or white tees will be placed between the actor's feet. Other small white squares of paper, often a folded drinking cup, bound with a cross of black tape, will be thrown down on the ground to mark the position of actors' feet or where a horse must stand. Occasionally, a rock or a piece of twig will also be used out-of-doors so that it can blend into the natural foreground of the shot, if the camera is viewing the whole of the ground on which the actors are performing.

It is not always possible for the actor, although he may have clearly memorized where all his marks are, to find them without looking down for them, and yet, this should be avoided at all times. An actor must develop a periphery vision which will give him the ability to find many of the marks laid down for him without actually ever looking at them. But there are some instances where an actor cannot use his periphery vision to find those marks, and since it is very necessary for him to accurately step on top of them for the framing that the camera is trying to achieve, he must use another method, and this is called *dressing off.* By positioning himself to another performer, to an article of furniture, a table, a chair, or whatever it is, to either side of a doorway or an archway, in relation to an object, a lamp, or otherwise on a table or a desk, he can, with great accuracy, assume the correct position in the scene without ever having to have a mark placed either on the floor, or on a desk, or by the side of any other piece of furniture or object.

The actor, in grouping himself in this particular way within the scene, can feel a great deal freer in his movements, and rid himself of that natural awkwardness of any performer who has to move from mark to mark and be looking down to some degree or other to see if he has actually arrived at the position that he should be in. By *dressing off,* he will find that his whole attention can be given to the scene in which he is playing, rather than to mechanically trying to stand over marks which are placed on the floor.

DRIFT: *To move in or out of a scene, or through a scene, to another position in the set, without being obvious.*

An actor may sometimes be instructed to drift upstage in a scene. In this way, he can later be isolated by the camera and be photographed in a reaction close shot. There is another form of drift when playing in a scene with other actors. The camera might be moving in to get a closer shot of one or more of the other performers, and, as the camera does move into the scene, it will bypass that particular actor who has been instructed to drift out of the scene, and in this particular instance, the actor must ascertain from the camera operator at what point in the camera movement he will be going out of the side of the frame, and assist, by a movement to that same side, the movement of the camera centering on other players in the scene. It is essential that any actor instructed to drift in this manner does so in a smooth manner so that he merely fades out of the side of the frame, instead of almost literally jumping out, as it would appear on the screen if his action of drifting should, in any way, be jerky or swift. (See: *Bleed*)

DUBBING: *The post-production synchronization of a voice not originally recorded in synchronism with the picture track showing the lip movements of an actor in a scene.*

The above is the purely technical definition of dubbing, and we might extend that definition in this way for the performer himself: the recording in a dubbing studio, under perfect conditions, of an actor speaking his lines in a scene in synchronization either to a sound loop previously recorded on a soundstage or on location, and subsequently, not considered good enough for the final film, or to the movements of the actor's lips in the visual image of that same scene, projected, simultaneously, on the screen while the actor is rerecording his lines.

There are many methods of dubbing. Fundamentally, they are all the same, except that the mechanical procedure of dubbing varies from studio to studio. Most studios, when the actor arrives to dub, or loop, as it is sometimes called, will provide him with a set of earphones and his lines on a lectern in front of him, and then project on the screen the loop, a small segment, sometimes only a word or two, or part of a sentence from a scene, which he will have to dub. He will listen to the sound through the earphones and watch the image at the same time, and rehearse to see if he can catch the same inflections, mood, and pace of the line as it comes to him off the screen and through the earphones. When the man in charge of the dubbing session is satisfied the actor has caught the tempo, and is matching the words that he is now speaking to the lip movements visible on the screen, he will take down, to a very low level, the volume of sound that is coming to the actor through his earphones. He will then roll a take on the sound recorder and attempt to have the actor perform the lines, so that later these lines can be matched, in the process of rerecording the whole film, to the visual image that is on the screen.

The actor may achieve this in his first take; it may take him several takes to achieve it. His timing might be too slow; it might be too fast. Usually, under this method of dubbing, lines will sweep from left to right across the image on the projection screen, and the lines that are for the particular actor dubbing the scene—and a line crosses the screen and strikes the right edge of the projection screen for every line spoken in the scene—when they do strike the right hand side of the screen, serve as a signal for him to commence speaking the appropriate words. Another company might use a series of dots which flash onto the screen in a count of three or four dots. They will be heard as they flash simultaneously onto the screen as a bump on the soundtrack itself, and after the last bump, the actor will speak on the next beat. In other words, it is both a visual and a sound cue to get the actor started in the right tempo for his line. That, fundamentally, is the method, with variations, for visual dubbing.

There is another method of dubbing used by several studios whereby the actor, in a recording studio, merely has the line come to him, either over earphones or over a speaker, and the minute the line ceases, he then repeats it. Each method has its merits, and each method has to be mastered so that the actor can dub without hesitation, rerecording his voice with the same artistic quality that he had when he first performed in the scene in the film itself. It is important for the actor, in such sessions, to be perfectly relaxed and to take absolute notice of whoever is in charge of the dubbing sessions, whether it is the producer, the director of the film, or whether it is a technician, who is qualified to supervise that type of session. Quite often such a

technically skilled person, as the latter is, is as fully qualified as
many producers and directors to give an actor some interpretive
instruction as well. The young actor should take good notice of
those people concerned in controlling a recording session and
endeavor to do what they suggest to him.

There are various other categories of dubbing. An actor may
be asked to dub another actor's voice. He may have to come
into the studio and watch the loops, and record his voice so that
it can replace the voice of the original actor in the scene. In this
instance, of course, the original actor must give his permission
to the producers to have someone else dub his voice, if it is in
the same language. Actors are regularly called in to dub a scene
in English which has originally been played in another language,
and this is a highly skillful business. It is engaged in in both
New York and in Hollywood, but it seems that the best exponents
of this form of dubbing, from one language to another, are in
Japan and Italy, where this multi-lingual dubbing is a very highly
specialized skill. Generally speaking, dubbing could be considered a rerecording of voice, accomplished by means of loops,
both sound and image, sometimes printed up together, sometimes
not, these loops consisting of short sections of dialogue, a word,
a short phrase, a short sentence wherever possible, and projected
in this composite print form while the actor himself, on a speaker
or on earphones, or a combination of both, is guided by a playback of the sound of the scene while he speaks his lines.

Another form of *dubbing* is the pre-recording of songs, rou-
tines for musical films, or for musical numbers in films. The song
or music is pre-recorded under perfect conditions, and then, during the filming of the scene, where an actor or an actress or a
number of people concerned in the scene must sing or dance,
they begin the scene with the playback of the particular musical number playing, and so synchronize their lip movements to
the words of the song, and their body movements, naturally, to
the music if they are in a combination song-and-dance number.
The two pieces of film are then matched together—the image
track and the sound track—and their composite print will then
make it appear that the performer was actually singing in the
scene that we see on the screen. While a scene such as this is
being filmed, a man or woman from the Sound and/or Music
Department, who is in charge of the playback, will stand and
watch the performer's lips to see that they are synchronizing

with the words of the song as it is being played, and will give the director an opinion in this regard as to whether the take should be printed or whether it should be taken again.

Every performer will, sooner or later, have to do some dubbing or looping. The first experience in this form of recreating a performance can be very nerve-racking, but the young performer should keep in mind that he should approach the matter in as relaxed a manner as possible, that he should ask advice at all times from the technicians concerned in the dubbing session, and, no matter how difficult it is at first to achieve the desired results, that he should, at all times, keep working at the problem until the best results are obtained from the dubbing session.

There is hardly any way for a performer to gain experience of dubbing until he actually has to do a session, but there are a number of ways in which a performer can prepare himself to a certain degree, for this particular, necessary, professional experience. I found that my lifelong habit of singing to a recording, whether it is a popular or operatic recording, and, on occasions, trying to synchronize my voice to the recording of an actor such as Olivier or Gielgud or such eminent actors in classical pieces, is a great help to being able to repeat one's own dialogue accurately in a scene. This is really just purely an exercise in either keeping to the music of a particular song, as one would when one is singing normally, or in catching the cadences of delivery of such eminent actors as I have mentioned. However, by the use of a tape recorder, it is possible for the actor to practice dubbing at home, at least vocally. The actor should take a tape recorder and record just his own dialogue in any scene that he chooses or has worked in, and then replay the tape recorder, and, while either listening to his lines over the speaker or on earphones, repeat the words along with the taped version. He will find that he will be able to match his words fairly closely to the voice that he has put on tape, and, in this way, clearly recall and match the particular cadence and pace of a line that he might either have acted or recorded several weeks, sometimes many months, before. You should try this method of exercising for dubbing—it is a sound approach. You will not be successful at first, but in its way it can prove to be a useful method of enabling the actor to approximate the conditions which he will face as far as the audio portion of dubbing is concerned.

ELECTRICAL CREW: *Those men, headed by a Gaffer, who are concerned with the lighting of the set and the equipment necessary to do so.*

The Gaffer is the person who, with the director of photography, lights the set from an artistic point of view. The "Best Boy" is his assistant, and is the person who sees that the lights, whether they are lamps indoors or lamps and reflectors out-of-doors, are placed in the right position and manipulated so as to light the scene for the very best results, photographically, as desired by the director of photography. These two men are assisted on the floor by a number of lamp operators who either work on the floor or overhead above the set; they are the only men allowed to manipulate the lamps, reflectors, or electrical supply on the soundstage or on location.

Along with the lamps, the electrical crew uses a number of other pieces of equipment either on the lamps themselves or in front of the lamps, to create certain lighting effects on the screen. Silks (half, single, double), and gelatins of various colors—these are circular in construction so that they can be fitted into a mounting in the front of the lamp itself—are used to create certain effects. Gobos, flags (pieces of three-ply, or frames covered with a black, opaque cloth material) are then adjusted in certain positions so as to correct the light patterns on the set and on the actor. Each one of the lamps is fitted with barn doors which can also, by adjustment, control the direction which the light will fall on the set or on the actors.

There will be occasions when minute adjustments of this equipment will be made so as to create a special effect on the performer's face and/or figure, and it would be wise for him to thoroughly note what the Gaffer and the Director of Photography are attempting to do, and so adjust his particular physical movements to their scheme of things in order to obtain the best effects photographically.

EXTERIORS: *Location sites or sets which have been erected out-of-doors, either on location or on the backlots of movie studios.*

There is another kind of exterior set that has been mentioned before in this section—a *green set*, constructed on a soundstage of a studio to approximate an outdoor location, where shooting out-of-doors, day or night, would be either too expensive or too difficult. Still another kind of exterior set is a Western street or a collection of house fronts or building fronts along a street, which are sometimes constructed within a studio. Many Western shows, to avoid inclement weather for some of the scenes which they have to shoot out-of-doors, have erected and maintained exterior sets on various of the soundstages in Hollywood.

EYELINE: *The direction and the level of the look that the actor takes when addressing any of his remarks, while on camera, to a character, or characters, who are off-camera, either to the right or to the left of camera, or above or below it.*

These particular eyelines will vary according to the distance that the actor is removed from the camera while making the shot, and according to the circumstances in which the actor off-screen is placed. For instance, in a close shot, with the actor looking virtually over the lens of the camera at a man sitting on horseback, to actually look at the man on horseback might be to look too far above the lens of the camera. It might be better for the actor off-stage to be placed at a certain height, a rung or two up a ladder or even straddling a short ladder, so that the look the actor on camera is giving to the actor off-stage, as viewed through the lens of the camera, appears a perfectly natural look. Then, too, when there is more than one character off-stage, speaking off-stage lines, and the actor on-stage has to speak to one or more of them, on each occasion he will be asked to look at that particular person, and his eyeline, the direction of his look as seen by the camera, will be checked by the operator, by the director of photography, and/or by the director himself, to see that the look is a natural one. Although the actor himself on camera often can be reasonably sure where he should look to the other players placed alongside a camera, the final decision on this is the prerogative of the director and the camera operator, and those two people will best be able to indicate to the actor the exact direction in which he should look.

For extreme close-ups it may be necessary for the actor to look within the area—to the side of the lens—of the matte box itself, and if such is the case, then a small chalkmark might be placed upon the serrated sides of the matte box, on which he can concentrate his attention in this extreme close look. The correct eyeline is what the camera sees, and not what is apparently natural to the actor that is on-camera.

FADE: *An optical effect achieved, either by manipulating the mechanism of the camera itself, or optically in the laboratory*

*during the processing of the film, such an effect occupying a
single shot.*

The shot in question gradually disappears into blackness, and
this is called a fade-out; or appears out of blackness, and this is
called a fade-in. Fade-ins are not very much used today, except
sometimes at the beginning of a film or at the end of a film. They
are sometimes used in the body in the cutting of the film to create a special effect, but the use of a fade today is most often
used very sparingly, and only when a special effect in the mood
of the picture is desired and can be best served by that particular optical process.

FAKE (MOVE): *To start to make a move away from a position in
a scene and then return immediately to the previous position
that the performer has occupied.*

In the continuing action of a scene, an actor may make such
a move and use it to build the pace of a scene. For instance, if
in a scene where he is in conflict with other players, if he starts
to make that move and then immediately returns to his previous
position, it can change and increase the tempo and the pace of
the scene, and so often add to the quality of it. This is in no
way a *false move,* which in itself is most often an error on the
part of the actor involved. A *fake* move is a deliberate move
where he seems to be going to do one thing and then immediately returns to his previous position to resume the flow of the
scene.

FAKE (PUNCH): *A punch which, from the point of view of the
camera, appears to be one that has landed solidly on the person
at whom the actor has struck.*

In all fight scenes staged for the movies, no punches actually
land on the actors, except accidentally, of course. The actor must
learn, when he is stepping in to do his close-ups or two-shots
with another performer or a stuntman, to be able to throw
punches with both hands that will completely miss the person
whom he is fighting with, but look to the camera as if the actor
had struck that person he is fighting. The person, in this instance, who appears to be struck, will have snapped his head
back at what appears to be a telling blow, thus "selling" the
punch.

The angle at which the camera is set in these instances is
highly important to gaining the best results from such an action.

The actor will find that a punch in depth, that is, from the camera away into the background of the scene or towards the other actor is not an effective one. The actor, in throwing a punch with his right hand or with his left hand, should take that hand wide to either left or right, and swing it across the other actor's face, leaving a good margin of space between where his fist will travel and the other actor, and this will look, to the camera, as if the actor, with his back or with his face to the camera, depending upon the set-up, has actually struck the actor who is facing him. The same would apply to any other form of blow delivered to another performer. For instance, if the blow is a karate chop, it should be pulled up without in any way actually striking the other person; if it is a kick, in a similar way.

There are many trade tricks to the construction of stunts and their execution, and the young performer should endeavor to learn them all. He can best do this by being in scenes with stuntmen, and by discussing with them at every opportunity the various ways in which he can throw punches, make kicks, karate chops, take punches. Stuntmen are experts at all of these and when they are working with actors, they are only too willing to explain to the young performer how he can acquire these skills.

FALSE MOVE: *A move not related to the action of the scene or the pattern of camera movement, which has been decided upon by the director and the performer and the camera crew.*

A false move is a movement or a gesture that diminishes the meaning, the significance, of the character at that particular moment in the scene, or which misleads the camera into a premature move. The pattern of the blocking out in a scene is designed not only to provide the actor with a set of movements which will carry him naturally through the scene, but that these movements will also serve, in their minutest details, as cues for the camera crew, whether they are operating a camera on a tripod or on a crab dolly or on a Chapman boom, thus enabling them to anticipate and begin a movement of the camera when it has to cover a particular actor who is in motion by himself or along with other actors with whom he may be moving in concert. It is important that the actor, once having established a pattern, stick to that pattern, so that the camera crew can anticipate and move with him in concert. A false move that is made at that wrong moment can throw the whole pattern off, and make the obtaining of the shot impossible.

However, the skillful actor can make use of what might be called a *true false move*. By this, I mean that when the actor knows that he is going to move, he can, out of the corner of his eye, see where the camera is and begin his movements in such a way that he will be leading the camera and the camera can easily frame him. A movement should always be a fluid one. A true false move, in essence, is one where the actor begins his move, hesitates a fraction of a beat, and then leads smoothly away in the direction of the next mark he should hit, rather than making a quick, arbitrary move to take him from one spot to the next. In other words, there is a slight hold, or beat, just prior to making the move, a preparatory hint of an imminent body gesture, the actor's move, which not only prepares the actor but enables the crew to "wind up" the ensuing movement of either the crab dolly or the Chapman boom, which will then place the camera in such a position that it ideally can frame the actor in his movement. A false move is an error on the actor's part; a true false move is the finesse that the accomplished actor can acquire, and so make even smoother the concert of his movements with those of the camera itself. Be sure, as an actor, to tell the camera crew exactly how you plan to make your move—and *then stick to it!*

FIND THE LENS: *An actor who, working in the background of a scene, with other actors working between himself and the camera, must find a space between those actors in the foreground through which he can clearly see or find the lens of the camera.*
     The actor does not necessarily look directly into the lens of the camera, which is an unforgivable fault in itself, but by positioning himself in such a way, he makes it possible for the camera to see him clearly in the scene without either one or the other of the foreground actors blocking him from the camera's view. This is an essential part of the actor's craft, to be able to do this, purely from the point of view of the overall grouping in the framing of the shot that is being photographed. The actor, too, while performing under these circumstances, must be sure that his movements and gestures do not, in any way, distract from the main body of the scene, but merely serve to supplement them.
     There are some actors who, working in the background of the scene, get up to all kinds of tricks to attract attention to themselves, which in itself is unprofessional, and very unfair to the players who are carrying the scene in the foreground of the

scene. However, upon direction from a director to attract attention to himself, the actor is at liberty to do so, and the director may have in mind, at a certain juncture in the scene, to "pop in," as it's called, and secure a closer shot of the actor in the reaction that he is having at that particular moment in the scene.

Many famous actors were notorious for their distracting movements and gestures in scenes. On the other hand, there were some superb actors, such as Louis Jouvet, the distinguished French actor, who sometimes deliberately placed himself in the background of the scene when he was performing in and/or directing a film, so that by a change of focus or by what he was doing in the background of the scene, the attention was drawn to him, and therefore, a subsequently separate close shot could be obtained of him and later cut into the main body of the master shot that was then being photographed in its entirety. However, the actor, in general, should, in a group scene when he is working in the background, work as if he were in an *ensemble*, and only do what is absolutely necessary for his characterization. In all regards, his work will be checked and supervised by the director, and whatever the director asks him to do in the part is all that the actor should do.

FISHPOLE: *A long pole from which a microphone is suspended, the pole placing the microphone in such a position above the scene so that it can provide the best pickup of sound.*

This pole on which the microphone is suspended is sometimes referred to as a *bamboo* because, in the early days of film-making, a long, stout bamboo pole was sometimes pressed into action in place of an orthodox microphone boom, in order that the mike man, the manipulator of the microphone itself, could be able to place, from a distance, this particular instrument in delicate and close proximity to the actors in the scene. Today, the microphone fishpole is usually made of aluminum, and the pole itself can be telescoped to a shorter length or extended to its extreme length, some twelve to fifteen feet. Fishpoles are often used on location, particularly in terrain where it is not very easy to place or push the orthodox microphone boom into place, and particularly by small or medium-sized units on location, where the size and weight of an orthodox boom would prove inconvenient, and where, for the scenes being shot, a fishpole serves the same purpose as the orthodox microphone boom would.

FIRST TEAM (SECOND TEAM): *The players directly involved in any scene in a film, whether they are the stars or the supporting players, are usually referred to by the director, the assistants, and the crew, as the first team.*

In essence, they are the people principally concerned with the shot which the unit is trying to obtain at that particular moment. The people who are standing-in for them, their *stand-ins*, are generally referred to as the *second team*.

Often, in a new set-up for a shot, the principals of a particular scene are asked to go through their particular movements which have previously been blocked out by the director, along with the actors, and to assume positions in which they are then marked on the floor or on the location site by one of the members of the camera crew. After these positions have been decided upon, the camera is set into its position, on a tripod or on a crane, ready to move over terrain on tracks or on the boards laid down for a dolly. The second team is then called in to take the place of the first team. The second team will stand on and/or move to the various marks that the principals in the scene will move to during the actual filming of the scene, and in those marks, the second team are lighted by the director of photography and his Gaffer. When the lighting has been set, the second team will be dismissed and the first team called back onto the set.

When the first team comes back onto the set, as experienced actors, they will move to the marks they have been assigned during the rehearsal (and these will have sometimes been adjusted and changed in the lighting of the scene) and there the director of photography will be able to check them once again. When he has checked the lighting of the scene, with his Gaffer and Best Boy, and it is to his satisfaction, he will announce that he is ready to shoot the scene.

In this particular period of time, since the lighting has been achieved with the insertion of the second team into the set, and then, finally refined by the first team taking their positions, the first team, the principals in the scene, should check out the sources of light, the particular problems involved, if any, and so be equipped, in the playing of the scene, to take the greatest advantage of the pattern of lighting that the director of photography has created for them in the scene. This period is the final rehearsal period before a take and the earnest professional actor will take full advantage of this particular period of time in which to make those final adjustments to the technical demands that the medium is now going to make upon him when the take is attempted.

FLAG: *An opaque, rectangular piece of three-ply, or other material of varying lengths and widths, used by the electrical crew and placed between a light source and the set itself to create a certain lighting effect, either by eliminating the light source from certain sections of the set, or the performer's figure and face, or by directing the remnant of the light which can pass around that flag onto a certain portion of the set, or onto the performer himself.*

A flag is one of the many pieces of equipment which are used by the electrical crew to create certain effects in the lighting pattern, as desired by the director of photography, and as created for him by his Gaffer and Best Boy.

FOLLOW FOCUS: *The continuous change in the focusing of the lens of the camera, which is brought about by the relative movements between the camera and the actor, moving in his performance of the scene; necessary when the distance the actor is from the lens is greater than can be accommodated by the depth of field afforded by the lens of the camera.*

The following of focus is the function of the first assistant cameraman, who is number three man on the camera crew, ranking behind the director of photography and the operator. The technicalities of following focus, of which the first assistant cameraman must have a fine and specific knowledge, is not the concern of the actor. The concern of the actor, when he is marked or taped in his various positions by this first assistant cameraman, who is responsible for the focus, is that he should ascertain the limitations in which he can work, or give some indication to the first assistant cameraman of any variations that he is likely to make in the performance of the scene, so that the assistant cameraman can adjust the focus of the camera to accommodate those movements of the actor. In other words, the actor is not a singular person working on the set; he is a person who must be in constant contact with the members of the crew, in order that the technical problems that they have to solve will be understood by him. He must endeavor in the performance of his part to work with them in a way which will obtain the best possible results, shot after shot.

FRAME (LINES-IN-OUT): *A frame is an individual picture on a strip of film.*

Frame lines can be defined as those horizontal bands between frames of film, which divide one frame from another, on a strip of film. The term *in-frame* infers that the four frame lines encompass the action and the performers. In the same way, the term *out-of-frame* infers that the action of the scene, or that of an individual performer, has moved out of the picture seen by the lens of the camera, or *framed* by it.

It is important in every shot that the actor ascertains the limitations of the frame, as dictated by the lens of the camera which is being used for that particular shot. He should, in every instance, ask the operator the limitations of the frame, i.e., the exact line of the top, the bottom, and both sides of the frame of the shot. In that way, the actor will have no doubts about the area in which he must perform, whether it is a wide area, as in a long shot, or a confined area, as in an extreme close-up.

In these variances of framing, the actor, in a long shot, will have a great deal more liberty of movement not only in the space that he can occupy, physically, in the shot, but in the energy of the movements which he may make at that distance removed from the camera. When confronted with an extreme close-up where the framing may only encompass from above his eyebrows to the bottom of his chin, and on the sides, from just either side of where his ears are, the actor necessarily is confined within a closer frame, and the camera being that much closer to the actor, and subsequently a much larger image being projected on the motion picture or television screen, his acting can be modified, compounded, refined, since it becomes a more personal image than when he is performing in a looser, wider, long shot. The actor, by observing his image on the screen in the various films or TV segments, in which he has performed, can gauge the impact of his image in various kinds of shots. Mentally and physically, he will then be able to control his performance during the playing of any part, so that he fills out the space he occupies, whether it is a long shot or a close shot, to the fullest extent, and with the greatest exercise of artistic discretion.

FRAMING: *The act of adjusting the gate mechanism of the camera to bring the film running through the camera into frame.*

There is a secondary definition of framing, which is: the setting up of a camera in such a way that the image framed by its lens is precisely that required by the director for the shot which he has in mind. The director of photography will always select the lens which he feels can obtain the best results in each particular instance.

The technical aspects of framing are, in the main, the concern of the technicians operating the camera and the director of photography. The actor must only concern himself with the *limitations of the framing* which are placed upon him as regards his movements in the shot which is to be taken.

FROM THE TOP: *This directive to an actor means to begin again from the beginning of a speech or the scene which is being rehearsed or shot.*

Often, a director will request his actors to take the scene from the top, i.e., to start from the beginning of the scene and rehearse it or begin acting it in an actual take. If the whole of the scene does not go to his particular satisfaction, he might request another take, and, once again request the actors to start the scene *from the top.* If, during the course of the scene, there is something wrong with it, and he doesn't wish to shoot the whole of the scene, he may ask for another take of the portion that was not to his satisfaction. This is called a *pick-up.* If, in the breaking up of the scene, the actor is then photographed at close quarters, and in the course of the close-up, bobbles a particular speech, the director might instruct him to go from the top of that particular speech which he bobbled, or to begin the scene again from the beginning, or *from the top.*

GAFFER: *The head of the electrical crew or the chief electrician, who is responsible, under the direction of the first cameraman, or the director of photography, for the lighting of the sets.*

The Gaffer is the man responsible for the artistic placement of lights in a set. He will issue his instructions, as to where those lights are to be placed and aimed, to the Best Boy, who will then instruct the various lamp operators on a soundstage, or lamp operators or others of the electrical crew who handle reflectors out-of-doors, and see that the wishes of the Gaffer are carried out. The Gaffer, in his turn, is working in conjunction with the Director of Photography, and it is these two men who ultimately decide the exact placement, the ratios, the quality of the light which will be used in the set itself. The arrangement of the lights, and the balancing of their power as to the amount of

candle power that is being poured into a set, and the subsequent
calculations that the director of photography must make to gain
the correct exposure for the film which he is using in his camera,
are matters which do not necessarily concern the actor. Each
Director of Photography, along with his Gaffer, have different
ideas on how a set should be lit, on what the balance of key light
to other lights should be. It is simply up to the actor to observe
the lighting at the various spots where he is to perform in the
scene, and to take full advantage of the effect that has been created for him. If he thoroughly observes what the lighting pattern is, and uses it to the very best advantage, he will find that
he has earned the approbation of both the Director of Photography and the Gaffer. These men will always strive to do their
best, not only from their own point of view, but—once aware that
the actor himself understands what they are striving to do, and
has done his best to take advantage of it—*for the actor.*

GEAR BOX: *The gear box is the motor which drives the mechanism
of a camera, and is located on the right side of the camera.*

It is enclosed in the outer casing of the camera itself in all
self-blimped cameras. Often, an actor will be directed to take
a look, during a scene, in the direction of the gear box. The actor
who is off-scene may be placed either in front of it, if it is possible, along side it, or behind it. When instructed to look at the
gear box, the actor should know where it is, and so be able to
direct his look at it without hesitation. This is a simple directive
which should be immediately understood and acted upon by the
actor.

GET INSIDE IT: *To play the part with more understanding and
with more believability.*

Often, in the course of the rehearsal, an actor, for a number
of reasons—lack of understanding of the part, lack of preparation, that natural nervousness some actors have during a rehearsal
period, which does not enable them to perform as they would
wish or had prepared to—sometimes inhibits his performance in
such a way that the playing of the part is definitely not to the
satisfaction of the director. In such an instance, the director
might suggest to the actor that he try to *get inside it* more, and
so take on more of the characteristics of the part which he is
playing. The actor will then have to work more vigorously at

what he is doing. He will have to stimulate his imagination, discover other things that he can do with the character, settle himself into it, pull the character around him so that it is covering his actual self, and only revealing the character to the director, and subsequently, the audience. When a director instructs or suggests that an actor should *get inside it* a little more, he definitely wants the actor to disappear into the part, to become the character, to think from inside-out, rather than from outside-in. This will often necessitate the actor running over in his mind all the many things he can do, or has planned to do with the part; he may have to take a short walk around the soundstage, mentally, at least, and, taking another deep artistic breath, plunge once more into the playing of the character, try to present it in such a way that his own personality is lost in that of the character itself. This must be done quickly, under most circumstances. The actor should select some salient facets of the character that he wishes to emphasize, and so work from there until he has pulled all the pieces of the part together, and is thoroughly *inside* the character, as requested by the director.

"GIVE HIM A HAIRCUT!": *A direction given by the director of photography to his operator when he wants to obtain the biggest impact possible of the image on the screen, and especially when he doesn't want any clearance in his composition above the performer's head.* (See: Crop)

GOBO: *A wooden screen, usually made of three-ply, or a similar rectangular construction of stout steel wire, covered with a black, opaque, cloth material, which is so placed, supported by a century stand, or similar piece of equipment, that it screens the light from one or more studio lamps, thus preventing it from shining on the lens of the camera.*

There are some gobos, and they come in many sizes, which are permanent fixtures placed upon footstands or rollers so that they can be pushed into place. Otherwise, gobos are attached to a series of adjustable stands, and can be placed at varying angles, and at various heights, according to the demands of the lighting of the set. *Gobo* is a general term, and these particular pieces of equipment are sometimes also referred to as flags, targets, or scrims, although a scrim, in the general usage of the word, is an area of gauze stretched in a wire frame, and so placed between either the sun, or a light, and the performer, so that the light source is diffused.

GRIP: *The person who, on the studio set or on location, has charge of minor adjustments and repairs to properties, to camera tracks, and the like.*

A Grip will also be in charge of manipulating a crab dolly, and the arm of the larger camera boom, such as the Chapman boom. The Grip is generally considered to be the "muscle" of any film set.

HANG IN THERE: *In general, this directive means that the performer should keep up his energy in the scene, that he should hold on to the emotions, the pace of the scene, that he should not let go in any way, that he should maintain his control of what he is doing in the particular scene he is playing.*

There is an additional meaning to this term: that the actor should give even more energy and vitality to what he is doing. It is an expression used when an actor is working in a highly emotional scene, and the actor is instructed by the director to "hang in there," i.e., to keep playing the scene at full pitch, to keep emotions high, to run right through the scene without any slackening of energy in his playing.

HANG IT ON!: *To perform or act to the fullest extent of one's capacity.*

This is somewhat a similar term to *hang in there.* The expression is also often applied when horsebacking in a scene. If riders are coming into a scene fullpelt at the gallop, it is often referred to as *hanging it on.* When an actor is performing this particular piece of action, he may be with a number of stunt boys who will say to him, "All right, fella, now let's *hang it on!*" which means that they want to gallop right into that scene as fast as the horses can run, and either pull them up or dash through the scene, whatever the action demands.

HAIRDRESSER: *A woman who is engaged to style the hair of both the male and the female players; to adjust, block, fit, and keep in order, during the course of the day, various wigs that actors may use in the film.*

Actresses employed in a film will find that their call is usually a good deal earlier than the other performers for that day, if their hair has to be dressed at the studio. There are some actresses who prefer to do this themselves, at home, and come to the studio with their hair in rollers, later to have it combed out and set by the hairdresser, but the custom is as a general rule, that the actress will come to the studio, have her hair shampooed, set, and dried by the hairdresser, and then proceed into the makeup department to be made up by a makeup man.

It is sometimes necessary for men's hair to be dressed, curled, or otherwise styled, and this is also the function of the lady hairdresser. In the instance where a man might have a toupee applied, he will, on some occasions, do that himself, or allow his makeup man to do it for him. However, it is usual, in the wearing of wigs by an actor or an actress, to have these wigs cared for by the hairdresser, who will place them on a block and stretch them back to the shape of the performer's head after each day's use, cleaning them and resetting them, so that they are in perfect order.

HIGH HAT: *A small aluminum tripod of fixed height, which can be attached to the floor of a soundstage, or to any place where it is desired to set the camera as low on its mountings as possible.*

A high hat, attached to a small, square piece of five-ply, is often used out-of-doors to place the camera as low to the ground as possible. A similar mounting for a camera might be inserted down into a hole dug in the ground, in order to have vehicles, trains, livestock, etcetera, pass overhead.

HONEY-WAGON: *A large, mobile trailer containing several dressing rooms, usually with individual toilet facilities for the performers who occupy them, and with other toilet facilities, on both sides, for the members of the production crew.*

These dressing room-trailers are very well fitted out for the comfort of the actors, and are maintained by the person in charge of them so that they are always scrupulously clean, and warmed or cooled, according to the time of year. Of course, under other circumstances, where it is not possible to bring in this type of equipment to a certain location, the actor will have to make do with other facilities which may not be quite so luxurious. However, every effort is made by most production units to see that these facilities are available for the performers, and for the crew, according to the dictates set forth in the contract which the Screen Actors' Guild, and other Locals have negotiated over the years for the protection and personal welfare of their members.

IN DEPTH (WORK IN): *To move on a line directly away from the camera.*

For instance, you may shift out of a fifty-fifty shot—a shot where two actors virtually face each other in a line horizontal to the camera itself at some distance removed—and then move upstage, or away from the camera, but still observing the line extending back to the camera, which would, in essence, clear the upstage actor of the performer who has remained downstage.

There is a secondary definition of *in depth,* and this is a term which the director may use to instruct the actor to *work more in depth,* as regards the character he is playing. It is similar to suggesting that the actor *get inside his character* more, that he extend his imagination to bring additional facets of the character to the surface, and display them in the scene.

INKY-DINK: *The popular term for a miniature, incandescent lamp, which is sometimes placed on a stand in front of a stationary camera, and so set as to shine in the actor's eyes, the front of the lamp itself often being covered with a small gelatin.*

INTERCUT: *The action of an editor in making an assembly of shots, or of placing one or more shots into the strip of film which contains the master shot.*

Another secondary definition of intercut would be when the editor inserts a piece of film into another, for the purpose of emphasizing a certain piece of action, and therefore, the use of the term then means to intercut from one particular piece of action to the other, as directed by the producer and the director of the film, while viewing the rushes, or assembled footage, in a projection room.

INTERIORS: *Those sets erected within a soundstage.*

A Western street set, which is, strictly speaking, an *exterior,* when it is built within a soundstage is sometimes referred to as the *interior* set, but in cinematic terminology, an *interior* refers specifically to a bedroom, a kitchen, a living room, a foyer, a corridor, and such like sets, all of which have been erected within a soundstage to be used during the course of the film. There is another kind of *interior*, which is an actual interior, i.e., when the film is being shot in the interior of an actual, standing house, hotel, motel, auditorium, etc.

In all screen plays, you will see the abbreviations *Ext.* and *Int.* Naturally, these two terms refer to *Exterior* and *Interior*. On each shot, too, the time of day will be noted—dawn, morning, late afternoon, dusk, etc.—and this is a guide, when reading the script, to the technicians concerned to prepare for the lighting of such a scene.

INTERVIEW: *When a performer is called to a studio and with the casting director, producer, and/or director, discusses the possibility of his playing a certain part in a film.*

It is not always the case that, when an actor goes for an interview, he will have to read for the people concerned. An interview often serves the purpose of introducing a young performer to his prospective employers, or of refreshing their memories of an established performer. Sometimes, people interviewing merely want to refresh their memories of the actor's personality, and see, in some instances, both with women and with men, how they have stood the passing of the years.

An interview is mostly conducted in a rather casual, informal manner, on a perfectly friendly basis, whether the interviewee is known or not, to those interviewing him or her. The young performer should endeavor, on these occasions, to be his own natural self. Most casting in Hollywood is done according to the type of person, and how he or she looks.

There have been agents who will advise their clients, to *dress for the part.* This can pay off in certain circumstances, but, as a general rule, I do not advise this, because it seems to make the person concerned more of a singular type, or even an eccentric, rather than a professional actor. I always prefer to go to the studio in the clothes that I would wear in the course of the day, in any case, and I advise all young professionals to go to an interview as they themselves would dress under normal circumstances, and to present themselves in their natural aspects. I believe that it is better for the young performer to be recognized for his own natural characteristics, rather than to dress for par-

ticular parts, on a singular occasion, in a specific manner. Under
the latter circumstances, the various people interviewing the performer really are unable to decide what his *true* personality is,
as opposed to the various characterizations which he might be
able to attempt.

In the matter of interviews, I do believe that a certain
conservatism is required of the actor; if the persons concerned
believe that he can play the part, they will be able to discern
that by talking to him in person, rather than seeing him as some
startling individual who presents himself in the form of a beatnik,
surfer, a cowboy, an Indian, or suchlike character. The young
performer should be recognized as an individual who is capable
of either playing himself, or various other characters that could
emanate out of his own particular professional acting ability, and
not just as one singular character, despite the fact that, at that
particular moment, that *"character"* might possibly get him the
job. It is the long-term view of this profession, and the establish-
ment, of a certain personality, professionally, that is most important to the young performer.

K.D.'s: *Small, canvas-walled dressing rooms which are erected
either within a soundstage or on location, sometimes with a ceil-
ing, and sometimes without, in which performers can dress during the day's work.*

There are rare circumstances these days where such dressing
rooms, known as canvas dressing rooms, and foreshortened to
K.D.'s, are allocated to principal or supporting players. Usually,
these players are supplied with mobile dressing rooms, either
for themselves personally or in the aforementioned honey-wagons.
However, K.D.'s are still used at times on location to provide a
form of dressing room for the extras or atmosphere players.

KEYLIGHT: *The main light used for the illumination of a subject,
usually the actor, in the scene to be shot.*

Out-of-doors, the primary light is the illumination afforded by
the sun, and indoors, a major light, an arc or a senior, takes the
place of the sun and becomes the actor's keylight. In a group
scene, there might be a number of keylights, according to the
amount of actors in the scene. In a two-shot there are generally
two keylights which will strike upon the actors concerned. In
a close-up the keylight is singular to the actor concerned in the
scene.

LENS: *A basic photographic lens consists of a piece, or series of pieces, which are called elements. These are of a transparent substance, bounded by two curved surfaces, usually spherical, or consisting of, on the other hand, a curved surface and a plain. On a motion picture camera, converging lenses are used, which form real images of greater or lesser magnification.*

There are, essentially, two main categories of lenses: 1) *Long-focus lens*: these are lenses of a longer focal length than normal, and consequently, give a greater than normal magnification. Into this category would fall a telephoto lens; 2) *Short-focus lens*: these are lenses of shorter focal length than normal, and consequently, giving a lower than normal magnification, and a wider field of view. These lenses are often referred to as wide-angle lens.

The technical construction of the lens itself, and its manipulation by the members of the camera crew, is not important to the actor. However, he should discover, by discussion with the camera crew, just what the depth of field and focusing possibilities of each lens is. Having ascertained and set that in his mind, he can perform with a greater freedom within those limits.

LET ME HAVE 50 PER CENT (MORE, LESS): *A directive often given a performer by a director, in order to bring out a fuller performance, or to modify a performance that is too large for the screen.*

The percentage named by the director will give the actor some indication of how far he is falling short of a satisfactory performance, or how much larger than life he is performing, and so therefore has to change what he is doing in order to satisfy the director. It is a matter, then, for the performer to adjust quickly to this particular directive, and either fill out his part more satisfactorily, or to compound and modify it, so that, finally, his performance has the qualities the director is looking for.

LIFT IT: *Directive sometimes given by a director to an actor, when the scene in which the actor is playing is "flat."*

There will be times when a scene has been rehearsed (even sometimes rehearsed too much) and it is playing flatly. Somehow, the scene has lost its bounce, and in asking the performer to *lift it*, the director wants him to play the scene with a great deal more vitality, so that the original sparkle, the pace, the tempo, the overall brilliance of the scene, is regained and maintained and the scene finally ready to be photographed. To *lift the scene* is usually a simple adjustment for the actor to make, and simply requires a fresh and energetic approach to the playing of the scene, so that the flatness that has crept in, from perhaps over-rehearsal, is eradicated, and the scene is presented in a fresh and interesting manner.

LIGHTING (GENERAL): *The illumination of a scene or a set, which is to be photographed by a camera.*

It is the general concept of the Director of Photography, and his Gaffer, that the scene to be lit should be thought of as being totally dark, so that its appearance to the camera is created solely by the color and the disposition and the intensity of the various lights, which these two men arrange to fall upon the scene. It is by the arrangement of these sources of light and darkness, of the contrast in the intensity of the colors in the set itself, that the actual physical entity of the scene is created, and the mood for the particular scene in the film established. The performer should take a good look around the set when it is lit, and at the lighting which is to fall upon any particular scene in which he plays. He should endeavor to feel the atmosphere created by the lighting, and so help that atmosphere to *tune* his acting, until his performance matches into the total, overall effect that the lighting has created within the set itself.

There are a number of kinds of lighting which a performer will notice on any set:

1) *Backlighting*: this is lighting from behind the set, or behind the performer, and toward the camera. The actual light source itself is shielded, slanted, if necessary, so as not to shine into the lens in any way. This method of backlighting increases the lighting contrast up to the extreme condition of silhouette, i.e., no front light at all, on the set or on the performer.

2) *Crosslighting*: the kind of lighting that is intermediate in its direction and its effect between the front lighting and the backlighting. Crosslighting will serve to model the set and the performer, picking out particular features, so that they can be clearly seen on film.

3) *Eyelighting*: this is usually accomplished by a small light, an *inky-dink* or a *baby*, as they are called, directed into the performer's eyes to accentuate or highlight the expressions in them. The *inky-dink* has been discussed previously in this section.

4) *Frontlighting*: this is the main lighting of a set, directed onto it from behind and beside the camera itself, i.e., from the front of the set. From this position, is also stationed the keylight, which is the main light shining into the scene, and illuminating the performers within that set. The greater the proportion of frontlight, the flatter, in general, will the lighting be, i.e., much lower in lighting contrast.

5) *Highlighting*: this is a special source of illumination applied additionally to a small area to create a specific effect. It might be directed onto a performer's hair, it might be directed onto a position where his hands are functioning, so that they are illuminated in the correct balance, and can be photographed as a distinct point of a scene.

6) *Toplighting*: this is light which is thrown down from sources mounted above the subject, either from behind or in front of the set or the performer, and serves to increase the apparent intensity of an overhead lamp, or such kind of fixture.

LINING-UP: *The process by which a cameraman sets up his camera to cover the desired field of view in the upcoming shot.*

Lining-up is also that term applied to the adjustment of the monitor-viewfinder to correct for parallax, i.e., the adjustment of the viewfinder so that it will see the exact same framing as can be seen through the lens of the camera itself.

LOCATION: *Any place, other than the studio, or studio backlot, of a film producing organization or studio, where a film is being shot.*

The actor, when he goes on location, will find there are some necessary adjustments that he must make. Apart from an adjustment to different living quarters, if he should be staying on location for any length of time, he will find, in working out-of-doors, that not only will his style of acting necessarily change, but that even his attitude to playing will be a slightly different one.

The various conditions of weather are such that an actor working out-of-doors must take care that his voice remains in good shape. The conditions under which locations are sometimes shot involve extremes of heat and cold, dust and dampness, and these conditions will affect the actor. In rehearsing out-of-doors, he must be careful to protect his voice so that it remains in good shape for the *takes* themselves, particularly if he is involved in any scene of a high emotional range, or in one where he is required to lift his voice high above the normal level. Then, too, the conditions under which he must physically perform, the varying terrains which he will encounter out-of-doors, will require him to adapt easily to walking, moving, and/or riding over surfaces that are uneven, to say the least. The actor out-of-doors must learn also to conserve his strength and vitality. He will have to build, and subsequently draw upon, a greater store of energy than would be required of him in a normal day's shooting on the soundstage. The length of the day out-of-doors, and the physical demands that location often makes upon the actor, will tire him a great deal more than a normal day's shooting indoors, and it behooves him, after a day's work on location, to see that he gets to bed early, and does his preparation for the next day, rather than staying up until all hours of the night, as is sometimes the inclination when actors and crew are on location.

On particularly hot days, on location, in summer, and especially out on the desert, the actor would be wise, between shots, to rest up in the shade, and to conserve his energy. In extremely cold weather, he should keep himself warm and limber, so that, when called upon to work, he will be able to do so with ease. Acting out-of-doors usually requires a great deal more concentration on the part of the performer than when he is working in an interior set, and a slightly "bigger" style of acting that fits him into the space that he is occupying, which out-of-doors, of course, is a larger one.

If the actor has to handle livestock or horses he would be best advised, when he first arrives on location, to ascertain which horse has been allocated to him, and to see that his reins, his stirrups, and equipment on the horse is adjusted to his comfort. He should then take the horse and try it out, see how it performs, let the horse get used to him, and let himself get used to the horse. If there are any other forms of physical movement that he must do in the course of the day's work, he should find the time to investigate where these will be done, and, if possible, to pre-rehearse them, so that when he comes to do the shot, he will have an acquaintance with the problems involved. In other words, out-of-doors, the actor will find various areas in which he must make adjustments, and it is up to him to think ahead in these areas, because, working out-of-doors, there is only a certain amount of light during the day, and every moment of it must be taken advantage of. The actor who has prepared his work ahead will find that it will be easier on himself, and that the people concerned, from the producer on down, will appreciate an actor who has done this pre-preparation and thereby made everybody's work that much easier.

LOCK INTO IT: *An instruction given to the performer, by the director, when the director does not feel that the performer has absolute control over the scene, that the scene itself is loose or flat, and needs locking into to bring it together into a cohesive playing whole.*

A scene, when blocked out and rehearsed, will sometimes move along at a pace, or with a lack of vitality, which causes it to fall far short in its overall effect of what the director desires. It just may be that the actors are not *standing over* their material, and that all they need to do is to *lock into* the scene, and play it forthrightly, and, in so doing, bring the scene to life. It usually merely requires a deal more energy from the players in the scene, and a more direct application of their craft to the scene, which will then bring it up, and so give that necessary spark to the scene which will enable it to play satisfactorily when a take is attempted.

LOOP: 1) *A slack section of film which is allowed to protrude several inches from the magazine of the camera. In this way a certain play is provided when the film is being pulled from a continuously moving feed-reel by the take-up reel of the magazine itself, and then moved intermittently, through the means of a moving sprocket, through the gate of the camera;* 2) *A continous band of film which passes through a projector, and is consequently shown on a screen, or a film reproducer, such as a Movieola viewer, in this way repeating a piece of action, and/or sound, over and over again. Loops are used in this way as guide tracks for dubbing, or as a source of continuous sound effects in rerecording.*

You will see the purpose of the loop, in the first definition if you will observe the camera assistant threading a fresh magazine of film into the camera. The loop is necessary so that it can be fed through the mechanism of the camera itself, and this loop provides the necessary slack that can be drawn down by the moving sprocket mechanism of the camera, through the gate of the camera, so that the film is exposed. The second definition of loop will be obvious if you take a look in the projection room of a dubbing studio, whether it is a combination of image and sound, or purely a sound dubbing session, where only the sound itself comes to the actor, and he repeats the lines after each loop of sound. The projection room will be festooned with the clusters of loops, sorted out and ready to be run for each actor when he reports to a Dubbing Room at the appointed hour.

LOOPING: *A session in which a fresh voice track is recorded, so that it may be synchronised at a later date with the original picture image.* (See: *Dubbing*).

LOOSEN THE FRAME: *The action by which a player, or players, move in depth out of a shot which frames them tightly, into other positions whereby the framing of the shot becomes looser.*

With a performer in a tight close-up, or two performers in a tight-two, the frame can be loosened by either of the individual performers, by one performer and then the other, or by both performers, moving in depth, i.e., away from camera, in the scene, and taking up other positions in the midground, or even in the background of the set itself. In this way, the frame, in varying degrees, according to the amount of movement that the performers do in the scene, is *loosened*.

The director, in viewing the scene through the viewfinder or the lens, may decide that the framing is a little too tight, as far as he is concerned, and suggest either that the performers are placed further back from the camera, or that the camera itself is moved away from the performers; in both instances, the frame would be loosened. Primarily, the actor should be concerned only when he is instructed to loosen the frame, and in this particular regard, his movements to the specific spots which will be worked out and marked, for him, are his primary concern. In the playing of the scene, he must proceed to those designated marks, and assume them, so that the subsequent framing of the shot is to the director's satisfaction.

LOT: *General term for a motion picture studio, e.g., the MGM lot, the Warner's lot, the Twentieth Century-Fox lot. To be on the lot means to be working or visiting at the studio.*

LOOKS: *Those certain, specific spots toward which, when playing on camera, and addressing dialogue, or reactions off-camera, the performer will have to look, i.e., in varying degrees above the*

lens or to right or left of camera, or specifically to other perform-
ers, off-camera.

There will be times when a performer will be directed to look, (above or below):

1) Toward the *viewfinder*: the optical instrument attached to the left side of the camera, directly on a line with the lens. This viewfinder is used by the cameraman to monitor the shot when the film is actually running through the camera. The viewfinder is an easy point of reference for the actor to direct his attention to, and the performer off-camera will be standing, in many instances beside or directly behind the viewfinder, and can speak his off-camera lines to the performer on stage.

2) Toward the *gearbox*: the oval-shaped motor and gear housing on the camera right side of the camera.

3) *Camera left or camera right*: right and left of a camera can be determined quite simply by thinking of the camera as a person facing the performer, i.e., when you are on-stage and facing the camera, your left is camera right, and your right is camera left. According to the correct look required of the onstage performer, which has been decided upon by the Director and the camera operator, the other performer or performers will be placed off-stage, i.e., off-camera, at certain positions either at camera right or camera left, and at certain heights, whether seated or standing or on horseback, and it is important that the actor on-camera looks directly at the designated spots, or at the eyes, or some pertinent part of the performer off-camera, in order to give the illusion that he is looking at the correct spots for his off-camera looks.

If a performer is in such a position in a scene that he must be looking down for part of the scene and then look up to catch the eyes of another performer, or to attach his look to a certain designated spot, or to a then as-yet-unseen or unnoticed off-stage performer, then prior to the commencement of the scene, he must rehearse his particular look, so that his look will go directly to that spot, or to the eyes of the performer who is reading the off-camera dialogue to him. A wavering, uncertain look will register just that *on camera*, and *on film*. The performer must rehearse these looks before the scene commences, so that they have a fluidity and so that they *look real* when actually filmed.

MAKE-UP: *Those colors, or special pieces of rubberized material, or hair pieces, which are attached to a performer's face, hands, and body, in order to create the exterior aspects of his character.*

The everyday make-up for a performer in films is a simple matter, as far as actual application is concerned, but the specific colors to be used are dictated by the kind of film which will be used in the shooting of the actual film or TV segment. The make-up colors differ according to whether it is black-and-white or color film.

The make-up is applied to the performer by a make-up man, the performer never making himself up, as he does in the theatre. A performer, by watching these make-up men do their work, can gain a great knowledge of what is necessary for his own facial needs, whether in a straight part or in a character part, and can, with due discretion, advise the make-up man in the course of the many parts that he may play. However, it is for the make-up man to make a decision on what materials will be used, and since he is a specialist, he should be allowed to make-up the actor without undue comment or interference.

MAKE-UP MAN: *A technical expert who applies make-up, special pieces, and hair pieces, to the performer's face and body.*

Make-up men are specially trained by their Guild in their craft, and, in conjunction with the Director of Photography, decide what range of colors will be used on each performer. The kind of film being used in the shooting of the particular motion picture or television segment will dictate this choice.

Make-up for films is a specialized art, in that it creates a great deal more naturalness than in the theatre. Whereas theatre make-up often requires a heavy application of grease paint, the make-up for films is a much lighter, transparent coloration of the skin, and it is advisable that, once it has been applied, that the performer himself, does not, in any way, try to add to it. This applies to both men and women, because the make-up men themselves are especially trained to know the density of the make-up necessary, and any addition to this can spoil the effect when filmed.

It is important, throughout the day, for the performer to check his make-up to see that it is in good order, and if it is not, to report to the make-up man and ask him personally to make a correction, whether it is in the coloration or in the attachment of various pieces to his face, hands, etc. It is especially important

after a break for a meal, where make-up may have been dis-
lodged by that particular function, to report to the make-up man
immediately upon return to the set, and have him adjust, or
freshen up, the make-up of the performer. By so doing the performer is ready immediately to work on the set, secure in the fact
that his make-up is in the very best condition to be photographed.
The make-up man on the set will keep a constant check on each
performer's make-up during the course of the day, and will either
powder it down and keep it smoothed out, or add the necessary
tiny touches to it to freshen it. He may also have to apply a
certain combination of witch hazel, lanolin, etc., to simulate
perspiration on the performer's face, and this is his particular
job, and is best left to his discretion. If you feel, rightly so, that
your make-up is not in perfect condition, it is your responsibility
to call this to the attention of the make-up man, and have him
make the necessary adjustments for you. It is, by far, best to do
this in a break in shooting, or immediately after a meal break,
rather than to hold-up production, and have it done either while
a shot is being rehearsed or being taken.

MAKING NOISE ON LINES (BUSINESS): *So manipulating properties,
or otherwise making movements, that create noises which interfere with the perfect recording of the lines that the actor is speaking.*
   The use of certain properties, and the carrying-out of certain
movements in a scene, will most certainly create noise. It is important that the performer separate the noise created by this
use of properties, or the performance of movements, so that they
fit in between the lines that are spoken by himself and/or other
performers. In this way, each particular, actual sound of the use
of properties, or that of movements will remain separate from
the lines themselves, and in no way override or meld with them.
   This is a matter of timing by the actor. If, for instance, he has
to put down a cup and saucer on a table, both of which may
rattle, then this action must be completed during a pause in the
speaking of lines. Another instance may be where the actor has
to return a sword to a scabbard; he must so time his action that
the sword is returned to the scabbard when no lines of his own,
or of the other performer's, are being spoken. Similarly, with the
closing of a door, the performer must so time his action that the
closing of the door is a separate sound entity, isolated from the
lines spoken either by himself or by other performers. In this

way, if the extra sound itself, that of a cup and saucer rattling, of a sword going into a scabbard, of the door being closed, does not sound right, or is too loud or too soft, then in the rerecording of the soundtracks, in order to obtain the final soundtrack, these separate sounds can be placed in among the lines that the actor, or actors, have been speaking in the scene which has been filmed. Otherwise, if one sound overrides another, it is not possible to do this separately, and both soundtrack and sound effects track must be rerecorded separately, then placed in the whole film, a much more complicated process than that when the actual sound itself is recorded on the set, and the actor, by his skill, has kept all the sounds quite separate, and so enabled them to be recorded perfectly.

MARKS: *Chalk, tape, wooden T's etc., which are placed upon the floor of the soundstage, or on the location site, to indicate the positions that the performer must arrive at, in order to accommodate the camera framing and focus in those particular positions.*

MATCHING: *Repeating exactly the actions which a performer has made in a master in every necessary, subsequent shot filmed to complete a sequence.*

Because of the many angles which are taken of a scene, during the course of shooting a film, it is of paramount importance to *match* your actions in every angle that is taken of the scene in which you are performing. For example, if in the master shot, you light and smoke a cigarette, or pick up a cup of coffee, or tie your tie, at a specific point in the action, in every other shot following this one, in which that same piece of action is photographed again, from a different angle and with a different lens, the performer must duplicate his actions exactly and precisely at the same time as he did in the master, i.e., he must match his actions.

There must be no variations from this unless the director decides that a certain part of the master shot will not be used, and that other shots—two-shots, close shots, extreme close-ups—will be used instead of certain parts of the master. If such is the case, the actor will not need to match his actions in the subsequent shots and will have the freedom to perform these shots differently to the master. But remember, it is only after the director has decided that certain portions of the master shot will not be used, and has given the actors permission to play the subsequent shots in a different manner, that the actor may disregard the obligation of *matching* his actions.

MATTE: *A matte is a light modulator, which, in various ways, offers an obstruction to the passage of light on its way to form a photographic image. Matte is almost essentially a mask, in the fact that in its usage, it masks out certain areas, and only leaves a visual possibility of the recording of the remaining area.*

MATTE BOX: *A pyramidal, boxlike structure mounted in front of the camera lens, and designed to hold camera mattes, used in trick photography, as well as filters. It also contains a permanent bellows arrangement, and the matte box itself is usually combined with this permanent arrangement and with a sun or light shade, which is attached over it, in order to deflect the rays or light from the sun, or from a lamp, which might shine into the lens.*

The matte box, is, in itself, adjustable, and is able to be slid along on two runners at the bottom of its structure. Its application to the camera is taken care of by one of the camera assistants, and any lights that may be shining into it are checked out by the Gaffer, and Best Boy, and those lights corrected, so that they do not shine into the lens. The actor need not concern himself with this piece of equipment except when he may be directed in a shot, being situated close to the lens itself, to direct his look to a certain point within the matte box. The actor should request that a small chalk mark, a small circle or an "X," be placed upon the inside of the matte box, so that he can, without fail, direct his look to that spot.

MATTING DOWN: *The process of masking, or blocking out, part of the image, as in a monitor viewfinder, by the insertion of certain masks, each of which corresponds to the lens being used. This process of masking adjusts the view through the monitor-viewfinder to match that obtained by looking through the lenses of different lengths.*

The small viewfinders often used by directors, if they are manual, will be masked in a similar way by small insertion plates. If they are automatic viewfinders, these maskings are obtained within the mechanism of the automatic viewfinder itself, by the adjustment of the casing of the viewfinder, in the same way as the f-stops and focus footage are obtained on a camera lens mounting.

MICROPHONE(s): *A device whereby sound waves are made to produce substantially equivalent electric waves, thereby recording the various sounds on the set so that they may again be used in the final complete film.*

There are a number of types of microphones, and each one is used for a specific purpose. The technicalities of these microphones need not concern the actor, although a knowledge of their limitations can be very useful to him. The actor primarily must concern himself with giving the necessary volume to his voice, required of him by the Sound Mixer, so that a good recording of his voice can be made. The actor's voice, if it is too soft or too loud in volume, can be adjusted within a certain range, by the Sound Mixer himself, who will bring the voice up or tamp it down purely mechanically with his recording equipment, but if the actor allows his voice to drop below the recordable level, or, in certain circumstances, if the actor shouts above a reasonably recordable level, he will find that the Sound Mixer will ask him to adjust accordingly. Then again, during the various movements that will be made in a scene, there will be times when the actor, facing away from a microphone, will have to *pitch* his voice a little louder, so that some record of his voice can be obtained at that particular moment, when the microphone cannot be placed to advantage on the set. The performer will find, upon examination of the movement pattern which he has to make, and after observing the positions in which the microphone can be placed during the course of the scene, that he himself may have to make various adjustments in his positioning, in order that his voice will be recorded properly. These are matters for the director, the performer, and the Sound Mixer, and his Mike Man, to work out, and there is seldom any difficulty in solving these problems once you are on the set. An actor should not be adamant to the *extreme* following a request of him to *project* his voice. There are certain limits, artistically of course, but beyond those reasonable limits, he is creating a problem for himself. If his voice cannot be recorded properly, part of his performance will suffer thereby. He should endeavor, in every way, to take advice from the director, and from the Sound Mixer, and so insure that the whole of his performance is as perfect as possible.

MIKE MAN: *A familiar term for that technician who controls the physical movement of the microphone(s), in the studio or on location, either by means of a boom or a fishpole.*

The function of the Mike Man has been touched upon before in this Terminology, and the actor should only concern himself with the problems facing this technician to the extent that the actor can, by positioning himself properly in the scene, facilitate the solving of these problems for the Mike Man. The simplest way out of any sound problem, for both the Mike Man and the actor, is for those people to combine their efforts to solve the problem, rather than one or the other insisting upon it being done in a certain way. Usually, it is the Mike Man who will do everything possible to solve the problem for his crew, and it is up to the actor to realise that he must adapt his performance at times to take care of the exigencies of certain unusual situations.

MIKE SHADOW: *A shadow which may be cast by a microphone onto a performer, or some object or the set, in the field of view of the camera.*

Microphone shadows must be eliminated before shooting a scene by altering the position of the microphone, the placement of the camera, or the lights shining into the scene. This is usually a simple adjustment, which is the concern of the crew members involved in these operations.

MIXER: *The senior member of a Sound Recording crew, who is in charge of the balance and the control of all sound, which is to be recorded on a set.*

The Sound Mixer controls both the microphone placements and the sound recording equipment from his console, and also is the one responsible for quieting the set with buzzer and bell, and for starting the mechanism of the camera, and the sound recording equipment, so that, ultimately, both machines are brought up to synchronized speed, and the filming of the scene can commence.

MONEY IN THE BANK: *A slang term generally denoting a large close-up of the star, or stars, of the film.*

This term is not greatly in usage today, but will sometimes be heard in referring to that kind of shot which, when projected on the screen, will ensure a great impact on the audience for the male or female star involved, and so therefore, be an important shot in the film itself.

MONTAGE: *A type of cutting method using numerous dissolves and superimpositions of a number of images, which are allowed to follow one another rapidly in a strip of film, in order to produce a generalized or a specific visual effect.*

This form of cutting is used in various types of films. It has been used extensively in newsreel editing, and in documentary features. It has been used, quite often, too, in motion picture features, and, as a general rule, is used to illustrate the passage of time, or to show a series of events in rapid, compounded, and condensed order, or to create a certain mood in the film itself. Montage can also be used to demonstrate the inner thoughts and feelings, or the reactions, of various of the characters in the film, according to the styles and desires of the director of the film. Today, montage is not used as often as it used to be in either silent films or early sound films, but is still, if correctly used, an effective way of achieving the above mentioned results.

M.O.S.: *This is the accepted abbreviation for without sound.*

The *M.O.S.* term is said to have evolved in this way: in the early days of Hollywood, a certain film director, of supposedly German extraction, always pronounced *without sound* as *mitout sound*. Whether it is true or not, the generally accepted way of indicating (on a slate or in recording such an instruction in the notes of a script) a scene that is shot without sound is: *M.O.S.*

MOVIEOLA: *The trade name of one kind of portable, motor-driven film-viewing machine, used primarily in viewing film which is to be cut together and the subsequently assembled footage. The name itself, Movieola, is often applied, generally, to any such machine, regardless of what its trade name is.*

MULTIPLE CAMERA: *The use of more than one camera in shooting a scene, all cameras involved rolling simultaneously.*

Quite often more than one camera is used to cover action scenes. This has long been an accepted way of shooting, so that a stunt or a particular piece of unusual action can be covered from a number of angles by various cameras—BNC-Mitchells, NC-Mitchells, Arriflexes—all of which can be set on a tripod, or hand-held, in the case of Arriflexes.

There are other uses of multiple camera, however, in the film business today, which you should also know about. Please refer to the diagrams: Figures A, B, C, and D.

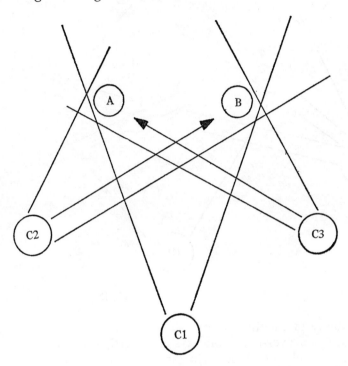

Fig. A

Generally speaking, in live television, from its inception, the use of three cameras or more for drama and comedy shows was the rule of thumb. The use of three cameras running film instead of tape became the accepted practice for filming many of the half-hour comedy shows. The primary object was to achieve spontaneity of performance and this method of shooting certainly provided the ideal conditions for this. Let us first look at Figure A. You will see, in Figure A, that the set-up is for a two-shot, and that I have illustrated the use of three live-TV cameras: camera C1 takes a full-on view of the two players, A and B. At the same time, while camera C1 is viewing A and B and throwing its particular image on the monitor screen, camera C2 and camera C3 have wheeled into position, and each has either the

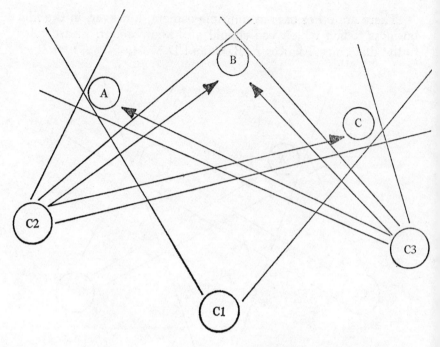

Fig. B

possibility of shooting an over-the-shoulder shot or a single. C2, shooting an over-the-shoulder shot of AB, favoring B, and also able, by a change of lens, to give the director a close-up of B. C3, shooting an over-the-shoulder BA, favoring A, and at the same time, by changing lens, able to get a close-up of A in the scene.

In the filming of certain shows in Hollywood—primarily, filmed comedy shows—at least three cameras are used to cover the action. These cameras are synchronized, are all rolling film, *not tape*, and only one sound track is recorded for use on any one piece of film used from any one of the cameras, and subsequently cut together to make the final, complete scene. You will see this clearly illustrated in Figure B, with three players, A, B and C. Each one of the three cameras, C1, C2, and C3, can be mobile. They can be on a crane or a crab dolly. However, usually, the main camera, C1, will be the mobile camera, and the other two cameras, C2 and C3, will be in a position to pick-up the shots required of them. Camera C1 will have a general view of the scene and be able to cover it according to the demands of the director, fully seeing players A, B, C in the scene. Camera C2 can also achieve, from certain positions, a three-shot, slightly raked, of A,B, and C. It can also achieve an over-the-shoulder of A and B, favoring B, or obtain close-ups of B and C. Similarly, camera C3 can obtain a three-shot of C, B, A, raking across this particular scene. It can obtain an over-the-shoulder of C and B, favoring B, or it can obtain close-ups of B and/or of A. This is a general, typical set-up for the filming of a comedy show, pre-rehearsed and then shot in scenes, successively, in front of a live audience, their laugh track being recorded simultaneously and not added later from a *can*.

In Figures C and D, you will see examples of the use of multiple cameras in the filming of motion pictures or TV segments. Two cameras, *sometimes more,* are often used today to cover a dialogue scene. First, let us look at Figure C. You will see that there are two players concerned, A and B. A makes an

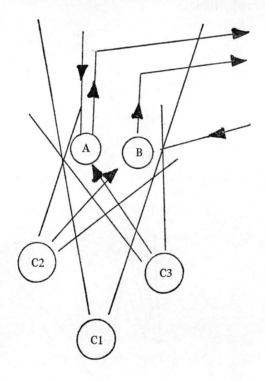

Fig. C

entrance into the scene, B joins him from camera right, and they both exit upstage, camera right. Camera C1 can cover the entrance of A and the later entrance into the scene of B, holding the two of them in either a fifty-fifty or a two-shot, covering the scene until they exit. At the same time, camera C2 will be obtaining a close-up of player B, and camera C3 could, if used, obtain a close-up of player A.

Figure D illustrates a more multiple set-up, player-wise, because we have players, U, V, W, X, Y, and Z. You will see from the position of camera C1 that it can obtain a loose rake shot of U, V, and W. Camera C2 is focused on W and can obtain a close-up of that player in his W1 and W3 positions, throughout the whole of the scene. Players X, Y, and Z are out of the scene, but may have to contribute dialogue to the scene, and so therefore, are placed strategically out of camera view at camera left so that the players U, V, and W, on camera, can turn and play to them or direct looks to them.

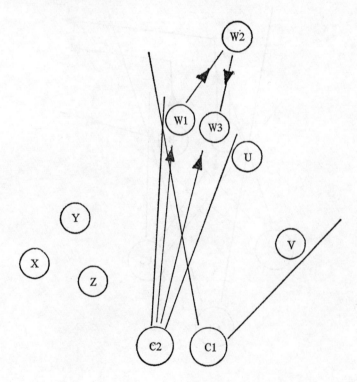

Fig. D

You may ask: "Which of the two cameras should player W concentrate on in Figure D?" Here, the situation arises that two cameras are covering him, C1 in a loose three-shot, and C2 in a single. From personal experience in just this kind of a multiple camera set-up, I have found that it is best to play the part fully, subtly compounding reactions so that they readily register for the close-up camera, C-2, and yet while moving from W-1 to W-2 and then back to W-3, filling out the scene in the way that would be normal for camera C-1. The player cannot divide his attention and play alternately to one or the other camera; he must simply play the scene as it stands.

Referring again to Figure C, where both A and B, or A, or B, is covered by a close-up camera(s), C-2 (C-3), the actor, in playing this particular scene, must realize that the camera at C-1 covers the entrance of A and B into the scene and their exit, and that once this has been obtained on C-1, although the scene itself will play right through, the shots obtained by cameras C-2 and C-3, whether they are over-the-shoulders or singles, will be used to *cut into* the master obtained by C-1. Similarly, in Figure D, the close-up obtained by camera C-2 will be cut into the film obtained by camera C-1, and complemented by other shots on U, V, X, Y, and Z, in various combinations, either in two's, in three's, or in singles. Therefore, the player concerned with a two-camera set-up should primarily concern himself with playing the scene quite fully, letting the cameras take care of the recording of the scene.

It has often been contended, and I have stated it in this book, that the larger the image on the screen, the more the actor can compound his performance, and make it less broad, but in this particular situation, with multiple cameras working, it is most necessary that the actor simply play the scene as it has been written to play, knowing always that the camera set-ups will take care of the image that the director requires of the scene. The player must not fall between the two stools of being concerned that in one shot he is looser in the frame, and in another, very tight in the frame. He must only concern himself with playing the scene.

NAIL (ACTOR): *A director may sometimes ask a performer to nail a particular part of a scene, whether it is a speech, or a movement, or a gesture. In other words, "imitating" the actual action of driving a nail into a piece of wood, the actor, in saying the speech, making the gesture, completing the movement, should be decisive, even aggressive, and so make a point at that particular juncture in the scene.*

NAIL DOWN (ACTOR-SCENE-CAMERA): *To make sure that there is absolute control over the actor, on his mark; the scene itself, as it is played; or the position of the camera.*

When it is requested that an actor be *nailed down,* it means that his position is final and definite, and a point of critical focus. Some obstruction may be placed in front of him, a desk, a piece of equipment, a sandbag on the floor, some form of specific mark, to which he must definitely adhere, and accurately take his position at during the course of the scene.

If a director should ask an actor to *nail down* a scene, it means that the actor should play his material so definitely that there is no mistaking his intention in the scene itself. If the Director of Photography requests that a camera be nailed down, it means that the camera itself must be rendered immovable. If the camera itself is on a crab dolly, it can be placed in position by using a plunger which acts as a brake. The dolly cannot be moved without lifting that plunger. The same thing would apply to the larger camera cranes and booms. Such a piece of equipment would be set into position, chocks put under the wheels, and the driving mechanism of the vehicle itself turned off. If the camera is mounted on a tripod, similarly, *nail it down* is a general term for saying the camera must be placed exactly on that spot and not moved under any circumstances, once the Director of Photography has ascertained the correct and accurate set-up for the shot in question.

N.D.: *Abbreviation for nondescript.*

This term is usually applied to horses used generally in a film. Special horses are used for the main characters in a particular film. These might be horses of outstanding color, or configurations of color, such as an Arab, a palomino, a paint pony, an Appaloosa, etc. All horses required, on the day's shooting will be listed on the back of your call sheet, specifically under the heading of *livestock.*

N.G.: *This is an abbreviation for no good.*

If a particular take does not turn out well, the script girl, or boy, will mark opposite that take: N.G., and after that, the reason for it, *camera movement, actor fault,* or whatever it happens to be. All of this is noted so that the producer and the production staff can see the reason why a certain number of takes were necessary for any one scene. Needless to say, it is best for the actor to make as few mistakes as possible, and so avoid the marking down of *N.G. (actor)* at the end of any take which is not successful.

ON A BELL or ON A LIGHT: *Red warning lights, or bells, or buzzers, turned on both within and without the soundstage, or location site, to insure complete quiet during rehearsals or actual shooting.*

ON CALL: *An actor engaged on a film, although not specifically given a start time for the next day, will be considered on call if there is a possibility of his being used at all in that day's shooting.*
It is the duty of the actor to remain at his place of abode, so that he can be readily called by the assistant from the set, if he has been told that there is a possibility of him being needed on that particular day. Sometime during the course of the day, he may be able to obtain an assurance from the assistant director that he will definitely not be called that particular day, and he may then consider himself *off call.*

ON THE NOSE: *An act, a specific performance in a scene, the day's work itself which is completed to the full satisfaction of everyone concerned.*
When an actor's performance is judged to be perfect, it could be termed to be *on the nose.* In other words, he has fulfilled all the requirements that the director has asked of him in the scene, and performed to the ultimate of the director's satisfaction. If a day's work or the complete film is finished on schedule, then it could be referred to as having been completed *right on the nose.*

OPEN UP SHOT: *A director asking the performers to face more towards camera, their original positions in the setting-up of the shot having been a fifty-fifty shot, i.e., each performer facing the other on a line horizontal to the camera.*
There are, of course, as can be seen by watching films and TV shows, any number of variations of this particular shot. These variations will be decided upon by the Director, the Director of Photography, and the performers themselves, who, when assuming this particular position following a master shot, can exercise

their artistic discretion, and enable infinite variations of the basic
shot to be set-up for the very best results in the scene itself.

OUTTAKES-TRIMS: *Rejected shots, or takes of a single shot, which
do not find a place in the completed version of the film.*
    I am sure that most performers have heard the term *the face
on the cutting room floor.* This is a colloquialism for outtakes or
trims. Of no concern to the actor, technically, since it is the
producer, director, and/or editor, who will make the decision
on the acceptance or rejection of these particular shots, it is,
however, very important to the performer, in the course of his
work, that he learns to protect himself in the making of all shots.
If he has not matched to the master in the subsequent shots, he
will find that some of his best work, in the closer shots, cannot
be used if the actions that he has committed in them do not
match with that of the master shot. Therefore, the actor must
be careful that he observes this principal of matching, unless it
is otherwise decided by the director, because he will find that
many of his best shots, those shots which can show him off the
biggest and the best, on the screen, will not be used—and he will
surely become *the face on the cutting room floor.*

OVERLAP: *The directive, do not overlap, given by a director, or by
a Sound Mixer, to a performer, means not to speak, or in any way
vocalize during the utterance of another performer's dialogue.*
    Sometimes, in a scene where a group of players are concerned,
and the director is not seeking special coverage during that portion of the scene, an overlap of dialogue may work very naturally
and well, but it is best not to overlap on any occasion during the
performing of a scene, because if coverage has to be secured on
that particular section, it is not possible to use any of that footage. *Not to overlap* is *most important in close-ups.* When one
performer is onstage, and the other performer, or performers,
are off-camera, and they are playing a scene, it is important that
neither the on-camera performer, nor the off-camera performers,
overlap any parts of their lines. It is imperative that a clean
sound track is obtained of the performer on-camera. This is one
of the most important parts of acting for the screen, and must
be observed and obeyed explicitly *at all times.* There is a way
of insuring that, irrespective of your position in the scene, either
on-camera or off-camera, that you will not overlap at any time.
If you are on-camera, and you are waiting for a line off-stage,

and it is delivered to you, let the line finish completely by taking a beat after the completion of the line, before you commence speaking your line. Keep your attention wherever it needs to be placed, take the beat, and then go freshly and cleanly into the line that concerns you at that moment. Similarly, when you are off-camera, be sure that the performer on-camera has completely finished his dialogue, give yourself a beat, and then say what you have to. In this way, the two voices will be kept separate on the sound track, the one on-camera being the most important one for later it can be inserted cleanly into the body of the film, without any problem during editing.

PAN—PANNING: *The movement of a camera in a horizontal plane in order to reveal a set or as it continues to frame a performer(s) moving left to right, or right to left, across a set.*
 When a performer moves from one position, across the set, to another position, and a camera stays framed on him, the movement of the camera is called *panning.* The geared head of the camera itself makes it possible for the camera to follow the actor easily, but, once again, there are limitations on the speed with which the actor may move, and in these particular instances, it is best that he control his movements with consideration for the Camera Operator, so that both of them can "be together." Then, too, it is important for the actor to make a decision on the exact moment that he is going to move, and keep to it. If, in some way, he can indicate, by a preparatory movement to the Camera Operator, his ensuing movement across the stage, so much the better. Above all, he must not make a false move, because, in this instance, that would have the Camera Operator *leading* him too much, and so cause a final irregular and rather jerky movement of the image on the screen.
 There are one or two special uses of panning. One of these is the employment of what is called a *swish-pan.* This is a movement when the camera itself is swiftly panned away from the action of the scene itself, so that the images on the screen consequently blur. This piece of film is cut into another *swish-pan,* which then resolves into another scene. You have seen the use of this swish-pan method to create a transition from one scene to another, in a number of current television shows. This is a purely technical device used by the director, upon the instigation of the producer or the cutter or the writer of the script, and is of no concern to the actor per se.

OVER-THE-SHOULDER (SHOT): *The positioning of two or more performers with the camera angled over the shoulder of one (or more) performer(s), so that the other performer, or performers, in the shot are clearly visible.*

This particular set-up is sometimes called a *reverse shot*. It is often so designated because, in setting up any over-the-shoulder shot, a similar shot will be set-up next over-the-shoulder of a performer who was in the previous shot, facing the camera. In the second over-the-shoulder set-up, or reverse shot, the face of the performer, whose back had previously been to the camera, can now be seen by the camera. There are several variations of the over-the-shoulder shot—the shot can be more open, or it can be very tight. In the latter, only a portion of the side of the head of the performer whose back is to the camera is visible on one side of the screen, while the face of the performer facing the camera occupies the greater part of the frame.

PARALLEL: *A fixed platform, usually constructed out of tubular steel, to which a wooden platform can be affixed. The parallel can be set up in the studio or on location to raise the camera, and the camera crew, above the ground, in order to obtain certain high shots.*

PICKUP: *The starting of a scene at some point other than the beginning, or top, of the scene.*

A scene may have been played through and a particular error on the part of the actor or the camera may have nullified its complete success. The director will decide to *pickup* the scene at a certain point, in order to secure, with the certainty of being able to use the greater part of the previous shot, another take of the same scene which, when both takes are cut together, will provide him with a complete shot. He may only have to pickup certain portions of the scene itself, a speech or two. The shot will be given a new number, and will be called a *pickup* shot. When the performer is confronted with this particular kind of shot, he should activate his imagination, so that he can begin the scene, rather than from the top, from the particular point designated by the director, and so play the scene in the same way as if he has commenced it from the beginning.

PICK IT UP: *A direction sometimes given to a performer, by a director, when the pace of the scene is lagging.*

Sometimes the pace of a scene will slow down, and the scene will lose its impact. In this instance, the director might say to the actors, in general, or to a certain actor, specifically, *"Pick it up!"* It generally means, in this sense, simply to pace the scene in such a way that it has the original vitality envisioned for it. Secondary use of the term would be the directive: "We will *pick it up*" from a certain point. See: *pickup,* which has been explained in the previous term.

PICK-UP PLACE: *A certain spot, within the confines of the studio itself, or en route between the studio and the location site, at which the transportation of the studio will stop to pick up actors to be used in that day's filming.*

When going on location, it is customary for actors to be asked to report at a certain spot within the studio, where transportation will be waiting to take them to the location site. On certain other occasions, when the actor concerned might live much closer to the location itself, and if the production staff, with due allowance for Transportation Guild and Insurance Coverage regulations, feels that the actor is a responsible person, the actor will be allowed to drive his own vehicle to an intermediate pick-up place, a certain designated corner, or perhaps even the outskirts of the location site itself, and there park his car, be picked up by the studio transportation, and driven into the actual location site itself. It is important, when the actor is accorded this privilege, that he is on time at the pick-up place, and ready and able to be transported to the location site.

The various Insurance Companies which insure actors for Production Companies and the members of the Transportation Guild have laid down certain regulations which must be observed by the studio, in the transportation of actors, and when an actor is granted the privilege of driving his own vehicle to a certain point near the location, he must acknowledge this courtesy that has been extended to him by the Transportation Guild and the production staff of the unit for which he is working, and make sure that he abides by all the directions that are given to him as to how far he may drive his vehicle, and where he may park it. Having done this, and arrived at his pick-up place, he should have all his gear ready at hand, his vehicle locked, if necessary, and be in readiness, and waiting, for the station wagon or stretch-out, or whatever vehicle is sent to collect him and convey him to the actual work-site.

PLAYBACK: *A recording of certain music or song(s), which will be amplified on the set while a particular musical sequence in a film is being photographed.*

The music or the song(s) has been recorded prior to filming. This is called *pre-scoring*. The music track is *played back* through loud speakers on a sound stage, thus enabling the performers, the singers, the dancers, to perform to this music while being filmed by an N.C. (so-called *noiseless* camera, i.e., an unsilenced camera). Scenes so shot are later synchronized with the original recording, which has been made under perfect acoustic conditions, and the two strips of film cut together into the final, assembled footage.

In charge of this playback equipment, on a sound stage, will be a member of the music department, and the sound recording crew of the unit itself. An additional member of the staff of the studio may be present—one of the technicians from the dubbing stage—who will stand by and give his opinion to the director as to whether or no the actor has synchronized the words, which they have sung while the scene was being shot to the pre-scoring of the sound track itself. This playback is used for the many shots required for the sequence being filmed, whether it is in an establishing or long shot, a master shot, or in the closer shots, which are necessary to give coverage to the scene.

POST-SYNC: *To record at a date later than the actual filming the voice of a performer, in synchronization with the visual image, so that the new sound track can be matched to the filmed image, and cut into the final, assembled footage.*

This method of *post-syncing* has been discussed under the heading of *dubbing* and *looping*. The expression *post-sync* is, of course, short for *post-synchronization*. Sound effects are also often redubbed in a post-synchronization session as well as speech.

PRINT!: *A directive used by the director only when the shot is to his satisfaction.*

By the use of this expletive, the director indicates that the shot has been completed to his satisfaction, and by it, he authorizes the script girl to make a note to that regard in her script-notes. He directly orders the camera assistant, whose duty it is to make a note of each shot on a list which he keeps in an invoice book, to have the particular take printed, or processed, into positive film (as opposed to raw stock, or negative film, which is used to film the picture), and then sent from the laboratory to the editor and his cutters, to be used in assembling the first rough cut of the sequence in the film itself.

PRODUCER: *The person who has the ultimate responsibility both for the original shaping of, and the final outcome of, a film.*

There are various categories of producer: executive producer, producer, and associate producer. An executive producer is sometimes only a titular producer, representing the financiers of the film. A producer is the man who is personally responsible for seeing that the original idea gets on film. An associate producer, sometimes one or more, is an assistant to the producer, assuming various tasks which the producer delegates to him. The duties of a producer are, in the main, the same for a feature film or a TV series, but despite different procedures, dictated by the form of a feature motion picture or the segments of a TV series, it is usual that the producer is the one who, beginning with an original idea, either a story or story idea which he himself has written or created, or a previously purchased written piece of material, such as a novel, a play, or a short story, a magazine article, by writing it himself or by employing a writer, shapes that material into a screenplay, and a final, shooting script.

In television, it is often customary for an executive producer to be in charge of a unit, and to oversee the preparations, in every way, of each segment in that particular series, and for him to deputize to one or more producers the actual work of being on the floor of a soundstage, or on location, while that segment is being shot, of watching its dailies, and of working with the director, if he is granted a first cut, and with the editor to assemble footage, so that the executive producer can finally give his opinion on that assembled footage. The associate producer, both in feature films and in television, is an assistant to the producer himself, and carries a deal of responsibility in this particular regard, serving, as he does, as a liaison between both the executive producer and the producer, and the production staff itself—in particular, the production manager, and the editor, who is assembling the final cut of a feature film or a TV segment.

There are many duties which the producer(s) must carry out, and an understanding of these duties is useful to the performer, in his day-to-day work.

PRODUCTION MANAGER: *That person, a member of what is called the front office of the unit that is shooting a film or TV segment, who, with his staff, has broken down the original script into a breakdown, scheduled it into an order of shooting, and made the many preparations necessary to see that every department concerned with the making of the film has fulfilled every requirement of them that the shooting of the film will demand.*

His daily duties are the making of a call sheet for the succeeding day, of gathering all the time cards, production reports, script reports, etc., together, and in general, keeping the whole production flowing as to whether or not the requisite number of pages are being shot on that particular day, what shooting is upcoming, both in the studio or on location, for the following day; in other words, this is the *gang boss* of the unit itself. He is the one concerned with all the physical aspects of the making of the film, and must control every department head to see that he is doing what is required of him. (See: Unit Manager)

PRODUCTION UNIT: *That group of people consisting of a director, camera crew, sound crew, electrical crew, etc., which works on a soundstage or on location to shoot an assigned picture, or section of a picture, or segment of a TV series.*

The performer in films will soon acquire a knowledge of the various departments which make up the composition of a production unit. He should then acquire a knowledge of their function, and of the particular way in which they will contribute to his own particular performance. On every unit, he should do his best to familiarize himself with, at least, the heads of each department, so that he can address them properly and courteously, call for them, ask for their services whenever they are required. This, first, out of common *professional courtesy,* and secondly, because he *should know who the department heads are,* so that, if necessary to his performance, he can *quickly ask* for them, and tell them what he requires.

PROJECTION (CHARACTER): *The clear definition which a performer must make of the character he is playing, so that it is easily recognizable, in the scene being rehearsed or shot.*

When the actor has done his necessary preparation, he must so exercise his craft that the character becomes slightly larger than life, and is, therefore, projected as a definite personality.

Actors who mumble to themselves, play too much inside themselves, cannot hope to project a character which will make an impact on the screen. By the application of the right methods of preparation, and by the right techniques, while working, an experienced performer can, with a few strokes of his imagination, create the beginnings of a character. Having sketched in the main, broad outlines of a character, he can proceed to refine him, creating a full, rich characterization.

The director may ask the actor to project the character a little more, and in this instance, the actor can be sure that he has not been successful in outlining the character so that the director has a clear idea in his mind of what it is going to be. The actor, too, should be careful to project his character in the rehearsal period, and not just simply hope that it will *happen* when he gets on camera. It sometimes does, but it is far better to project a character as fully as possible in the rehearsal period, so that it can be judged by the director, instead of the actor waiting until a take is attempted, in the hope that the full projection of the character will then emerge.

PROJECTION (REAR): *This is a method of projecting a strip of film on a screen, situated behind the area where the performers are, so that the performers appear to be in the actual place depicted on this strip of film.*
The projector for this method is placed behind the screen itself, and the camera which is photographing the scene, is aligned in a straight line with the projector, and both motors, of the projector and the camera, are synchronized, so that the image on the screen, flickering as it does, will match with the movement of the gate of the camera filming the scene.

There are many limitations on the movements of actors in rear screen projection, and they must be observed rigidly by the performer. He may have to move in certain areas only; at other times he may have to sit in the interior of a vehicle, and control that vehicle by manipulating the wheel of an automobile, and the gears. It is a difficult form of acting which requires the exercise of a very lively imagination, but, if the scene is fully understood, the director has given explicit instructions, and the actor has discussed the scene fully with him, then the actor himself should have no problems in settling into this form of scene, and playing it as fully as if he were in an actual automobile, or within an actual set, or location site itself.

PROJECTION (VOICE): *For a performer to so pitch his voice in volume that it can be heard at a distance.*

There will be occasions when the actor, photographed at a distance, will need to pitch his voice and to match the vocal effect to that of the visual image. There will be other occasions when he will be asked by the sound mixer, and by the director, to pitch his voice, that is, to project it, a little more than he is doing. They both may feel that the actor is too low in tone, not quite sharp and decisive enough in quality, to be recorded perfectly. In this instance, the actor should clarify the tone of his voice, and pitch it with a deal more edge, so that it can be satisfactorily recorded.

PROPERTY DEPARTMENT: *That particular group of men in a film production unit, headed by a Propmaster, who are responsible for the gathering and the giving to actors of the various properties which will be used in the scene.*

This department also includes set decorators, wranglers, animal handlers, and is responsible for the setting up of make-up tables, of a schoolroom, if necessary, of checking independent heaters in dressing rooms, of setting up wardrobe racks, and checking the dressing room set-ups, if they are not contained, as they often are, in mobile trailers.

PROPERTY MAN: *Depending on the size of the unit, and the demands of the production itself, the property man No. 1 will be the Propmaster, and will be assisted by the assistant propman.*

In particular circumstances, these two men might be assisted by extra propmen. The duties of the propmen are to deliver the properties onto the set, or to the actor himself; to, in certain instances, load and unload revolvers and guns, which may be used in a scene, to hand out special pieces of equipment, to supervise, where necessary during a scene, the refurbishing of special pieces of equipment, such as cigarettes, cigars, food, coffee, etc., which may be used by actors in a particular scene.

PROPS: *Those many various articles used in some manner, shape, or form, by performers in a scene.*

The performer will have these properties handed to him, on a soundstage or a location site, and will be responsible for them, in some instances, during the course of the day, and in other in-

stances, only during the course of the scene, when such properties will be immediately handed back to the propman to be refur-
bished and held until the next take comes up. In every instance,
where a property has to be used by a performer, he should
acquaint himself with it, and spend the necessary time rehearsing with it, whatever it may be, so that when it comes to using
it in a scene, the performer is adept, easy, and familiar with the
particular article, and will cause no hold-up to the scene itself
because of his inability to handle such a property.

PUSH BACK (CAMERA): *When an actor, by a movement to the
camera, makes it necessary for the camera to move away from
him and settle into another position, so that when the actor has
occupied his next position, the focus will be correct. This move
by the actor is termed pushing back the camera.*

In a scene involving continuous movements between performers and the camera on a soundstage, the camera will usually be
mounted on a crab dolly and the studio floor, if necessary, covered by five-ply boards. This will enable the crab dolly to move
smoothly and with great mobility in a variety of directions. On
location sites, this is also quite often done, but, mostly, the shot,
in this instance, would be obtained in a travelling shot or trucking shot in which the camera, mounted on a crab dolly, a Chap-
man-Nike, or a large Chapman boom, would move along wooden
or aluminum tracks. A performer moving towards the camera,
would, by such movement, *push it back* along the tracks.

In each instance, when the move is to come at a certain point
in the script, the actor must make the move *exactly* at that particular point. He must also be careful not to make a *false move.*
He must cue the camera crew by some predetermined indication,
e.g., a gesture of his body in the direction in which he is going
to move, just prior to the actual movement itself, so that the
camera can start its movement a fraction of a second before the
actor makes his. In the most perfect cooperation between performer and camera, the camera should begin to move slightly before the performer moves, leading him by a fraction of a second.

For the actor to move first, and then push the camera back
seems to be the meaning of the term. It is virtually the reverse
in actual practice. The actor appears to make his move, the
camera moves away, and then the actor actually makes his move,
making it seem that the camera has moved away to accommodate

the actor's move, rather than the actor arbitrarily stepping forward into the camera, and the camera having to back away from him.

RATIO (FILM): *The relation, or ratio, of the width to the depth of the final projected image of the film on the screen, which has been governed, in the first instance, by the lenses through which the film has been shot.*

Prior to recent years, the standard framing was that achieved by standard 35mm film. There have been many changes since then, which have seen the development of Cinemascope, widescreen, and similar methods of shooting and projecting of film. Nowadays, there are other systems in vogue which use 65mm and 70mm film, and these are each designated by the trade names which have been given to them by the companies who invented these particular cameras and films. The technicalities of these ratios are not the concern of the performer, except in the regard that he must understand the framing of himself in any particular shot, and so therefore, set in his mind a clear image of what portion of the screen he occupies.

There is a secondary definition of Ratio (Film) and that is: the amount of feet of raw stock (*negative* film) that the director is permitted to expose through a camera to obtain a printable take. The average ratio varies according to the type of film—feature, TV segment—and to the attitude—financial and artistic—of the production company involved.

RATIO (LIGHTING): *The amount of light necessary from secondary lights used in a scene to balance against the key light of the scene.*

In this way a ratio is established, 1 : 3, 1 : 5, etc., and a general tone or mood of the scene is established by the application of light in these various ratios. Once again, the application of this kind of lighting, the technical aspects of it, are not the concern of the actor. He can clearly see the effect of the lighting on the scene, and so use it, in conjunction with his performance, to enhance the mood that is created.

The lighting is created in each specific scene at the request of the director, and by the director of photography, as indicated by the script. By observing the lighting of the scene, an actor can often gain a great deal of information which will be very helpful to him in the performance of his part. If he can absorb the effect of the lighting of the scene, and so translate it into terms of his own performance, he will find that that performance is immeasurably enhanced by this observation and application.

REEL (FILM): *The standard unit of film measurement; the amount of film which will project for ten minutes, i.e., 900 feet of 35mm film, and 360 feet of 16mm sound film.*

Standard reels are designed to hold these lengths of film, but will accommodate up to 1,000 feet of 35mm film, and 400 feet of 16mm film. According to the make of the camera, there are other reels designed, and sometimes in use, which will hold more, or less, than these standard amounts, but, for the most part, the reels seen in use on the cameras used in filmmaking today, are those of standard reel length.

REFLECTOR: *A square, reflecting surface composed of a thick board contained within a metal frame, and supported by a stand, which allows such a reflecting surface to be manipulated, such surface being covered on both sides with aluminum foil, one side containing foil that is softer in texture, and laid so that it appears to have a waving, fluttering effect, and on the other side, quite smooth. The "wavy" side creates a softer light, and the opposite side, which is sometimes referred to as a lead, creates a much harder light.*

The color of the reflecting material is usually silver, but sometimes gold is used. These reflectors are used to reflect, or direct, the light of the sun to that part of the scene where it is needed. Reflectors are used out-of-doors, where it is necessary to reflect the sunlight onto the actors or some part of the scene, especially where the location sight is such that a power source and lights are unable to be brought to that particular spot. However, reflectors are used, in the main, to supplement the lighting by lamps of a scene out-of-doors.

RELATING: *Indicating your awareness of another performer in a scene, without, in some instances, actually turning to him.*

This is accomplished by using your eyes, with an indicative look, or with a slight inclination of your head. *Relating* has been discussed before in this Terminology under the heading of *Downstage.*

REVERSE (SHOT): *That shot which covers the performance of an actor in the scene, from the point of view of another performer who has already had his performance in the scene recorded, similarly, from the point of view of the other actor in the scene.*

This is the same type of shot as an over-the-shoulder shot. However, a *reverse shot* may also be such that in a large, very complicated scene, a master may be shot from one side of a set or a room or end of table, and then repeated from the other side of the set or room, or from the opposite end of the table.

RIGGING: *The rigging of a set, within a sound stage or on location, is the placing of lights in their preliminary positions, prior to an accurate adjustment of them when the action of the scene has been blocked out, and the camera angle, or movement of the camera, has been determined.*

The rigging of a set entails both the placement of lights and/or reflectors on the floor of the sound stage or location site, and their placement, at various points of vantage, above the scene itself, whether on the sound stage or on location. With the setting up of the lights, there is also the laying out of cables, and this is all part of the job of the rigging, or constructional and electrical crews. Some studios, in the changeover of sets from one day to another, employ special construction and rigging crews.

RISE UP INTO (OUT OF) SHOT: *When an actor, from a position below the bottom of the frame, takes a position which brings him up through the bottom of that frame into a set position within the frame itself.*

An actor who has been seated in one shot, and now must be photographed in a standing position, may be asked to *rise into the shot.* He may have been seen either seated or spread-eagled on the ground, and now must come up into a set shot, which will photograph him at a certain distance, and so achieve a specific effect desired by the director. There will be another term applied to an actor under similar circumstances, that is, he will be requested to rise up *out* of the shot. In this instance, being photographed in a certain position, either seated or sprawled on the ground, or seated on a rock, etc., in a close shot he will be asked to *rise up out* of that position. In the succeeding shot, he will most likely be asked to rise up *into* that shot.

It is important for the performer to complete the necessary dialogue which he has in the shot when he is seated before rising up through the top of the frame, and, similarly, when rising

up, into a shot, not to begin speaking until he is firmly and se-
curely in position, and correctly framed in that particular shot.
If he should speak while rising up into frame, or rising out of
frame, it makes it impossible for the editor to use the dialogue
which he has spoken. It is always best for the performer to finish a speech and rise out of a shot, or to rise up into a shot, and
then begin speaking.

RISER: *A small, flat platform or box similar to an apple box, which
is used to elevate an actor in a scene.*

Often, a stand-in, in lieu of wearing specially constructed
boots to match his overall height to that of the man for whom
he is standing in, will use a small riser to elevate himself to the
height of the performer for whom he is standing in. Risers are
used to build slight platforms for performers to work on, under
certain circumstances, or for a camera operator to stand on when
the tripod of the camera has been raised to a height which
makes it difficult for him to either manipulate the controls of the
camera, or to view the action through the viewfinder. A riser
might also be used to elevate a property in a scene, perhaps a
lamp standing on a desk, to a height at which it will fit better
into the framing of the shot.

ROCK IN—OUT: *Used to describe a performer who moves out of
the side of a frame, or the top or bottom of a frame, or in depth
in a scene, so that he is out of frame or out of focus.*

The moving out of the side of the frame, the assuming of a
position where a performer is subsequently out of focus in a
reasonably loose shot, can sometimes be accommodated by the
camera operator himself, or by the use of a different type of lens,
but rocking in and out of frame, or focus, is something that the
performer must take care of himself in close-ups, because especially where the focus is critical, it is extremely important that
the performer locks himself into position in the shot, and so enables the camera operator and the crew to achieve a perfect shot
of him.

RUSHES: *Prints of the negative film exposed in a single day of
shooting, rushed through the laboratory the same night, and delivered to the studio the following day, so that these prints may
be viewed by the producer and his staff.*

Rushes may be picture, sound, or a composite of both, and are often called *dailies*.

SCENE: *A small portion, often part of a longer sequence, of the shooting script of a film.*

A scene, in itself, implies that it is a complete entity, but in actual usage, a scene may be one of many which goes to make-up a particular sequence in a shooting script. This scene, in whole or part, will be recorded in either a complete or progressive master shot, progressive meaning that the master shot itself may be broken into two or more sections. This particular master shot(s) will then be broken up. Other shots will be taken in various set-ups of certain sections of the scene—closer two-shots, over-the-shoulders, close-ups, etc., the camera in these shots always being placed in a closer proximity to the performers concerned than in the master shot. These shots, when cut into the master shot, will lend emphasis to the scene, according to the desire of the director.

SCHEDULE: *A listing of the order in which scenes, from the shooting script, will be shot, not necessarily in the order in which they are written down in the shooting script itself, but according to the dictates of the breakdown assembled by the production manager.*

When a breakdown of all scenes in the shooting script have been achieved, these scenes are listed on thin strips of cardboard, with every detail concerned in the scene printed upon these strips, and the strips then assembled into an order which the production manager believes will be the best for shooting them as far as a sequence of sets and locations are concerned. When this board has been completed, according to the number of days it is believed that the film will be shot in, a series of printed sheets are assembled, which set down, in detail, the information contained on the board, i.e., on each individual strip that has been set on the board—scenes, cast, equipment, number of pages to be shot each day, and various other pertinent information. This schedule, when mimeographed, is then given to each member of the cast, and the key personnel in the crew.

SCOOT IN: *A quick, urgent movement of the camera on either a dolly across boards, or on a boom along tracks, so that the cam-*

*era is brought into close proximity with the performer(s) in the
scene, or an object of especial interest and importance.*

In other words, in this particular camera movement, a similar
impression to a *zoom* is obtained, and this can be brought about
particularly well by a skillful operator, a grip, pushing the camera mounted on a crab dolly and settling it into position. At a
given signal, either from the director of photography or the director, or on a pre-planned move to a position by a performer,
the grip can put the dolly in towards that particular finishing
spot, and so achieve a particular camera movement on the screen
that is akin to a *zoom shot.*

SCREEN PLAY (SHOOTING SCRIPT): *The final form in which the
story to be filmed is placed on paper.*

The writing of a screen play goes through certain phases.
Whatever the original material may be, an idea, a short story,
a novel, a play, it is usual to write first what is termed a *story
outline.* This is a rearrangement of the original material into a
form which is considered the best line for the final film itself
to take. It does not deal, in great detail, with the many facets
of the story itself, but merely outlines the general story line, so
that everyone is clear how the original material is to be adapted
into a film.

The next step is to develop a full *treatment* of the story outline. In the treatment, the story outline itself is extended, dialogue added where necessary, either from the original material
or by writing dialogue for the additional scenes which have been
woven into the story outline, and now into the treatment. Once
the treatment has been finalized, then the screenplay writer will
take that material in the treatment and so place it on the page,
describing the scene, telling what the characters do in the scene,
writing the dialogue for the scene, in far greater detail.

When this first draft of the screen play has been achieved,
then that particular draft may go through many versions, until
finally, a shooting script is arrived at. The shooting script will
have each scene designated and numbered, and will contain,
basically, an extension of the material in the first rough draft,
polished, altered in such ways as has been decided upon by the
producer, the director, and the writer concerned. There is a
certain basic form for setting down this material, which you will
find repeated many times in all kinds of screen plays, but there

are certain writers, and certain directors, in preparing their own scripts, who, sometimes, will use variations of the basic form. However, as a general rule, the final shooting script is that script which can be given to the production unit, the staff concerned with breaking down and scheduling it, of costing it, of budgeting it, so that it is ready to be cast, and put on the sound stage for filming.

SCREEN PLAY WRITER: *That person who is responsible to the producer to set down, usually in final shooting script form, a story which is to be filmed.*

Screen play writers work in various ways. In motion pictures, they may be asked to adapt a story, a series of articles, a book, a play, into a shooting script, and will proceed, in their own way, to either outline the story, so that it is clear to everyone concerned, or go directly to a treatment, or take the original material and shape it immediately in a shooting script form. Depending upon the ability and reputation of the writer, he may proceed in any number of ways. There is no set form; every writer has his own method, and will pursue it.

In television, the procedure is much the same. An idea is suggested for a segment, that idea is developed by a writer into a story outline or treatment, and he is told to proceed with the shooting script by the producer concerned. However, in all matters of writing for motion pictures, or television series, there are certain rules laid down by the Writers' Guild of America West which limit the amount of time that a writer can be engaged to do certain sections of the writing that will result in a shooting script, and certain remunerations are set down as minimums to cover this work.

In other forms of writing for films, documentary, industrial, and the like, there are other rules, regulations, and remunerations laid down, and the method of work will depend upon the producer and the writer concerned. A documentary or an industrial may require a certain amount of research, of actually visiting a certain area or plant, and acquiring the necessary material on which the script will be based. However, fundamentally, the pre-requisite of writing for the screen is to have a basic original idea and/or some written matter, and so develop it until it is synthesized into a final shooting script, which can then be handed to the production unit involved, and subsequently "shot" upon a sound stage or upon various locations as a film.

SCREEN TEST: *A short scene, usually from the film about to be made, in which a performer, under consideration for casting in a certain part, is given the opportunity to demonstrate his potential.*

A screen test is usually not the exact filming of the scene as it will eventually be done in the film itself. The set is often a makeshift arrangement, but the purpose of the screen test is to see if the player concerned can give a performance in the particular part. Everything possible is done so that the performer will look his or her best.

In preparing for a test of this nature, the performer should seek to understand his character completely. He should regard the test-scene as if it was a scene that he would be doing in the course of the making of the particular film, or even in the course of making any film. The pressures involved in the making of a screen test, where being cast in the part is the end result and all important, places upon the player additional strains in excess of what he would encounter if he merely was playing the scene in the course of a normal filming. However, the player must approach his task in exactly the same way he would normally, and endeavor to present himself in the very best and most favorable light, while making a screen test.

There are other kinds of "screen" tests which the performer may be involved in. There will be tests where his costume will be photographed. These are, in no way, a test of the performer, but merely to see how his costume and make-up look under certain set and lighting conditions. However, the performer must know how to show his costume off, and also his make-up, in these particular tests. The performer, for a costume test, may be asked to walk about the stage, to make certain turns so as to display the costume. Similarly, in displaying make-up, particularly a wig or a beard, the performer must be able to rotate on a certain spot on the test-stage, so that the make-up, the wig, beard, etc., is shown to fullest advantage.

SCRIM: *When a flag is made of some form of translucent material, usually of a fine gauze, it is called a scrim.*

A scrim is used to partly cut off, or dilute, partly to diffuse, the source of light near which it is placed. Its effect is, thus, between that of a gobo and a full diffuser. There is a small scrim called a *finger scrim*, which can be placed very delicately to diffuse a performer. The action of adjusting this finger scrim is termed: to *feather*.

SCRIPT: *The usual term for a screen play, or shooting script.*

According to what is being filmed, whether it is a motion picture script, a television segment (and both these scripts are very similar), or a documentary, an industrial film, etc., the form of the script will vary according to the dictates of the producer and the director.

It is wise for the performer to enclose the script that is given him in some sort of cover, and to keep a pen or pencil handy so that he can make a note of any changes that are made on the spot, during the rehearsal of a scene, and have a clear and accurate record of them. During the course of filming any motion picture or TV segment, he is also likely to receive *revised pages*. These are pages, which, for some reason or other, have been changed in one way or another. They are mimeographed and handed to the actor, either to show a revision of a speech or an action on a certain page in the script or to give him additional scene pages, which will be filmed in due course. The actor should immediately place these pages in his script in the right order, discarding the old pages so that at all times, he keeps up-to-date on everything that is being done, or will be done, in the film.

SCRIPT SUPERVISOR: *The person who is responsible on a set, or on a location site, for keeping an accurate record of all scenes, and all takes of scenes, which are shot, of recording various technical notes on them for use by the production staff, and later typing up all this information into a form that will be used by the editor and his cutters in assembling the film.*

The duties of a script supervisor, whether a man or a woman, are multiple. He has to time each particular take, and make a note of it. He has to keep a record, progressively, during the day, of the number of the script pages shot. He has to note accurately the movements of the players in the scene, not only their physical movements from one spot to another, but those tiny, little intricate movements of the hands, for example, when handling properties, and the exact moments in the scene at which those movements were made and/or those properties were used, in order that accurate matching can be achieved in the following shots.

SEQUENCE: *A section of a film which is more or less complete in itself.*

At one time, in the early days of film-making, such a sequence might have begun with a fade, and ended with a fade. It is more customary nowadays, that a sequence begins out of a dissolve, and ends going into a dissolve. However, depending on the style of the director and the writing in the script, there are many other devices to begin and end sequences. Sometimes, as has been discussed, a swish pan is used; more often, a direct cut at the conclusion of the sequence leads into another sequence, for particular reasons of shock, emphasis, relationship, etc.

However, a sequence is regarded as a complete entity in itself, within the framework of the shooting script. In terms of writing, we could say that a shot, a separate shot within the scene, could be taken as being equal to a sentence; a scene, within that sequence, to a paragraph; and the whole of the sequence to be the same as a chapter in a book.

SET: *Some type of artificial construction, either on a sound stage or out-of-doors, which forms the scene of a motion picture shot, or series of shots.*

SET-UP: *The setting-up of the camera in a certain specific position from which to shoot the shot.*

Each time the camera is placed in another position, it is regarded as a further *set-up*, and this is noted by the script supervisor who makes record of this information.

SETTLE IN: *In order to settle in to a shot, the performer must approach his mark at the normal pace demanded by the required action of the scene, but, instead of stopping abruptly, exactly on the mark set down for him, he slows his pace as he approaches the mark, and eases into, settles onto, that mark to assume his correct position for the camera.*

SHAVE: *To pass very close to, or around, a piece of furniture, etc., in a set, when making a movement in a scene.*

SHOOT AROUND: *When a performer must leave a sound stage for some particular reason, is ill, is late arriving on the set at the beginning of the day, or upon returning from lunch, the director will often shoot around him.*

The director will film those parts of the scene in which the performer is not actually on camera. Those particular portions of the scene in which the performer is physically and visually concerned will be filmed later when he is able to return to the sound stage.

SHOOTING SCRIPT: *The so-called final working script of the film, which details the shots, one by one, in relation to their accompanying dialogue, movements, etc., within each scene.*

The term itself, *shooting script* or *final working script,* is misleading in the essence that once this state of the script has been achieved, there will be numerous other changes made, either prior to the production beginning or during the course of the filming itself. These changes, whenever dictated, are then inserted into the body of the script itself, and the revised pages or changes are sent out to each one of the performers in the film itself, not just to those who are immediately concerned with the scene, but to every performer who is listed as a character in that particular script.

SHOT(s): *A portion, or all, of a scene which is photographed from one set-up of the camera, or during the course of a camera movement in filming the scene.*

Shots are listed and indicated in the script according to the camera angle, the distance between the camera and the subject, or the subject matter of the shot. The following are a list of the various shots that will be encountered in any script, and in the course of filming:

1) *Close Shot*: A shot taken with the camera close, or *apparently* close, to the subject or performer(s), in the scene.

The close shot itself may have varying degrees of framing, ranging from a shot which includes the shoulders of a performer to an extreme close-up, where only the performer's face, from the forehead to the chin, or merely a portion thereof, might fill the screen utterly.

2) *Dolly Shot*: A shot in which the camera moves supported by some form of crab dolly or large boom, either on a series of smooth boards or on a camera track, from one place to another, in order to photograph the performers in their movements. This shot is sometimes called a *trucking* or *tracking* shot, but the most common usage is *dolly shot.*

3) *Establishing Shots*: Long shots, usually of exteriors but

sometimes of a large set constructed within a sound stage to represent either an exterior of a building or street, or of a set, such as a large ballroom, hotel foyer, etc., in order to establish the whereabouts of the scene itself and show the dimensions of the set.

4) *Fifty-Fifty (50-50) Shot*: A shot in which the performers stand relatively face-to-face on a plane horizontal to the camera itself, some distance removed. There are variations of a strict fifty-fifty shot, in which the performer may slightly open up to the camera, but this will be at the jurisdiction and upon the decision of the director himself. The strict application of the term fifty-fifty is *actor facing actor*, or *eyeball to eyeball*, as it is sometimes called.

The basic fifty-fifty shot is one performer face to face with the other, both being on a horizontal plane exactly equal to the lens, but:

(1) From this basic shot can evolve an open two, i.e., the performers can angle themselves in varying degrees so that they reveal more of their bodies to the lens; in other words, *open themselves* to the lens.

(2) There can be a 50-50 favoring one performer more than the other, i.e., one performer faces camera, still on a horizontal line with the other, but with the other performer still facing the actor who has opened himself to the camera.

(3) There are many variations possible to the 50-50 shot, but all such shots must evolve from the performers first standing equally on the cross of the "T," facing each other, with the stem of the "T" extending straight to the lens.

5) *High Shot*: A shot which photographs a subject, or performer(s), from a height.

This type of shot can be taken from a platform, a parallel, from the elevated arm of a Chapman boom, or from an airplane or a helicopter.

6) *Insert Shot*: A shot of an object—a newspaper heading, a photograph, any object being used in the scene that needs to be emphasized. This close shot of the object is then cut into the sequence to point up the significance of the particular object in the scene. A similar emphasis can be gained by *zooming*.

7) *Long Shot*: A shot in which the object of principal interest, either a vista, a mountain, a building, certain phenomena

(natural), or a performer, is, or appears to be, far removed from the camera. This can be achieved by either separation of camera and subject, and the use of another lens, often a 20mm or a 25mm lens, at a distance not quite so far removed from the object.

8) *Low Shot*: A shot where the camera is pointed up at the subject, often from ground level.

This shot is sometimes employed to make performers, or structures appear larger or taller, or to gain certain effects, as when horses or cattle should stampede over the camera, and can be seen literally jumping right over the camera, or the spot at which the camera has been placed, often in a small, concealed pit down in the ground.

9) *Master Shot*: A shot in which the scene is photographed in its entirety, from the *top* or start of the scene right through to its conclusion.

There are several ways of photographing a master shot; either a master can be filmed from one particular angle and at a distance that serves to show the set and the performers fully, the camera being set in that spot and not in motion, or the camera can be in motion with the performers, moving and settling into various (camera) positions. The blocking-out of the scene will be such that both the performers and the camera come to a stop at certain times in the master. The sections of the master which take place at these particular spots can be covered later and cut into the master shot by the editor.

Except in action sequences, it is very rare, whilst the camera and performer are in movement, that another shot in which other performers are not moving will be cut into such a scene—with the exception, of course, of a pure *reaction shot* by other characters to the ensuing action, should this kind of a shot be necessary.

10) *Medium-Close Shot*: A shot intermediate in distance between a close shot and a medium shot.

11) *Medium-Long Shot*: A shot intermediate in distance between a medium shot and a long shot.

12) *Medium Shot (Mid-Shot)*: A shot which shows a person at full height, or views a scene at normal viewing distance.

The above three shots are not often listed in scripts today. Their choice of usage, as far as set-up is concerned, is that of the director, or director of photography, and, in general, these particular usages of shot have gone slightly out of fashion. A screen writer might only depend upon simpler forms of close shot, long shot, establishing shot, angle, etc., to list the different shots in his script. Abbreviations of letters, such as M.C.S. for medium-close shot, C.S. for close shot, C.U. for close-up, are not often used in American scripts today. They are sometimes still encountered in English and European scripts.

13) *Moving Shot*: A shot from some form of vehicle, such as a truck or an automobile, a stage coach, or an airplane. Some interesting variations of this shot have been obtained by affixing a camera to the front of a ski or a surfboard, or underwater sleds.

14) *Over-the-Shoulder Shot*: A shot in which the camera is set so that it can shoot over one performer's shoulder, including a portion of his head and body, into the scene, usually onto another player(s) facing the camera.

There are many variations of the standard over-the-shoulder shot, as has been explained under this separate term in the Terminology itself.

15) *Pan Shot*: A shot in which the camera pans across the set, either following a performer, or simply to show the extent, or the details of the set itself.

16) *Pick-Up Shot*: A shot, not necessarily another fresh angle, where the scene, instead of being commenced from the top of the scene, is picked-up at a certain point, in order to cover some small deficiency in the previous taking of that scene. A pick-up shot is simply another take. It will be given a different number on the clapperboard, e.g., Sc. 8A (instead of Sc. 8), Take 1.

17) *P.O.V. Shot*: A shot taken from a player's point of view to reveal (with or without including him in the shot) what he sees in the scene.

18) *Reaction Shot*: A shot, usually taken in close-up, which can be inserted into a sequence, with dialogue or without, to show the effects of any actor's words or actions on the person being photographed.

19) *Reverse Shot*: One of two complimentary shots necessary for the coverage of a looser two-shot. In other words, this is the angle opposite to one already shot, and a reverse shot in this sense is really a matching over-the-shoulder shot, or single, etc.

Sometimes, when a camera is in movement, and settles

over a performer's shoulder onto another performer, the over-
the-shoulder shot has already been achieved by the placement
of the performers and the placement of the camera, as they
both come to a stop in motion, and then proceed with the
playing of the scene. Therefore, the reverse shot, or the
matching over-the-shoulder shot to that, will then be taken
to match in to that previously obtained over-the-shoulder
shot, which was part of the master shot itself.

20) *Two Shot*: A shot containing two characters who are
placed, as a rule, fairly close to the camera. The term *three-
shot* has a similar meaning. The two shot itself usually will
show two players not quite face to face, as in a fifty-fifty, but
rather more open to the camera. The camera will be positioned either dead center, looking squarely at the two performers, or slightly to one side, and favoring one of the performers should the director consider that character more
important than the other in the scene. The performers themselves, by varying their positions to the camera, can assume
any number of variations to that basic two shot.

There are several other kinds of *two-shots*: when the two
players face the camera square on, or stand facing the camera
with one performer behind the other and cleared to the
camera.

21) *Zoom Shot*: A shot taken with a zoom lens.

This shot is achieved by having a performer come into a
certain spot, and then, the moment that he has reached that
spot, or even during the course of reaching that spot, have
the camera zoom into him, and hold him in a greatly larger
magnification. Other ways of achieving this type of effect
would be to have the camera *dolly* move in as fast as possible and settle in close to the actor, or to cut from that first
shot, where the actor rides in or walks in, to a close or even
an extremely close shot, of the performer himself.

SILENT BIT: *The performer doing a piece of business, in a scene,
without lines, or an atmosphere player who has been directed to
perform a certain piece of business, and not speak.*

In the case of the performer, this is merely part of his performance overall, but in the case of the atmosphere player, who
has been engaged merely to serve in that function of *atmosphere,*
and will be paid a basic amount of money for doing just that; if
he is asked by the director to perform what is termed a *silent bit,*

then his salary for the day is subsequently adjusted. If however, an atmosphere player is called to the stage one day, and is made-up and in costume ready to perform his silent bit, even if it is rehearsed, *if it is not filmed*, he will only be paid his basic daily rate, and not the agreed-to salary for the silent bit which he was to have performed.

In the case of the performer, he should take every advantage of the atmosphere player, doing these silent pieces of business, and integrate the atmosphere player into the scene with him. On the other hand, the performer must, in no way, request that the atmosphere player do special pieces of business with him, or utter any lines, without first conferring with the director, and the assistants, as to whether or not this is permissible in the economics of the budget of the film that is being made. If a decision is made to use an atmosphere player in a *silent bit*, then the performer is at liberty to work within those limitations with the atmosphere player, and so gain the benefit of his presence in the scene.

SILENT CAMERA: *A camera which is designed for silent shooting, i.e., merely the shooting of the action of the scene without sound being recorded at the same time. This camera is an unsilenced camera, and its mechanism is noisy. It is referred to as an N.C.*

You will have encountered references to various cameras, and initials which designate them, such as B.N.C. and N.C. B.N.C. stands for blimped, noiseless camera, and N.C. stands for noiseless camera. The blimped, noiseless camera is self-blimped, encased within a solid casing, and the noiseless camera itself can be silenced to a degree by the use of a barney. However, the B.N.C. is the essentially silent camera. It is fully blimped so that its mechanism cannot be heard, in any way, as the dialogue of a scene is being recorded. The N.C. without a barney is an extremely noisy camera and can only be used to film dialogue scenes in an emergency. Such dialogue recorded would provide only a guide track for redubbing at a later time.

SLATE: *A manual clapperboard, or an automatic slater, which is exposed to the camera to record details of the director and cameraman, the scene number, the take, day or night, and so on, and to provide a means of synchronization for the editor when cutting the film.*

Slateboards, clapperboards, and automatic slaters have been discussed, in some detail, in another section of this Terminology.

SLOW MOTION: *The motion of film in a camera which is run faster than the standard rate, therefore resulting in that action filmed appearing slower than normal, when the film is subsequently projected at the standard rate of ninety feet per minute.*

Slow motion is often used to demonstrate certain movements which otherwise could not be analyzed if filmed at a normal rate of speed. Slow motion is often inserted into a film to create certain effects, to increase or enhance the mood of the particular scene.

The reverse of this is, of course, fast motion, and was often used in the early days of film-making to speed up the sequence and make it more spectacular, as, for example, the chases which the Keystone Cops of the Max Sennett comedies indulged in. The reverse procedure of slow motion is the way in which fast motion is achieved, i.e., the camera is run at a much slower rate, and when projected at a normal rate, or above normal, rate of speed, the entire action of the scene is speeded up.

The rate at which the film is run through the camera is governed by the setting of certain mechanisms in the camera itself which reduces or increases the rate at which the film will run from the feed reel of the magazine itself, through the gate, through the mechanism of the interior of the camera, and back into the take up reel of the magazine once again. These rates of speed usually range from twelve to sixty-four frames a second, depending upon what particular effect needs to be achieved. The standard rate of speed at which film runs through a camera is 24 frames per second.

Sometimes a certain spectacular stunt will be shot at a slower rate of film speed, that is, the speed at which the film will pass through the mechanism of the camera itself, so that, when projected at a normal rate, the stunt itself will appear to take place at a more spectacular speed. This governing of the mechanism of the camera to achieve these effects is of no concern to the performer himself. It is merely a technical device to enhance the particular action in the scene itself. The performer should behave in a normal manner, and the camera mechanism will achieve the results required by the director.

SOUND CAMERA: *Those cameras designed for sound shooting, that*

*is, the recording of picture while concurrent sound is being re-
corded by the sound equipment. These cameras are silenced by
blimps, of some form or other, or by barneys, so that the noise
of the camera mechanism will not be heard, and interfere, in any
way, with the perfect recording of the dialogue, or the sound
effects of the scene itself.*

SOUND CREW: *Those personnel of the production unit who are
concerned with the recording of sound and sound effects in the
scene being photographed.*

The Chief of the Sound Crew is usually referred to as the
Sound Mixer, and his assistant on the recorder is the *Sound Recorder.* There will be, in addition to these two men, a boom operator, who manipulates the mike boom and places the mike in
the correct position during the shot, and he will be assisted by
a cable man, and sometimes, a second cable man, whose duties
are to run the cables from the mixer and the recorder to the
microphone and the camera, so that the mixer himself can start
both the camera and the sound recorder, and synchronize them
before the scene is photographed. Other members of the Sound
Crew may be: the operator who looks after the playback machine, another operator who may take care of a P.A. (personal
address) system, etc. These men constitute the Production Unit
Sound Crew. There are other sound crews, whose duties will
be in the interior of the studio, and primarily concerned with the
post-synchronization, and these men, performing much the same
duties, are usually known as the Dubbing or Rerecording Sound
Crew. These men and their function have been discussed under
the heading of *Dubbing.*

SOUND EFFECTS: *All sounds other than voices which will be synchronized in the final sound track of the film. Also, narrative and
music which may be recorded on the final sound track of a film,
either while the shooting is in progress, i.e., concurrently, or later
laid in on a separate track during the rerecording session.*

Prior to the rerecording session, these sound effects usually
occupy separate sound tracks, called sound effects tracks, and
have been selected for the specific purpose of mixing into the
final sound track. However, it is also sometimes customary to
record a series of sound effects—wind, running water, horses'
hoofs, squeaking doors, etc.—while on location or in the studio,
and to store these tracks for future use in the rerecording session.

These tracks are called *wild tracks.*

SOUND EFFECTS LIBRARY: *A collection of the most commonly used sound effects which may be required by the editing department of a studio.*

These sound effects have been recorded over a period of time, and are indexed, or otherwise catalogued, so that they can be taken out and used whenever needed. These sound effects are most conveniently recorded on film for rerecording purposes, but are sometimes rerecorded from sound effects records, or from their recording, in the original instance, on magnetic tape.

SOUNDSTAGE: *A stage which is used for sound shooting and is acoustically soundproofed so as to isolate it from its outside surroundings.*

However successful the construction of these stages have been in the past in eliminating the general noises from outside, today, with the increase in air traffic overhead, it is extremely difficult to completely eradicate such a penetrating noise as that of a low-flying or circling airplane, and often work on some of the older soundstages has to stop because of this. There are other smaller and newer soundstages enclosed within a larger complex of buildings, such as recording studios, which, because of their smaller area, have been successfully soundproofed so that no sound at all from the outside gets to them.

SOUND TRACK: *A narrow band, at one side of the sound film, which carries the record of the sound of the scene photographed.*

In certain instances, in the use of certain types of sound, several of these bands may be used to record the sound, however the general classifications and technicalities used in sound recording need not concern the actor.

SOUND TRUCK: *A mobile conveyance containing sound recording equipment.*

SPECIAL EFFECTS (SP-EFX): *Trick effects which are artificially achieved.*

Special effects crews are in charge of all effects needed in filming—explosions, small arms effects, fires, floods, etc.—but the term *special effects* was originally coined to cover such optical matters as split screen photography and other forms of matting, of the shooting of models, and of the combination of foregrounds and backgrounds, and what are sometimes referred to as *glass shots*. However, of recent years, the term, *special effects*, has become a generic one for the unusual physical effects or photographic tricks, that are performed by a special crew, either on a soundstage or on location, or in conjunction with split screen, etc.

SPECIAL EFFECTS LIBRARY: *A library in which special selections of film are stored, which can be drawn upon to be cut into films or TV segments. This film is stock effect of fire, flood, tornado, and so on, shots, and can be used to supplement the main body of the film which has been shot.*

SPEED: *The correct speed at which the camera mechanism is designed to run film for a time depiction, cinematographically, of action. This speed is ninety feet per minute, or 24 frames per second.*

The cry *Speed!* means that a sound and/or other camera (N.C. etc.) has reached synchronous speed with, if sound is to be recorded, the sound recording equipment. Otherwise, it simply means the camera(s) has reached the correct speed for filming. It is a signal for the director to call Action!—for the scene to commence.

SPEED UP (ACTION): *To increase the pace of the action of the scene itself, so as to give more vitality to the scene.*

SPEED UP (CAMERA): *The speeding up the film while shooting a scene so that when projected at the normal rate, the effect will be a slower motion than is normal.*

This particular action of *slow motion* is, and can be, used in certain instances, by a director to emphasize certain moods within the structure of the film itself. You have seen this technique of shooting used in certain commercials, and in certain art films which have been produced in Europe, in particular, to create a certain mood sequence within the body of the film. The action of slow motion, in itself, creates a certain somnabulistic dream mood, which when used judiciously, can artistically isolate that particular portion of the film which is played in that fashion.

SPOT LAMP(s): *Focusable lamps, the beam of which can be narrowed to a fine beam or spot, or widened, in contrast, to a flood, which illuminates the whole of the scene generally. These lamps are often designated as spots.*

The use of such a lamp was often seen in the theatre, where, thrown from the front, it illuminated the single acts in front of the front drop. It is used today in movies, in those particular scenes which require this type of illumination. It is rarely used in the general lighting of any specific scene for a realistic movie, although it should be noted that the focusing of all lamps used in moviemaking can be controlled, the beam flooded or narrowed according to the dictates of the Gaffer and the Director of Photography.

STAGE (ACTOR'S BUSINESS): *The blocking-out, or the designing of the movements, and personal business that the actors will do in the course of performing the scene.*

When the performer is deciding upon his physical movements in the scene under the guidance of the director, this is generally referred to as the *blocking out* of the scene, but any specific action, such as riffling through the pages of a book, lighting a cigarette, drinking a cup of coffee, eating a meal, making a telephone call, should be referred to as the *actor's business.*

STAGE (AREA): *The floor of a film studio on which the shooting of the film takes place is called a stage.*

Today, since we are shooting sound films, this particular kind of a stage is always called a *soundstage,* with one exception: if there is a series of actions to be filmed which will be synchronized to a playback, the area in which this is performed can simply be called a stage, because there is no necessity for a soundproofed soundstage. This is sometimes the case when shooting a musical dance sequence, in which the players synchronize their singing and their dancing to a playback, or in the instance of shooting various types of *musical* films, made especially for filmjukeboxes, and the various short featurettes which are sometimes used as program fillers for TV. These short films generally feature singing, instrumentalists. While being photographed in various locations, the performers synchronize their movements and their voices to a sound track, which has previously been recorded, and which is played to them on a playback machine during the course of the scene. Vocals for commercials are almost invariably filmed in this manner.

STAND-IN: *A stand-in is a person, male or female, who stands in the performer's place on the set after the scene has been blocked out, while the lights and camera moves are being finalized for the next shot.*

The stand-ins employed on the set will usually observe the general blocking-out of the scene, by the director and the principals, and when that has been completed, they will step into those positions, however many, which the principals in the scene will occupy, and so remain there or move from one mark to another while the director of photography and his lighting men set the lights for the scene. A good stand-in knows how to duplicate the positions and the actions of the principals, so that there are few adjustments to be made later on when the principals come back to those positions.

I make it a rule to step into the scene a little earlier than necessary, i.e., before the first team is called back on the set, so as to help out the director of photography and his lighting man as much as I can. I do this especially in close shots, where the lighting is more tricky. However, if my stand-in is competent, I take the advantage offered me to rest, particularly between set-ups of scenes, and then just step in for the final adjustments. The actor, when he has been called back into the scene, should take notice of the lights as they have been set, and endeavor to take advantage of them. In instances where there are either tricky or difficult positions to assume, or movements which the stand-in cannot duplicate as accurately as the performer involved in the scene, I make it a rule to ask the stand-in to allow me to do my own walk-throughs, for the lighting crew. In this way, too, I make the task of the director of photography and his lighting men that much simpler, and ensure that the lighting in the scene is absolutely right for me.

STAND OVER: *When an actor has perfect control of the material in the scene, his movements and his lines, he might be considered to be standing over his material or the scene.*

You will find the term *stand over* discussed quite thoroughly by Stanislavsky in his book *An Actor Prepares*, and I will not go into the details of it here. Simply, if a performer has made his preparation properly, and has so rehearsed his scene, with the director and the other players, that he has control of it, he will always have the satisfaction of *standing over* his material, of knowing that he will be able to perform the scene as he had planned.

STAY WITH THE MONEY: *In a scene, particularly an action scene, the use of this expression means that the camera operator has been directed to stay with or follow the most important player in the scene.*

It often happens in an action scene, especially a fight scene, where the action itself is not likely to be confined to the exact marks that have been placed on the floor, or sometimes even within the limitations of that particular area of the set or location site in which the action or the stunt has been staged, that the director will suggest to the camera operator that he *stay with the money*—simply, that he should follow, irrespective of what else happens in the scene, the actions of the principal performer.

STEP BACK: *To take a 'position,' both physically and mentally removed from the performance of the actor himself, so that he can quite objectively look at what he is doing in the scene, and so make the necessary corrections in his performance.*

I should think that this term was derived from the stage, the theater, in that a performer there, under direction, is sometimes unable to determine whether or no he is doing his work correctly, and so therefore, in his mind, has to *step back*, even step physically away off the stage, and so, reconstruct in his mind what he is doing there within the confines of the stage. In other words, he constructs for himself what he is doing, runs it through his mind, makes his decisions as to how he is presenting the part on the stage, and then once more stepping onto the stage area, is able to get inside the character, and present it in the correct fashion.

STEPPING ON LINES: *When a performer begins speaking his lines before the preceding line, addressed to him or in the scene, is completed.*

This is the strict definition of *stepping on a line*, and it is best to avoid it in playing a scene unless specifically indicated in the script or requested by the director. There will be occasions when a film director may instruct a performer, according to the composition of the scene or according to the pace necessary in the scene, to *step on* the end of another performer's line. When this is done, either there is, in a general scene, an overlapping of dialogue which will not be covered singly, the scene playing in this particular fashion, better than any other way, or by playing the lines in this way allowing no pauses between lines, the general pace of the scene is stepped-up, thus enlivening the whole of the tempo of the playing within the body of the scene itself. However, unless specifically instructed to do this, the performer should endeavor *not* to step on anyone else's lines, because it is quite impossible to cut from a scene in which lines are stepped on to those other scenes, the singles, the close-ups, in which there must be no over-lapping, every line spoken being kept separate from those of the other performers. (See: *Overlap*)

STOCK FOOTAGE: *Those sequences of film, in a film library, each sequence consisting of certain shots—geographical establishing shots, certain historical material, often purely newsreel footage, and other general footage, viz., street scenes, park scenes, general panoramic shots, etc., which are likely to be printed and used again in other productions over a period of time.*

There are specialized film libraries throughout the world, in every film center, and these libraries have a mass of material from which all manner and kinds of film can be drawn, not necessarily just those listed above, but in an almost unlimited amount of categories.

STOCK SHOTS: *Shots which are kept in stock, or in a film library, for general studio use.*

It may be, in a certain type of film or in a television series, that there are certain necessary shots which are repeated, particularly in a television series, week after week. These shots will be either selected from a film library at the beginning of the series, or especially filmed for that particular filmed or live television segment, and then placed away to be used when they are needed. Openings or titles, identifications for breaks in the scenes are also shot and filed away for continuous use week after week during the run of a TV series.

STORY BOARD: *A series of sketches of the action of the story to be filmed.*

Most often, story boards are utilized for the creation of animation films, and they are assembled to illustrate the story line, captioned, and serve as a general outline of the projected film. Walt Disney Productions deal in story board assembly greatly, as do Hanna-Barberra for their cartoon series. These story boards or rough assemblies of film are used later when the performers come in to record their dialogue.

However, there is another kind of story board, which is put together in a similar way, but in the sense of pre-preparation, where the set-ups of a major film to be shot are sketched out by an artist, in conjunction with the director, so that the director, and the director of photography, will have some idea, previous to the commencement of actual photography of the film, of what set-ups will be used in the day-by-day course of the filming. One of the most famous practitioners of this method of shooting is Alfred Hitchcock, who was at one time one of the most skilled art directors for films.

STRETCHOUT: *A large station wagon which can transport a dozen or more people to a location site.*

A stretchout is a specially constructed vehicle, sometimes with doors on one side only, capable of transporting at least a dozen people and their luggage to location. They are primarily used, from the pick-up point at the studio, to take actors and technicians from the studio to a location site outside the city.

SWISH PAN: *A type of panning shot in which the camera is swung very rapidly on a horizontal plane, from right to left, or from left to right.*

The processed film creates a blurred sensation when projected and viewed at a normal speed. This particular kind of transfer from one scene to another was, I should think, first instigated to produce some kind of shock, or to give an impression of rapid transfer, i.e., speed.

TAKE: *Each performance of a certain piece of action. All successive takes are numbered from one, onward, and these numbers are changed prior to the commencement of each take, on either the slate board itself, or the automatic slater.*

TAKE CAMERA (FRAMING): *To move into, or assume, a position, from a previous position, in a scene when the perfomer, or performers, who have been with you have left the scene, such a movement putting the performer squarely into the center, or near center, of the framing of the particular shot.*

This is usually a move dictated by the director so that the camera can isolate the performer in the scene, sometimes dollying in to secure an even bigger shot of him. It is important if the camera is moving to the performer that the performer remain on the spot he has assumed, after everyone else has left the scene and he has *taken camera*. It is also important, whether or not the camera is moving, that once the actor has assumed that final, last mark in the scene, that he take his look, i.e., assume his eyeline, exactly as directed, and hold it until the director calls *Cut!* If the performer has any doubt as to what exactly he should be doing under any of these circumstances, he should discuss it with the director, get a clear picture in his mind, and so be able to create the exact effect that the director is striving to achieve.

TAKE CAMERA (ACTOR): *When the performer moves out of the scene and takes a position which will give him a view of the scene as the camera is seeing it.*

This may mean just standing in close proximity to the camera and watching what the director is suggesting the actor does in the scene, or it may mean looking through the viewfinder, or the lens itself, to see exactly what the director intends that the performer should do.

During rehearsals of the scene, or sometimes even during the filming of a scene, after the take has been stopped, the director will sometimes step into the set to demonstrate a move or a piece of business. At this point, he may say to the performer, whose place he has assumed, "Take camera." This means that the performer should simply view the scene by placing himself next to the camera, thus enabling him to understand the problem from the director's and the camera's P.O.V.

TARGET: *A type of gobo, which is even smaller than a flag. It is circular in shape, and from three inches to nine inches in diameter. Half-targets are semicircular.*

Targets, as with flags and the other equipment which the electrical crew use, are placed in position between the lamp and the performer to create certain lighting conditions. Their use is a matter for the electrical crew and need not concern the performer, except when he is placed in or out of a light, and must take advantage of that lighting factor for the performance of his scene.

TEA WAGON: *A small, wheeled console, i.e., sound console, used by the Sound Mixer when controlling the sound on a soundstage.*

This particular console varies from a small portable to a larger, more permanent fixture on the stage, but is always "mobile," and can be transported quite easily from set to set, or from soundstage to soundstage. The mechanism of the console controls the operation of the camera, of the sound recording equipment, and of the lights, buzzers and/or bells, etc., which are activated to call for quiet or indicate the end of a take on a stage.

TELEPHOTO LENS: *A lens, of any construction, which is capable of extremely high magnification.*

A telephoto lens enables the camera to be removed, often at a great distance, from the scene itself or the performer, and by its removal from that particular scene, to photograph without distraction the scene or the performer in the scene. A further extension of the telephoto lens is the zoom lens, which, when adjusted and focused to its extreme focus, i.e., furthest removed from the performer himself, as far as the image is concerned, enables the scene to be shot from a more considerable distance than the more orthodox lenses.

TIE DOWN (ACTING): *A decision to do what has been achieved up to a certain moment of rehearsal.*

In other words, the scene has progressed to a certain point, which is to the director's satisfaction, and he may instruct the actors to *tie down* the scene as it is at the moment. He means that, as far as he is concerned, the scene is playing well, and that the actors should conform to what they have achieved to that moment, and so, *tie down* the scene, and play it in its present form.

TIE DOWN (CAMERA): *To indicate that the camera, having achieved a certain perfect framing of the scene to be shot, should be immobilized in the position it is now in; the term also infers that the scene is ready to be photographed.*

Depending on how the camera is mounted, whether it is on a tripod or whether it is on some form of dolly or boom, a perfect framing having been achieved, to the satisfaction of the director of photography and/or the director, the instruction to the crew is to *tie it down,* simply meaning that the camera should set firmly in that designated position, ready to record the scene from that particular spot.

TIGHTEN THE FRAME: *To play in closer proximity to the other performer, or object, or a portion of the scenery, in a scene which is being photographed.*

It may be that one player is closer to the camera than the other, with another performer in the midground of the scene, and the director will instruct the performer in the midground of the scene to come in closer, i.e., move forward to, or into a closer proximity to, the player in the foreground. The action performed in this instance will tighten the frame. The focus is changed as the player in the background comes forward, and settled on the two players as they position themselves in the foreground of the shot. The result, on film, is that the *frame will be tightened* around the two performers in the foreground.

In the instance of *loosening the frame,* the opposite applies. If two players are in close proximity in the foreground of the scene, and the director instructs the performer to loosen the frame, that performer, so instructed, must move in depth, directly or on a slight diagonal, away from the other player. The camera will adjust to make a new framing, and such framing, with a concurrent adjustment of focus, split between the two players, will *loosen the framing* on those two players.

TILT: *To so point the camera down or up so that the angle seen on film is changed.*

Tilting the camera is a movement of the camera in a vertical plane, and is in contrast to panning, which is moving the camera from left to right, or from right to left, on a horizontal plane. Tilting, in itself, can serve to emphasize the height of the person who is viewing the foreground subject or object seen by the camera, and conversely, if the camera is tilted up, it increases the actual height of the person looking down at a subject/object or off to right or left of the camera at an object or a person who is placed off-camera. Down angles, or tilting of a camera, is usually used to emphasize the state of the subject, that is, the performer in the scene, or to give a view of an object in a scene. The tilting up of a camera is usually to create a certain stature for the person or the object viewed by a camera, and make it more menacing, more ominous, or larger-than-life.

TOO BLACK AND WHITE: *Playing a scene too obviously.*

Sometimes in a scene a performer will play a scene in such a way that his *highs and lows* of playing are too much in contrast to give the correct overall impression of the scene desired by the director. Also, the actor may have made his character too villainous or too heroic, so that the *in-between-qualities* of the character itself are not emerging. A director may say to a player: "You are playing it too black and white." He will usually mean that the actor is playing the scene too definitely from a certain point of view, which he believes is not *exactly* right. It is, therefore, up to the performer to smooth off the mountains and fill in the valleys, so that his performance balances out, and the correct contours of his characterization emerge: to gauge the range of the term correctly, the player must think purely in terms of *black and white* and the *gradations between.* There are, of course, many gradations between black and white, and the director is suggesting to the performer, in essence, when he says that his performance is too black and/or too white, that he wants him to find those other gradations in between and so *shade* his characterization to a perfect "tone."

TRAVELING SHOT: *A certain shot in which the camera, on its mount, either a dolly or a boom, moves bodily in relation to its object, i.e., the performer or the conveyance in which the performer may be traveling. In other instances, a traveling shot may refer to a camera in motion on a certain vehicle photographing an actor in motion by himself or in some form of conveyance.*

This particular type of shot is not a *dolly shot.* A dolly shot can be achieved in a number of ways, either on tracks or on boards, but a *traveling shot* is achieved by placing the camera in a moving vehicle, such as a specially constructed camera car (or even in the trunk of a car), a train, a helicopter, etc., alongside which the performer and/or the means of conveyance on which he is traveling, moves in concert with the camera and its means of conveyance. This shot is also sometimes called a *trucking* shot, but whatever term is used, it means a shot in which a performer in motion is photographed by a camera in motion.

UNIT MANAGER: *The person in control economically of a production unit, either on the soundstage or on location, acting as he does on behalf of the unit's producers; often called a Production Manager.*

The unit manager has many duties prior to the commencement of production, and these have been explained generally under the term of production manager. Essentially, the unit manager is the person who controls the physical and technical function of the unit, whether on location or on a soundstage. Having established a breakdown in the schedule, and having a budget to which he must keep, it is his job to see that the director and his assistants keep to the schedule and stay within that budget.

UPSTAGE: *That area beyond the midground of the set (in what may be referred to as the rear of the set) in which a performer may move or perform.*

The same terms apply on a soundstage as they do on a theater stage. When a performer is directed to move *upstage*, it means to move away from the audience.

There is a secondary definition of *upstage* which applies in much the same way as in the theatre. It can be sometimes detrimental to the scene if another player *upstages* his fellow performer, unless, of course, directed to do so. Such a move, conscious or not, can destroy the balance of the scene, as seen by the camera, and must be corrected by the director. If a performer is specifically asked to *upstage* another player in a film set, by the director, it is for the specific reason of directing attention, in the scene, according to the placement of the players in it. However, to deliberately upstage another player is inexcusable, and to do this will certainly evoke correction by the director himself. Basically, to offer an *area* definition of *upstage* could be to state that the actor is placed in the background of the shot. In films, to move *upstage* is a movement that the player makes to place himself further away from the camera than the performer who is playing in the foreground.

"UPSTAGING": *A kind of cheeky attitude off-stage, unthinking, often irresponsible, sometimes deliberate, of one performer to another, which is contrary to the etiquette expected of performers.*

I list "*upstaging*" as a *term* and put it in quotes, primarily because this type of behavior by one performer to another (or by a performer to one of the unit personnel) is an *unforgivable breech of etiquette* on a film set. It is an indulgence in bad manners, and an action of which a performer should never be guilty.

It is a form of rudeness, which the professional in the business will not allow, and will certainly correct as soon as evidence of it is noted. It is a form of personal behavior which is not adult, and the professional who indulges in it can hardly be expected to win friends and influence people.

VIEWFINDER: *An optical device, attached on the left of a camera, which provides an image approximating that which is seen by the lens, if such a viewfinder is corrected, as it should be, to parallax.*

When the camera is in operation, the viewfinder is used by the camera operator to monitor, i.e., watch the framing of a scene. At such a time, it is impossible for him to look directly through the lens itself, since the internal mechanism of the camera is *racked over* at the commencement of the filming of a shot by the camera operator to enable exposure of the film through the lens itself.

WARDROBE MAN (WOMAN): *That person, male or female, who is concerned with, first of all, the selection of wardrobe suitable for the performer in the film, in consultation with the producer and the director.*

When the performer has been set for a part, and is called to Wardrobe, it is most important for the performer, having read his script, to have some idea of what his wardrobe should be. It is quite possible that the performer, with intelligence, can make suggestions, both to the producer and director, and to the Wardrobe people concerned, as to what wardrobe he should wear in the film. The more experienced a performer is, the more he is able to offer certain suggestions in this regard.

During the course of fitting(s) for a wardrobe, and the ensuing discussions and decisions on that wardrobe, the artist should work closely with the producer, the director, and the Wardrobe man. Having decided upon the wardrobe that he should wear in the film, he should then see, each day that he works, that that wardrobe is in good shape, and if it is not, call it to the attention of the wardrobe man and/or the producer and the director, depending upon the circumstances. The performer is directly responsible for the personal care, during the day, of his wardrobe, and should give it every consideration. If there is anything wrong with the wardrobe, or if any part of the wardrobe needs adjusting, he should bring it to the attention of the

Wardrobe man, who not only will adjust the wardrobe as it is required, but will each day, if it is necessary, see that it is cleaned, and properly laid out for the actor for the following day's work.

The Wardrobe man is a highly skilled person and, if the performer knows how to work with him, will go to any lengths to obtain the correct wardrobe for the performer, and keep it in perfect condition for him. It is important that the wardrobe should match every day, according to the scenes which are being shot, and it is equally the performer's responsibility in the morning, whether he is served by a dresser or not, to see that his wardrobe matches, if he is continuing a scene, exactly as it did on the previous day's shooting, and if not, to bring it to the wardrobe man's attention. In other words, in films today, from the very beginning of wardrobing for a performer, the performer must be equipped to discuss his costume with those people concerned, and so keep an eye on his wardrobe throughout the whole film to see that it supplements his performance to the best advantage.

WILD LINE: *A line that is recorded quite separate from a scene, a line which may or may not have been previously performed, which will then, subsequently, be inserted into, or overlaid, on the scene which has been photographed.*

It may be that a performer in a certain scene, with other extraneous sounds evident during the scene—such as horses, wagons, etc., passing through the scene—will be required to record quite separately what lines he has spoken or should be heard saying, so that these can be mixed into the sound track of the scene at a later date. Usually, he will do this quite separately from the filmed action of the day, often directly afterwards, sometimes at the very end of the day. The microphone having been set up, the Sound Mixer will call: "All right—let's have quiet. This is wild line for production 9621," and he will then *cue* the performer. The performer will then say the line into a microphone suspended over him. He may be asked by the Sound Mixer to repeat the line several times, and if to the satisfaction of the Sound Mixer, the line(s) will be okayed and noted for subsequent printing among the rest of the sound recorded that day.

WILD RECORDING: *Any sound recording which is not made syn-*

chronously with a picture image is called a wild recording.

Various sound effects—random voices, unidentified voices, conversation from a gathering of people, crowd responses, etc.— are usually recorded *wild*, and later mingled with the final sound track. Any form of recorded sound, vocal or pure sound effect, capable of being *laid over* an image, without having to be lip-synced, is usually referred to as a *wild recording*.

This type of recorded sound is also referred to as *wild sound*. Wild sound, in itself, may be gained not only from extras and performers on a set, but also may be extracted from a sound effects or a sound library, or specially recorded at a later date, and subsequently rerecorded into the final sound track.

w.n.: *When a performer might be needed for the next day's work, but a time has not yet been decided when he may be needed for his next day of work, the actor will be designated on the call sheet as "W.N.," or will notify.*

Two similar annotations, *will call* and *no call*, may also be used after an actor's name on a call-sheet but these two terms do not mean the same thing as "Will notify." They signify that the actor is not to be used on the following day, a start time for the day after that has not yet been decided upon, and that some-time during the course of the next day, evening, or the following morning, the actor will be given his call by the assistant director. In the instance of a *will notify* call, it does not mean that the actor if he is not called that night must necessarily stay at home the following day waiting for the phone to ring, but it is always wise, in these circumstances, for the actor to ring the set or the office of the unit, if the actor is going to be away from his own phone for any great length of time.

w.p.: *Abbreviation often seen on call-sheets for location work, signifying weather permitting.*

W. P., or *weather permitting,* for which the initials stand, will often be seen typed or written on the top of the call sheet which designates the next day's location (outdoor) shooting. It means what it says: if the weather is fine, then the shooting will proceed; if not, then the unit will, necessarily, either wait until the weather clears or proceed back to the studio, at once, to film in the *cover sets.*

As stated above, the *weather permitting* call (designated as such on the call-sheet) signifies that all going well the following day, and the weather being good, the unit will shoot; if not, it will return to the studio and work in its cover sets. If, in this instance, the actor is not on call for out-of-doors, but could be used in a cover set, should there be a change in the weather, he should stay close to his phone and/or check with the studio to see whether or no he will be required to work. If, too, with a *weather permitting* call, and the actor has not yet left for the studio, and the weather should be such that it looks as if he will not be required to work that day on location and is not needed indoors on the cover set, once again, the actor, at that early hour in the morning, should call the studio to see whether or no he should either drive to the pick-up point for that day's location work, or to the location, if he has permission to drive there; in essence, making very sure whether or not he is going to be used that day in *any* capacity.

WRANGLER(s): *That person, or persons, who is concerned with the handling of livestock—horses, cattle, other animals (other than dogs), etc.—to be used in a day's shooting.*

Generally, the term *wrangler* applies to those very skilled horse handlers who will provide the horses for the principals, and other players or riders in a day's filming. These men will bring the horses from the stable where they are kept, and will provide them, according to the actor's capabilities in handling a horse, to those performers, who need to ride or handle those particular livestock in the scene. Wranglers are very skilled both in the handling of all livestock, and in judging the ability of performers to ride. Their knowledge of livestock, as well as their knowledge of the capabilities of riders, is immense, and the performer should endeavor, under all circumstances, to make a close acquaintance with these men, who can provide him with a horse and/or with knowledge that will stand him in good stead when he has to use a horse in a particular film.

All of the wranglers in the business have, in the course of the years that I have worked in films, come to understand both my ability and my limitations in handling a horse. There has never been a time when I have worked that I have not been provided with an animal that I could use very well, and very comfortably, in any of the scenes in which I have to ride, or perform certain stunts on horseback, in the course of making the films that I have in Hollywood. I would say as far as actors go that I'm considered a better-than-average rider. Fortunately, I've had the advantage of being around horses from an early age. I urge all actors to learn how to ride competently. There are many times in all kinds of films when an actor will have to ride.

Take advantage of the wranglers' knowledge of horses when on a film; they can teach you many things. Some of my best friends in this business are wranglers; try to make them yours.

ZOOM-ZOOMING: *The actual, or apparent, rapid motion of a camera towards its object is known as zooming.*

The use of the zoom lens today is primarily that of punching into a performer or an object by *zooming*, in order to create an increased interest by a tighter framing. The normal method of *punching up*, before the zoom lens came into use, was to dolly in rapidly, or to cut from a longer shot to a closer shot to achieve *emphasis*. Today, with a properly used zoom lens, which is used both with sound and without sound, a director is able to *zoom in*, to *punch up*, to a big shot of the performer or the object, and so create an immediate intensification of interest.

ZOOM LENS: *A lens of considerably variable magnification which enables zooming effects to be simply achieved by the manipulation of the focus of that lens, without moving the camera towards its subject.*

By the use of this particular lens, it is quite possible to show a person at a distance in a scene, and then, by the manipulation of the focus of the lens, to *zoom* in to a very tight shot, thus filming an intimate reaction of the person within the scene, without resorting to cutting in a separate shot. It is usually difficult, though not impossible, in this particular regard, to record sound in this particular type of shot, but the impression desired is usually the revealment of a subject—a performer and his specific reaction to the certain part of the scene. The main object of *zooming in* is usually to point up the presence or reaction of the performer in the scene.

The blocking-out of a scene from a screenplay which you will encounter in this section of the book, analyzed for you as illustrated in the four accompanying figures, is what might be called the *American-style* coverage of a scene, a method of shooting a scene which, basically, has not changed since the day D. W. Griffith shot his first close-up and cut it into the body of a master shot.

In American feature film productions today, under the increasing influence of the freer form of shooting scenes which European filmmakers have practiced for many years, some directors have departed in some instances from this basic coverage but, in filmed TV today, because of the size of the screen, the economics of the TV side of the film business and the desire of most producers to have a director deliver adequate footage to them so that only they, the producers, may later cut it, this basic coverage of a scene is the one you will be most likely to encounter.

The coverage of the example scene is simple in essence, although it does call for a two-part master of six moves by the camera and 14 additional camera set-ups to cover the scene completely. The average competent feature film director might use only two-thirds as many shots. An imaginative American or European director might need only half as many. Without being obliged to provide coverage of the scene for a zealous TV producer, I could quite easily, with the use of a Chapman boom, cover this scene in one complete master shot and need only another half dozen shots to provide exciting, additional coverage of the scene. However, I felt it best for the purpose of the student-performer to demonstrate a full orthodox coverage first, because it will provide a basis on which to think in more unorthodox, European terms in the future.

Having studied this basic coverage, make sure at every opportunity that you *attend and study* showings of the latest European films and those American ones which follow this more imaginative cinematic coverage of scenes. You will see how the basic form of coverage can be compounded and varied so as to provide some very exciting cinematic results.

In this section, the performer will be taken step-by-step through the setting-up, the staging, and the blocking out, of a certain scene. For this purpose, I will use an extract from a western screenplay titled *Slade McKee*. It has not yet been produced, i.e., filmed and was chosen specifically for this reason. In this way, the actor is freed from any comparisons he might make in playing material that he might have seen previously on the screen and will be able to take a completely fresh approach to the scene.

In the blocking-out of the scene, the various shots, the coverage of the scene, will be discussed in detail—the master shot(s), the two-shots, the over-the-shoulder shots, the singles, the close-ups, etc. First, the performer will be taken through the scene from a purely physical point of view; then from the interpretative point of view. He will be shown the many requirements of beginning a scene and carrying it through in every aspect until the director has thoroughly covered the material. I will deal with the preliminary preparation by the actor for the interpretation of the character, how to work on the sound stage with the director, the camera, the sound, and the lighting people, some of the many aspects of the day-by-day work involved in acting professionally for motion pictures.

The example scene, pages 188–191, is the version which we used in the Screen Actors' Studio. Here the performer can study the scene as a whole and not be, in any way, inhibited by the *form* of the screenplay itself. The actor and the actress will be shown, step-by-step, what will be expected of them, from the moment of being called for an interview, of being cast, and handed a script, of being wardrobed, until they go to work on the soundstage and *shoot the scene*.

Let's begin at the beginning. The telephone rings, and at the other end of the line is the performer's agent. He tells the performer that a certain producer and/or director would like to interview him for the part of "Slade McKee" in a film to be produced called *Slade McKee*. The agent, having told the performer of this interest in him, gives him the time at which he has to be at the studio. The agent assures the performer that he himself feels that the performer is right for the part, that the casting director has assured him that a definite interest has been shown in the performer by the producer and the director. If the agent has some knowledge of the character "Slade McKee," which he may have secured from having read the script or having secured the breakdown of the descriptions of the cast from the producer, the director, or the casting department of the producer's unit, he will be able to give the performer a more detailed idea of what the character is. With this information at hand, the performer, when he goes to the interview, can think himself into the right frame of mind to present himself in the best way possible to the people interviewing him.

Arriving at the studio for the interview, the performer will present himself to the casting director who will take him to the office of the producer and the director. There, the performer may be handed a script and given a certain amount of time to read it, if the producer or the director wishes him to read a scene from the screenplay itself. If such is the case, the performer, having been told which scene he will have to read, should then endeavor to concentrate utterly, solely, on that scene, to read it as many times as possible, to gain a good overall idea of what the scene is about, and the attitudes of the character which he is to "read," and to settle in his own mind the characterization which he would like to offer in the reading.

Ushered into the office of the producer and the director, the performer should endeavor to be as relaxed as possible, in order to show off, to the best advantage, his own natural aspects to those interviewing him. If asked to read from the script, as is likely, he should play the scene with the necessary animation, applying all of his intelligence to it, but above all must endeavor to perform the scene without any nervousness. He can help himself in this regard by reading the scene a little more slowly than he would under normal circumstances. Once having read it, if it is not quite to his satisfaction, he may ask can he read it again, and if the producer and the director wish this, and are interested in him as a performer, then undoubtedly they will grant that request.

A decision regarding casting a performer may be arrived at on the spot during the course of such an interview. Then again, it may be that, wanting to consider both the actor and other candidates for the part further, the producer and the director will simply thank the actor for coming to the interview. The performer now must wait for the decision of the producer and the director, which will usually be arrived at in the course of the next few hours, or days, or *weeks*.

Assuming that the performer is absolutely right for the part, and the producer and the director want him to do the part in the film, his agent will be notified of the decision. The agent will have discussed, prior to that time, with the casting people, the price that will be paid to the performer for his work in the film. This offer will be related to the performer by the agent, and if a mutual agreement is secured between these two people, the agent will get back to the casting director and/or to the producer and the director, and *set* his performer for that part in the film.

Under certain circumstances, the performer may be required to test for the part, and, if this is the case, the performer should refer to chapter 2: Terminology—*Screen Test* and make a careful note of the particular requirements which will be mandatory for him to observe in the making of this screen test. In making this kind of test, the performer will prepare and play the test-scene to the best of his ability, and, all going well, his selection for the part will follow.

When the performer has been cast, and the script has been handed or sent to him, he will receive a call from the production office of the unit concerned, either from the producer's secretary or from the wardrobe man in charge of dressing the film, and a certain time and place will be set for him to come to the Wardrobe Department where he will be fitted in the wardrobe suitable for the part he is playing. The actor may be wardrobed at a studio or at a regular costume company, such as Western Costumes, Berman's, etc. Such companies, or the Wardrobe Department of a studio, usually can supply the costumes needed for the show. If not, they will be made specially for the film.

When the performer reports for wardrobe, wherever the department is located, he will find that the wardrobe man and, sometimes, the costume designer in charge of the show, will be there, and will have a number of costumes laid out for the performer to fit. When the performer has been fitted into them, he will be required, on most occasions, to show them to the producer and the director of the film. As a rule, the performer can rely upon the good judgment and taste of the costume designer and the wardrobe man to provide him with costumes which are suitable to the part he is playing. However, if the performer does not feel that the wardrobe given to him is exactly right, he is entitled to discuss this with these two men and with the producer and the director of the film, and suggest various changes. The astute, knowledgeable performer can substantially supplement the judgments of the costume designer and the wardrobe man, and make very valid suggestions to the producer and the director, in order to gain for himself the very best costume possible for his character in the film. Having tried on the costumes and decided upon any adjustments to be made to them, the performer, the producer, the director, and the wardrobe man further discuss each costume thoroughly, and will arrive at a final decision as to the costume that the performer will wear, allowing, of course, for certain small adjustments which will be made at a later date for the wardrobe department by tailors, seamstresses, etc.

It may be necessary for the artist to go to the make-up department, in order to have fitted various wigs or hairpieces, to have a make-up designed for his character in the film. After this make-up has been created on the actor by the make-up man for the unit, the performer may have to, once again, go to the producer and the director, and show this make-up to them, and, between them all, come to a decision on what will be the final make-up for the part that he is to play. Once these two matters of wardrobe and make-up have been decided, the performer can feel free that both these functions will be taken care of for him by the personnel in charge of those departments.

In certain shows, such as Westerns, it may be necessary to take into account a number of other things. For instance, if a performer has ridden before and has a preference for a certain horse, he may ask for that particular horse to be secured for him for use in the film. The producer and the director may have certain ideas on various accoutrements of wardrobe that he should wear, such as a gunbelt and guns, etc. These are all matters for the performer to discuss with the producer and the director, and make a decision on, well before the date on which shooting will commence.

The performer will want to discuss, with the producer and director, as fully as he can, the character that he is to play. The character will be, to the knowledgeable performer, fairly self-evident from the script, but in the performer's preparation of the part, there will be many unanswered questions, and these unanswered questions must be discussed with the producer and the director, and decisions made on them, as best as can be, before the start of production. The general overall attitude of the character, his development, all of these things, are the performer's consideration, and where he has thoughts in this regard, he must bring them up for discussion so that the producer, the director, and the actor, can "kick them around," and finally come to some kind of decision so that the performer knows exactly what he will do during the shooting of the film.

The preparation of a part, from the first page until the last page of the script, is a very intricate process. The performer must read and absorb the script and understand the story completely, so that he can clearly delineate his own character, and see it in relation to all the other characters in the story itself. He must be able to make decisions on the physical aspects of the character, as to how he will conduct himself physically in the various action sequences throughout the screenplay. He must, of course, have a very clear conception of the thought-process of the character from the first page to the last page of the screenplay.

In preparing a part in this way, the performer would do well to make notes throughout the whole of the screenplay—yet, no matter how complete a preparation a performer may make on a part prior to the commencement of filming, he will find many questions still to be answered during the course of shooting. It is the actor's continuing task to solve the problems, answer the questions. The problem of *filling-out* a character during the shooting of a screenplay, with the schedule all jumbled about, can be solved by preparing the character in the screenplay as one would prepare a character in a play for the theatre. If the performer has done a good preparation and has asked and answered the necessary questions which have arisen about the character, at each juncture throughout the shooting of the screenplay, no matter what scene comes up to be shot, the character can be intelligently discussed with the producer and the director by the actor for each scene that is listed in the day's shooting.

The more intense and *in depth* a preparation the performer makes, the more questions it is likely that he will find to ask

regarding his character. In each day's preparation for the succeeding day's work, he will find he has certain questions to ask
of the director and the producer. He should ask them, if possible, prior to that day's shooting. There will always be a certain
amount of questions to be asked on the day of shooting, but the
actor will usually find that many of these questions are answered
very simply by working in the scenes themselves, with the other
actors. If there is anything that bothers him from the point of
view of delineation of the character, then prior to the actual
commencement of the rehearsal of the scene, the actor should
find the time to discuss this with the producer and/or the director, and so, be able to go into a scene thoroughly equipped to
begin his rehearsals on it, and not in any way waste time during
the shooting of the scene by holding up production to engage in
discussion or pose questions that should have been asked and
answered before the commencement of rehearsals for that particular scene.

Shooting a film, because of the jumbling around of the schedule, is not quite the same process of applying preparation in one
continuous stream as it is for a play in the theatre. In films, the
performer must be prepared to make immediate decisions on
character development, but if his preparation has been diverse
and in depth prior to the day of shooting, he will find that most
of the questions that come up can be answered fairly quickly
and decisively on the spot, which, to say the least, is one of the
main facets of the economics of film-making, both materially
and intellectually/artistically.

Now, having made his preparation and being ready to commence work on the film, the performer concerned will be given
his call for the first day of shooting. Upon arrival on location, if
it is an outdoor film and the location shooting is to be done first,
he will find that, having been made-up and wardrobed, he is
now expected to move into his first day's work without a moment's hesitation.

Formerly, the first day's work on location used to be rather
leisurely in order to get the performers and the crew into a kind
of tempo of film-making. Today, this is seldom the case, especially in TV. From the first shot, the pace is fast and unremitting.

If the shooting of the film begins on location, there is a
physical element which makes additional demands on the actor,
especially in conditions of extreme heat or cold, and the per-

former must be prepared to adjust himself to these conditions when working out-of-doors. Let us assume, for the sake of the scene from *Slade McKee* which we are going to discuss in this particular section, that, having done so many days location work out-of-doors, the actor and the company move to an actual out-doors set of an Army fort of the period, a standing set which contains a practical stable in which such a scene could be shot. Now, this scene, which is set in the interior of a stable and which contains a blacksmith's forge, could very well be set on a stage, but irrespective of where the set is, whether it is on a soundstage or out-of-doors, the actor faces the same problems. So, regarding this scene which we are about to discuss and dissect to find out what are the approaches of the various performers in it, the various set-ups of the shots, etc.; let us not think of it as either a scene that is necessarily to be shot on location out-of-doors, as it very well may be, or on the other hand, as a scene set on a soundstage. Let us simply think of it as a scene that takes place in a set, wherein the performer has to play a scene.

The scene that we will analyze, in its many parts, is from a feature screenplay, the story of which takes place toward the end of the Civil War, "on-the-Border," as it was called, in the southern part of what is now New Mexico. The scene occurs early in the screenplay.

Now, to help the performers prepare the scene, it would be helpful to know what has happened in the screenplay up to that point. Here is the story so far: Colonel Slade McKee, a Texan, who has fought with the South during the Civil War, having been captured and incarcerated in a Northern prison, and having attempted to escape unsuccessfully several times from this prison, has, upon an offer from the United States Army to serve as a scout on the border, accepted this offer and ridden West where his instructions are to report to the commander of Camp Courage. Camp Courage is a U.S. Cavalry fort situated in the foothills of the Almagre Mountains in New Mexico. Making his way to Camp Courage, Colonel Slade McKee is stopped by a band of Mescaleros Apaches, headed by their chief, Escalante, and his two sons, Congaros and Natako. When Escalante and his sons find out that Slade McKee is heading for Camp Courage to serve as a scout for the United States Cavalry, they are clearly disappointed in him and remind him that when he was first in the West, he lived with them, had a son named Asa by the chief's daughter, Aliope, and that they have always considered him a blood brother of the Mescaleros. McKee admires the Mescaleros very much and remembers the time that he spent with them, but his orders are to report to Camp Courage, and so he proceeds on his way. When he arrives at Camp Courage, he is met by an old friend, Cal Burke, an ex-prisoner like himself, who also has accepted the offer to serve on-the-Border. McKee is further surprised to find that the commander of Camp Courage is a boyhood friend, Charley Dunham, with whom he originally went to the West from Texas and with whom he enlisted in the United States Cavalry in San Francisco. McKee is greeted by Charley Dunham, who tells him the real reason why McKee was offered his release from the Union Army prison, in return for serving on the Border. It is simply this: the Civil War is almost over, treaties need to be made with the Mescaleros so that the territory can be opened for new settlers. Dunham has realized that, because of his personal attitude to the Indians, he never will be able to conclude a treaty, in his particular command area, with Escalante and the various other Apache chiefs. Knowing that McKee is a blood brother of the Mescaleros, he has requested his release from prison so that he can serve as a go-between for himself with Escalante of the Mescaleros. McKee is not very pleased to learn this, but since he has been released to serve on-the-Border, he decides to accept Dunham's offer, and see if Escalante and the tribes that he controls, despite the fact that previously the Apaches have been betrayed, on more than one occasion, in their dealings with the Whites, can be brought to a parley and a treaty concluded. Following this discussion, Dunham tells McKee that Carrie Fairweather, a woman whom Dunham has always been in love with but whom he knows once loved Slade McKee, is coming out to New Mexico. Story-wise here, when Slade McKee went West and lived with the Mescaleros, Carrie Fairweather, not hearing from him, in her disappointment, married another man, who was killed in the Civil War. She has a son, Ned, and is coming out to New Mexico to live with her father-in-law, Leb Fairweather, who has a ranch a few miles from Camp Courage. Dunham has written to her, and asked if she will marry him. He has not told her that Slade McKee will be at the fort, not being absolutely sure that she will become his bride. Dunham feels that he has a certain hold over McKee. If McKee refuses to serve with the

Cavalry or to take Dunham's orders, Dunham can send him back to Andersonville. Following the discussion between McKee and Dunham, a wounded trooper brings the news that the stage bringing Carrie Fairweather and her son, Ned, to the fort, has been overrun by Apaches. In the subsequent search by Dunham, McKee, and others for Carrie and her son, it is Slade McKee and Cal Burke who rescue Carrie and young Ned from the Indians, who have been led on their raid of the stagecoach by Natako. Taken to Camp Courage, Carrie and Ned are looked after by the wives of the officers there. That is a capsule outline of the story to the point where our *example* scene begins.

At the beginning of the scene, Slade McKee is preparing a horseshoe for his horse, and, in the first version, young Ned, Carrie's son, comes into the forge and talks to Slade McKee. The conversation is interrupted by his mother and he is sent back to his quarters, so that his mother can talk to her old flame, Slade, with more privacy. In the revising of this scene for an interested producer, it was decided that the boy, in this particular scene, was unnecessary, and that the scene should be solely between Slade McKee and Carrie Fairweather, thus resolving it into a conflict between these two characters who have not seen each other, except in the rescue scenes, for quite some period of time. Both have been in love with each other at one time. McKee has been with the Indians, the U.S. Cavalry and the Civil War; Carrie Fairweather has been married. We have a situation where they would both like to get together again, from a physical and sexual point of view, but they are still sparring with each other because Carrie Fairweather feels that McKee went off with the Indians and forgot her, and that is the reason why she married this other man; McKee feels that if she had really loved him, she would have waited for him despite his "marriage" to Aliope. From the moment the scene begins, there is this conflict between these two people, which promises a renewed intimacy in the future.

The outcome of the screenplay is of no account at this particular moment, but here are two people who have known each other, have been in love with each other, have been separated for many years, and now, having been placed in contact with each other once again, with Carrie coming back presumably to marry Dunham, Slade McKee being the man responsible for rescuing her from the Indians, here they are, alone and face

to face. It is a situation between two people who have much to
forgive in each other's conduct and yet still feel very strongly
attracted towards each other. That is the background of the
characters up to the starting point of the scene that we will
block out.

First of all, let's spend a few moments "discussing" the character of Slade McKee. Slade McKee, as a young man, was
brought up on a ranch in the Llano Estacado of Texas. At the
age of seventeen, along with his friend, Charley Dunham, he decided to head West. On their way through New Mexico, they
met up with a tribe of Mescaleros Apaches, whose chief was
Escalante, and whose sons, Congaros and Natako, were much
the same age as McKee and Dunham. McKee fell in love with
Escalante's daughter, Aliope, and elected to stay with the
Apaches while Dunham went on to San Francisco to enlist in
the United States Cavalry. After a certain period of time, Mc-
Kee realized that he could no longer live with the Mescaleros,
although by this time he had had a son, Asa, by Aliope, and so
he left the Mescaleros and proceeded to San Francisco, where
he himself enlisted in the United States Cavalry and later served
on-the-Border in Arizona with Dunham. At the outbreak of the
Civil War, Dunham elected to stay with the United States Cavalry and Slade McKee decided that he would return to Texas
and enlist with a Texas battalion to fight in the Civil War for
the South. In the course of the Civil War, McKee rose to the
rank of Colonel, and was captured and incarcerated in a prison
such as Andersonville, succeeded in escaping several times from
the prison, only to be recaptured. Towards the conclusion of
the Civil War, Charley Dunham learned that McKee was a prisoner. Now having assumed command of Camp Courage in the
Mescaleros territory of New Mexico, Dunham realized only too
well that a man like McKee could help him negotiate a treaty
with Escalante. Without revealing his identity, Dunham offered
McKee his freedom if he will scout on the Border for the commander of Camp Courage. McKee accepted this offer and came
to Camp Courage. Although he has never agreed with Dunham's
philosophy towards the Indians, having accepted the post and,
at the same time, the absolute authority of whomsoever should
be in command, he felt he should do his best to secure the successful signing of this treaty for Dunham. Having agreed to this,
he is involved in the search for Carrie Fairweather and her son,
Ned, who, on the way to Camp Courage, have been captured by

the Indians and taken hostage. When he and Dunham took a patrol out to apprehend the Apaches, it was Slade McKee and Cal Burke who managed to recapture Carrie and her son, Ned, from the Mescaleros, and so return them to the safety of Camp Courage. Meeting up with Carrie again, he has experienced a resurgence of the emotions that he had for her years before, but in the scene that we are going to analyze now, he is, although very attracted to her, not quite sure how he should go about courting her again. He is not certain of how she feels about him, and what her real reason is for coming out here to join Dunham. McKee is a man larger than life, wise, virile, tough but gentle, who, from his boyhood, led a very adventurous life. He has been in love with Carrie Fairweather at one time, has married and had a son by an Indian girl, has served with the United States Cavalry and with the Confederate Army during the War, and now has been brought back into contact with his old boyhood friend, Charley Dunham, and with the girl he once loved, Carrie Fairweather. As a man, he wonders just how much he should allow himself to become involved again with Carrie—and decides to play it cool.

Now, the character of Carrie Fairweather. She is a mature young matron who, as a girl, grew up with Charley Dunham and Slade McKee. At that particular time, she had been in love with Slade McKee, and had been prepared to wait for him to come back from his trip to the West and his service with the United States Cavalry, or to join him wherever he chose to settle down. When she heard that he had lived with the Mescaleros, married an Indian girl, and had a son by her, she had been vastly disappointed in him, and felt that he had deserted her. She had married a man named Clay Fairweather, a young man of no great courage who, subsequently, because of his cowardice, was killed during the Civil War. Having received a visit from Charley Dunham, Carrie had agreed to visit with her father-in-law, Leb Fairweather, who has a small ranch in the vicinity of Camp Courage, and so give herself a chance to consider becoming Charley Dunham's fiancee. On the way to the fort, her stage-coach overrun by the Mescaleros, she was taken hostage, subsequently rescued by Slade McKee. All of her old feelings for him revived at that moment. Being a much more mature woman now, vastly different from the youngster of sixteen who first fell in love with Slade McKee, she has an ambivalence of feelings regarding her supposed engagement to Charley Dunham and her resurgence of feeling for Slade McKee. The scene itself, which we are about to discuss, takes place fairly early in the screenplay. It is the first time, except for a brief moment or two during the rescue sequence, where Slade McKee and Carrie come face to face, and are able to talk about the many things that have happened to them in the years that have passed.

The foregoing is basically the bare facts, a sketchy outline, of the characters, as I drew them up before writing the screenplay. For the performers concerned, attempting to analyze and play this example scene without the benefit of having read the full screenplay, it is not necessary at all to adhere rigidly to the characterizations which I have offered you. There is no reason why a performer, actor or actress, should not create preparatory notes, a more detailed background, a more diverse, even quite different background, for the character he or she will play in the scene. Whatever the actual content and structure of any screenplay is, the performer should endeavor to fill out in detail, as much as possible, the *structure* of the character. In other words, an actor should construct for himself the entire background of the character with which he is concerned, noting down every possible facet so that he compiles a life history of the character that he is going to play.

I refer you once again, to a book which is considered the Bible of all actors—Stanislavski's *An Actor Prepares*. This book offers a theory of acting which I consider clearly outlines the basis for all fine acting. However, whichever way you choose to approach this particular scene in order to gather the background of the character, I must leave to you.

Now, if you will examine the diagrams of the scene, Figures 1 through 4, pp. 164, 173–4, which outline the physical *blocking-out* required within the body of this scene, and compare them to the simplified script version, on pages 188–191, you will see that each movement, in the diagrams, can be related to the simplified version of the same. You will see that each number in the diagrams is inserted in the script itself, indicating, according to the physical movements in the scene, where the character is or moves to at that particular time. You will see also in the master shots, Figures 1 and 2, and in the subsequent coverage of the scene, Figures 3 and 4, the approximate placement of the camera for each particular set-up, in order to obtain full coverage of the scene.

Now, in setting down the movements of players and camera,

Slade McKee   Figure No. 1

ILLUSTRATION OF BLOCKING OUT FOR FIRST PART OF MASTER SHOT

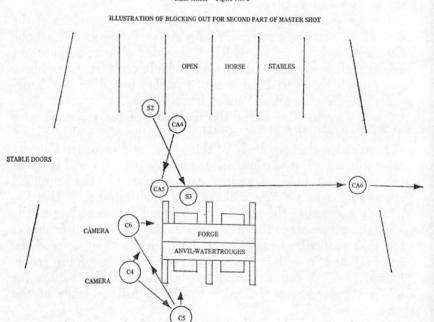

Slade McKee   Figure No. 2

ILLUSTRATION OF BLOCKING OUT FOR SECOND PART OF MASTER SHOT

in order to simplify them for the performer, I will show you first of all, in the first two diagrams, Figures 1 and 2, the movements in the master shot(s), which will cover the general action within the scene, and then you will be able to study progressively in further diagrams, Figures 3 and 4, (once again almost virtually adhering to the same basic pattern of movements as in the master shot(s) diagrams,) the necessary camera placements to *cover* the scene.

The master shot(s) will cover the whole of the scene from the beginning to the end, and will be discussed, in both parts, as a continuous scene, but when the separate masters are broken up into closer shots, i.e., close two-shots or over-the-shoulder shots, or singles, and those even closer shots, such as close-ups and big head close-ups, to provide emphasis, I will discuss, in detail, the reactions of the characters and the particular problems involved in each one of these particular shots.

To analyze each shot, the young performer will be asked to exercise his imagination. Each set-up must be carefully thought out, especially from a visual point of view, by the student performer in order to clearly grasp the problems involved. Undoubtedly, each performer will *see* shots in a different way. I only wish that it was possible to take an *actual filming* of this scene and place certain pieces of film down on this page, so that, from point to point, you could *see* what the scene "looks" like.

In analyzing the scene, you will find that the structure of it falls into three different sections: (1) the master shot(s); (2) coverage at certain points of the master shot(s) where the performer and the camera *are not in motion*; (3) those close shots, singles or extreme close-ups (also when the camera is not in motion), which will *point up* the scene.

In analyzing a scene in this particular way, we will be going into a great more discussion regarding each particular shot than would ever occur on a set. Once the performer has the knowledge to perform a scene such as this, and is able to take direction from his director, progressively, the process of playing becomes more automatic and there is often little or no discussion needed in the making of the scene. However, analyzing it from a beginning professional's point of view, this method I have chosen of breaking up the scene is the only possible way in which a young professional can thoroughly understand what is entailed in each particular set-up. Therefore, if it seems that the breakdown of this example scene from *Slade McKee* is overly detailed, once you have worked your way through this particular section of the book, it would be a very good idea to start from the beginning again, to read the scene afresh, taking the scene as a whole, thinking it through carefully, making notes for yourself concerning what you would be doing in the scene. If you are playing the part of Slade McKee, try to visualize the part—what he looks like, how he moves, the way he handles his personal properties —linking these to what he has been, what he is now, his thoughts and emotions during the scene; if you are playing the part of Carrie Fairweather, do the same. Make yourself a notebook based upon this scene which will provide you with a certain form of personal textbook. It can be referred to in the future, and so serve as a guide for all future scenes in which you will perform.

Basically, in performing for films, the young performer will find, give or take a really imaginative director or two, that there is a repetition of set-up, of physical behavior within a scene, with certain variations according to the content of the scene, the context of the material. If the performer can understand the basic structure of a scene, i.e., the overall scene itself, the writer's and the director's conception of it, the character that he himself must play, the character's relationship to other characters, and be able to accomplish the primary purpose of establishing the *geography* of the scene in the blocking-out of the master shot itself, so that the whole dramatic or comedic purpose of the scene, if shown in that particular form, would be clearly apparent to the viewer, then he will readily see that the *cinematic* treatment of the scene, achieved through the closer shots, which are used for emphasis to point up the emotional, the dramatic and/or comedic content of the scene, is merely an extension of this primary creative activity. This, then, is the basic overall structure of the scene which the performer must be aware of—first, the exposition of the whole of the scene, and secondly, the "fleshing-out" of the scene obtained by pointing up and emphasizing the scene with a selection of other closer shots, which, when cut together by the editor, will give the most interesting, the most effective delineation of the dramatic or comedic content of the scene itself.

If the performer can prepare his part in a *straight line*, so that he thoroughly understands the character within the scene, physically block out the scene with the director, so that his movements are correct, for the character, and so play it emotionally, that the context of the scene is revealed, he will find that every scene he plays, ever, no matter how long or how short it is, is composed, as far as cinematic technique is concerned, *with certain exceptions,* of a master shot, which covers the whole of the scene, and then a coverage of certain important points in the scene.

There are any number of ways to interpret a scene, but only one right one. Overall, it is the performer's task to have a clear grasp of the scene as a whole, to play it for its singularity or complexity of meaning, and then be able to repeat the scene in various other shots, according to the director's desire, so that the cinematic form of the scene can be photographed in its many parts, the film delivered to the editor, the physical form of the scene cut together, processed, and ultimately projected on the screen in a theater or on TV. Fundamentally, scene after scene, throughout a screenplay, *this is the best approach an actor can take to putting scenes together*: first, play the whole scene; then, repeat sections of the scene until all the necessary pieces of film have been shot for coverage. The actor's real satisfaction: to see all those pieces put together, and the final whole of the scene —or the film—reflect the quality of his personal artistry.

Now, to the actual, physical setting-up, or blocking out, of the scene from "Slade McKee." We will first go over the movements of all the characters, and the camera movements that will accommodate them during the master shots. We will then deal with the interpretive aspects of the two characters in the scene as a whole, and proceed to the breakdown or the coverage of the scene, by the director. At this point, I would like you to read, several times, the simplified version of the scene from *Slade McKee,* which appears on pages 188–191, so that you can refer to it as we move along. I should also like you to take a look at the four diagrams, figures 1 through 4. The Figures themselves will be discussed one by one; Figure 1 dealing with the first part of the master, Figure 2 dealing with the second part of the master, Figure 3, the coverage of the action in the background of the set, and Figure 4, the coverage of the action in the foreground of the set or the scene.

Let us now concern ourselves with the primary blocking-out of the scene itself, as illustrated in Figures 1 and 2. You will see that the first camera position, C-1, is designed to reveal a certain amount of the geography of the interior of the set itself. The camera is pointed towards Slade McKee, who is standing, working, at the forge in the center of the stables, and revealing in the background, the open doorway of the forge and the parade ground beyond. Outside of the forge, there would be the general activity of the fort itself, and this would be evident in the background of the shot, as the camera holds Slade McKee in the foreground of the shot, working at the forge. The actor's business would be so designed that shaping a shoe for his horse, he would take the heated shoe out of the fire, beat it into shape on the anvil itself, and finally cool it off in the water bucket. These particular movements, if taken from actor's left to right, would bring him into a fairly full-on position to the camera, and could serve to start the movement of the camera in the scene. The actor's first piece of personal business at the forge would precipitate a slight pushback of the camera, so that it could lead the actor as he moves from his first position to his second, that is, from S-1 to S-2, the camera preceding him to C-2 at an even rate, keeping him in perfect focus, until finally, the camera settles in C-2 and the actor in S-2.

Now, with the actor in position S-2 and the camera in position C-2, a different perspective of the interior of the set is obtained. As the camera is settling into C-2 and the actor into S-2, we would see Carrie in her first position, CA-1, in motion. The camera would have settled in C-2 before Carrie arrives at her second position, CA-2, just inside the stable, where Slade becomes aware of her for the first time. She would move into CA-3 after delivering her first line in the scene. Carrie's next movement, when Slade resumes his work on the horse's hoof, filing it, will then be to CA-4 and, in this particular position, the relationship of S-2 and CA-4 would require the third movement of the camera from C-2 to C-3, in order that the director may be able to have this part of the scene play in an open-two. He will, of course, later cover this set-up, but in playing the scene this way, and in later letting Slade McKee move out of the scene from left to right, that is, from camera left to camera right, he can set-up his first camera position for the second part of the master. You will see that all of these moves, both by the actors and by the camera, are clearly illustrated in Figure 1 on page 164.

It is quite possible that a scene such as this could be covered in one continuous master shot, the camera proceeding from C-3 back to the foreground, or downstage, of the set, and assuming positions that could photograph the scene through to the end of the shot, to camera position C-6 as illustrated in Figure 2 on page 164. However, this would require additional intricate camera movements, if a crab dolly is used as would most likely be the case in this particular coverage of the scene. In order to simplify the problem, the director might elect, as I have done, to shoot the master shot of the scene in two sections. He would carry the first part of the master up to the third movement of the camera, and then reset for the beginning of the second part of the master shot. Here I refer you to Figure 2. You will notice that the positions of the camera, C-4, is fairly relative to the position in Figure 1 of the camera position, C-3. However, with coverage at S-2 and CA-4, a fresh commencement of the scene from camera position C-4, to cover the second part of the master, is perfectly acceptable. The second part of the master, in this orthodox way of resuming the master shot, would commence on Slade McKee's move downstage back to the forge after his line, "It must have been," to Carrie. In beginning his move from S-2 to S-3, the actor pushes the camera back from its position of C-4 to C-5, where, in settling, it carries Slade McKee in the foreground of the shot at S-3, and allows Carrie at CA-4 to be seen clearly in the background of the shot.

The next movement is that of Carrie from CA-4 down to CA-5, where she virtually assumes a variable 50-50 shot with Slade McKee, i.e., a position of the two players which, in the playing of the scene, could vary between an orthodox 50-50 shot and an almost open-two. Toward the conclusion of the scene, where Carrie says to Slade, "See you at supper," and then makes a move from CA-5 to CA-6, just within the doorway of the stable itself, it would be necessary to counter the camera once again, from C-5 to C-6, to carry Slade McKee in the foreground at S-3 and Carrie in the background of the shot at CA-6, and to see her exit from the stable back through the grounds of the fort itself. This is, in essence, the same form of counter as in Figure 1. In Figure 1, the camera moves, or counters, from C-2 to C-3, that is, from left to right, as Carrie counters from right to left on the screen, diagonally from CA-3 to CA-4. In Figure 2, the counter is the reverse of this. The camera moves, or counters, from C-5 to C-6, that is, from right to left, and Carrie in her movement is virtually countering, from C-5 to C-6, left to right, across the screen. In essence, then, these are the physical movements required of the actor and the camera for the two parts of the master shot, as illustrated in Figures 1 and 2.

Now, before proceeding to the coverage of the scene, which

is clearly set down in Figures 3 and 4, let us concern ourselves with some of the interpretive aspects and the physical problems involved in the two parts of the master shot.

The performer in the part of Slade McKee will need to practice and develop a fluidity and a naturalness of movement in handling the forge itself, the bellows which will cause the fire to "hot-up," the tongs which will be holding the horseshoe itself, the placement of the horseshoe on the anvil, the beating of it with the hammer that will *simulate* the correct *shaping* of the horseshoe. These are not actions that can be accomplished instantaneously; the actor must find the time to practice these particular pieces of business if he has no personal acquaintance of them beforehand, and make sure that all of his actions are perfectly natural in the scene. Similarly, when he takes the cooled-off horseshoe and goes to the background of the scene to fit it onto the horse's foot, he must know how to pick up the hoof, how to place the shoe upon it, how to *simulate* or actually perform the actions of filing and shaping the horse's hoof and fitting the horseshoe to it, in the course of the performance of the scene. The actor can be readily instructed in this by those people best qualified on the set, the horse-handlers, the wranglers, who can show the actor what he should be doing in this regard.

For the sake of the set-up of the scene, what might be called the asthetics of the scene, the horses in their stalls would most likely be faced towards the camera and their halters secured to a rope strung across the front of each stall. The back wall of the stable might even be open or each stall have a separate dutch-door. The actor, in playing the beginning of the scene, will have to know how to pick up the forehoof of the horse. It can be done in two ways. Either it can be done with the performer's back toward the camera, that is, his own face toward the rear of the horse, in which case then, he must be able to pick up the horse's hoof by bending it up to him; or by facing in the same direction as the horse, and in another manner, picking up the horse's forefoot and placing it upon the front of his thigh. I would suggest this would be the best way to handle the horse's forehoof so that the actor is facing toward the camera.

The position of the camera at C-2 would be accommodated by taking out that particular dividing wall of the stable stalls, thus giving the camera a greater range of view and mobility. When Carrie comes into the scene and begins talking to Slade, the actor may have to move out, a foot or two, underneath the halter rope into a more *cleared* position. However, this need not prove necessary, depending upon the set-up of the scene.

Now, before the movement from S-1 to S-2, the performer, having prepared the horseshoe, must indicate, by a specific gesture, e.g., the cooling off of the horseshoe in the water-bucket, the holding of it in his hand again, or the taking-up of a file and paring knife, that he is preparing to move from position S-1 to S-2, so giving the camera a chance to lead away from him. In the course of the movement from S-1 to S-2, he must maintain an even pace so that the grip operator *pulling* or *pushing* the dolly, as the case may be, can keep at an even distance from him, thus enabling the focus to be maintained perfectly throughout the camera move.

With the camera in position C-2, where Carrie is now revealed in the background of the shot, she will be seen coming across the grounds of the fort and moving to her second position, CA-2. She will have been cued into motion, *through* what could be called position CA-1, by the director or his assistant activating a cue-light or calling directly to her when the camera starts to move from C-1 to C-2. She *must* be in motion as the camera is coming into C-2. At CA-2, since Carrie should pause to take in the scene, and say her first line, she must take a beat at that mark, CA-2, to allow any focus adjustment that must be made to be attained at precisely that spot, the distance between the camera and that spot having been measured by one of the camera assistants. The beat(s) taken by Carrie—before and after the line—is most important, particularly if the director wants to punch in at CA-2 for a single of Carrie. In my coverage of the scene, I have allowed for coverage at CA-2 and for a complimentary of Slade at S-2, camera positions C-7 and C-8, wishing from a directorial view to point up the renewed relationship of these two people and their attitude to each other as quickly as possible, at the very beginning of the scene. Before Carrie makes her next move, she should give to the camera operator working the focus some indication that she is about to begin, and then proceed evenly to CA-3, and, once again, *hit that mark*. There, because according to the lens being used on the camera the focus may have to be adjusted again, she should hold that position and then when she has to move to CA-4, once again assume her position at CA-4 accurately for the final focus in the scene as far as the first part of the master is concerned.

Interpretatively, the actress playing Carrie must convey to

the audience, as she comes into the stable, that her presence there is not accidental, but that she has come for a particular reason. When she comes into the foreground of the shot, it must be very evident that she *wants to talk to Slade*. On the other hand, Slade, seeing her in the background of the scene as she comes into the stables, *need not necessarily appear to pay attention to her* until she speaks her first line, but he must indicate clearly to us that he sees her approaching and give us a good idea of his emotions in that particular regard for a coverage single at C-8.

In the closer positions of S-2 and CA-4, when Slade reaches out to take hold of Carrie, giving the audience and her a clear indication of his feelings for her, it is an extremely difficult and delicate gesture for him to accomplish without appearing too blatant. Remember that they are not alone in the stable. In the background of the shot are other troopers working on their horses, as Slade later somewhat wryly indicates toward the conclusion of the scene. This moment requires the most sensitive display of *personal* acting between the two performers. The slightest gesture of Slade towards Carrie and her rejection of it by the smallest of moves away from him, can convey a great deal more than any larger gesture and/or reaction. It is important, too, that Slade, after his line, "It must have been," which is an indicative line in itself, should hold the look to Carrie and that she should return it before he moves out of the scene and back to the forge. In a scene like this, at its beginning, where a great deal is inferred and even more left unspoken, the performers must *fill out* the scene by the interchange of looks between themselves, and so, give the audience the chance to *think along* with them.

Referring again to Figure 2, which covers the second part of the master, you will see that the movement of Slade from S-2 to S-3 is a similar movement to his move from S-1 to S-2. In other words, he takes his look to Carrie after his line, "It must have been," and then begins his move, pushing the camera back from C-4 to C-5. The camera settling at C-5 reveals him at S-3, with Carrie at CA-4 in the background. It is quite possible that according to the position of the camera at C-5 and Slade at S-3, that Carrie at CA-4 may have to make a slight movement to her right to be absolutely sure that she is clear to the camera. This may not necessitate another mark on the floor for her. It is the performer's problem to see that they make that necessary miniscule move which composes them properly in the frame with the other player, according to the position of the camera. If she needs it, the actress should ask for another mark to be placed on the floor. Certainly check your adjustment of position with the camera operator.

Now, it is Carrie's turn to move to Slade McKee, from CA-4 to CA-5. In the later coverage of this shot, Figure 3, on this page, you will see that there is a shot—C-11—that covers her reaction at CA-4 to Slade's remark when he first arrives at S-3, which is, "I hear you're going to marry Charley." She makes her move, after that line, down to him, to CA-5, at a position camera left of the forge and inside the anvil, where Slade is reheating and reshaping the horseshoe. As I have said previously, she will virtually come into a 50-50 shot with him here at CA-5/S-3, and as the scene proceeds, according to how I believe they should play it, this position of the two players will change into an open-two from time to time.

From here on, almost to the conclusion of it, the scene itself becomes increasingly intimate in tone, and the business by Slade —of working on the horseshoe, of avoiding any overlap of sounds on the lines, of the use of the horseshoe to bring between himself and Carrie as a deterrent to her amorousness, must be timed

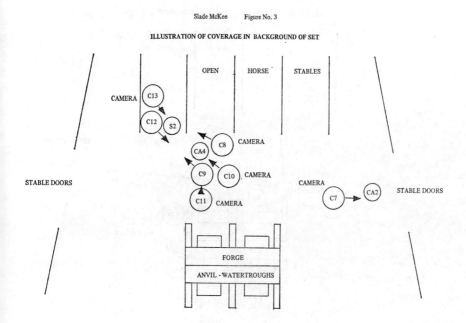

Slade McKee   Figure No. 3

ILLUSTRATION OF COVERAGE IN BACKGROUND OF SET

expertly. The next movement of Carrie is from CA-5 to CA-6. She says, "See you at supper," they hold a look for a beat, then, with a slight inclination of the head, a tiny smile, admitting her temporary "defeat" by Slade, she makes the move. As she moves, she must, in that beat, in the timing of it, give the camera a chance to counter from C-5 to C-6, as she walks from CA-5 to CA-6. There, at CA-6, she delivers the rest of her last speech in the scene, having "hit" that mark at CA-6 so accurately that the focus which will favor her there will be perfect on her in that position. At the conclusion of the line, she turns and walks out of the stable, thus concluding her part in the master shot.

You will see, in Figure 4 on this page, that there is a shot to be obtained at C-20 of Slade at S-3, which will be his last line in the scene, the close-up there matching the close-up of Carrie at CA-6, which will be covered from camera position C-19. Irrespective of these two shots, the final position of the camera at C-6 in Figure 2 could provide the final shot for the scene itself. It is quite possible that the cutter would go back to this shot in order to fade out, rather than on the single of Slade at C-20, depending upon the shot following in the script. The director

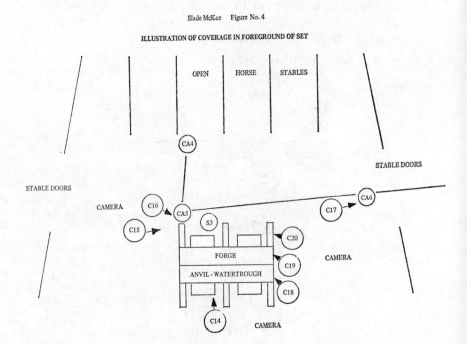

Slade McKee   Figure No. 4

ILLUSTRATION OF COVERAGE IN FOREGROUND OF SET

would give him this alternate: he has the conclusion of the shot at C-6 and will cover Slade for his single line in C-20 in Figure 4.

It will be seen in the discussion of the primary moves made by both performers in the blocking out of the scene—their interpretive gestures throughout the scene, the physical business with which they are involved—that it is very necessary for the performers to thoroughly set this business—each movement and gesture—so that when it comes to the coverage, which is indicated in Figures 3 and 4, the performer will be able to match, in those different angles, exactly what they did, physically, in the two parts of the master.

Essentially, in the two parts of the master, which are illustrated in Figures 1 and 2, the problems confronting the two performers are these: to so carry out their personal business that it appears natural; to move from position to position with an ease and fluidity which will enable the camera to assume without hesitation its subsequent position; to hit each mark accurately, as laid down in the blocking out, so that the focuses at those particular marks can be accurate; to, in close proximity to each other, anticipate, *virtually set-up*, the subsequent coverage of the scene without any drastic alterations of their positions; in short, to artistically simplify their movements, so that the coverage itself will not become more intricate than necessary.

I should like to elaborate on that last statement—I might even call it—*dictum*. If a player in a scene, which needs to be covered in order to provide emphasis in cutting, insists or persists in moving *erratically*, backwards and forwards, up and down, whatever, it is impossible to give that person proper coverage. Therefore, in a scene such as this, particularly in Figure 2 where Carrie and Slade are in close proximity to each other, an extreme turn away by Carrie to her right or a movement up and down in the scene to the background and once again to the foreground, would make it impossible for the director to cover her in other shots. Similarly, if Slade McKee, in his position S-3, were to indulge in movements which were unnecessary and distracting to the scene because of their multiplicity, unsuitability or ineptness, the director would be forced to stay with his master shot and have no possibility of shooting other shots and cutting together the scene, in the ways that I have laid it out in Figures 3 and 4. Therefore, the performer should make it a rule to simplify his movements in the scene, without restricting the artistic content of his playing, so that his performance serves to set-up the various other shots which are necessary for the coverage. Apart from all of this, during the course of the scene, it is the performer's task to play the character as truthfully, as realistically, and as convincingly as possible, moving in close harmony, both physical and mental, with the other performer(s) and the camera, so that the scene is completely believable. No small task for the performer to accomplish, but these are the basic essentials of accomplishing a perfect take of the blocking-out of the master(s), of playing each set-up for the scene itself. In this way, the scene has a pattern, it has a purpose, it can be covered, and all the shots obtained of the scene can then be placed together by the editor, in cinematic form, for the best possible effect.

There is a give-and-take between performer and director, between director and performer and camera, in every blocking-out of a scene, but the director will have the last say as to how he wants the performer to move, and it is then up to the performer to fulfill his character within the framework that the director has decided upon. Primarily, in the performing of the scene, the performers should stick to the decisions which were made in the blocking-out rehearsals and not attempt, within the body of the scene itself while attempting a take, to make any drastic changes in the major blocking-out of the scene. While a set-up is being photographed, there will inevitably be some slight, spontaneous, unpremeditated movements on the part of the performer which will not destroy the pattern of the shot, even, perhaps, add to it, but the performer should strictly discipline himself so that his business is regulated to his lines, and accurately performed, take after take, at every moment sticking very closely to the decided-upon pattern.

Now, let us proceed to the coverage of the scene as illustrated in Figures 3 and 4. You will see, looking at Figure 3, that the two players are primarily in positions S-2 and CA-4, with two pickup shots to be obtained: of Slade at S-2 and Carrie at CA-2, from camera positions C-7—the lighting being the same as for master shot—and C-8. They have already been covered in this position, S-2/CA-4, in the first part of the master shot from camera position C-3. You will also notice, in Figure 3, after obtaining shot C-8, that the next three camera set-ups will be C-9, C-10, and C-11 the reaction of Carrie to Slade at S-3. These shots would be shot in this order because the scene is lit in this direction, that is, the lights are aimed into the set and only need to be modified to light the performers in this particular way.

From the positions of C-12 and C-13 the lighting is reversed, and so the background behind these players from these camera positions will need to be lighted, and perhaps even a portion of a wild wall placed where formerly the crew and the camera stood, beyond the bounds of the set as illustrated in Figures 1 through 4.

So, in Figure 3, we have the first five shots to be obtained in the coverage of the background of this scene, at the beginning of this scene. C-7 and C-8 are singles of Carrie and Slade at CA-2 and S-2, respectively. C-9 would be an over-the-shoulder shot favoring Slade in position S-2. This particular shot will be so composed that portions of Carrie's face and body will be seen on the screen, on the right hand side of the frame, and Slade, in position S-2, will occupy the left side of the frame. This portion of the scene will be played the same way as it played in the master shot. The concentration of the two characters, one towards the other, is important. The matching of the business that Slade is doing with the horse's hoof is *all important*. The set-up for C-10 is a single on Slade and should place the business that he is doing *below the frame set in this shot*. However, it is necessary for him *to continue with this business, or to simulate it*, matching it to his movements in the previous shots, the over-the-shoulder shots and the master. Carrie, formerly in position CA-4, would now be placed on camera right where, alongside the gear box, she would deliver the lines off-stage to Slade at S-2, making sure that, in no way, does she overlap. Slade's gesture towards her, when he wants to touch her, would be made in her direction, equally the same as if he could touch her in close proximity, as in the master and/or in S-2/CA-4 from C-9. Camera position C-11, a single on Carrie at CA-4 after Slade has left the scene from position S-2 and moved back to the forge, leaving the scene camera right on his way to position S-3, would be picked up in this position. It is her reaction to his line, which he speaks in the foreground at the forge, saying to her, "I hear you're going to marry Charley." She would then move out of scene, also leaving the scene camera right. It is necessary for both players to leave the scene camera right, or to indicate that they are going to leave the scene camera right, because in the pick-up of the second part of the master, starting from C-4, you will notice that the camera is positioned slightly toward the left-hand side of the set, and therefore, the players, in movement, Slade from S-2 to S-3 and Carrie from CA-4 to CA-5 in C-11 must move left to right across the lens, therefore across the screen. In this way the movements of the players will "match" and do not "cross the line," a term which I will not go into here since it is primarily a cameraman's problem on set ups to ensure that the images photographed will match on the screen when intercut by the editor. The next two shots of coverage in this particular part of the scene would be C-12, a complimentary over-the-shoulder of S-2 and CA-4, where the camera position now favors Carrie. Camera position C-13 is a complimentary single to camera position C-10, a single on Carrie at CA-4, where Slade, in position S-2, would assume a position alongside the viewfinder, or camera left.

I have often been asked what adjustments in his acting a performer must make, from what he does in a master shot, to what he must do when he is involved in a close-up. This, I believe, can be explained simply in this way: using orthodox lenses, the closer the camera is placed to the actor, the larger his image will be on the screen; therefore, the stronger his impact is on the audience. Thus, the actor can afford to compound his performance, the closer the camera is to him, and introduce more subtleties into his expressions, his gestures, his vocal tones, than he would be able to use in the wider, looser, more removed master shot.

Now, let us refer to Figure 4, which covers the positions of the players and of the camera, for the conclusion of the scene, in the foreground of the set. You will notice that the movements of the players are quite simple: Carrie has moved from CA-4 to CA-5 in the master, Figure 2. Most of her playing for the second part of the master will be at CA-5 until she makes her exit, going to CA-6, and then leaving the stable. Slade is at S-3 throughout this part of the scene. The coverage in the foreground is quite complex. From camera position C-14, there is the single of Slade McKee at the forge, which would cover the line, "I hear you're going to marry Charley." The single on Slade could either be solely on him, or show, over his right shoulder, in the rear or background-left of the scene, Carrie at CA-4. If covered in this way, it would be a slightly looser shot, and Carrie, in the background, might readily be in a softer focus than Slade at S-3, unless the forge itself was pushed back into the set, so that the lens of the camera, whichever one might be selected, could, with its depth of focus, carry both Slade at S-3 and Carrie at CA-4 in suitably sharp focus. Camera position C-15 would cover the over-the-shoulder of Slade at S-3, with Carrie at CA-5, and allow the movement of Carrie from CA-5 to CA-6 to be carried, if Slade counted slightly to his right and camera slightly to *its* right, after she has moved past Slade. In other words, a similar shot, though contra, to that of the counter of the camera from C-5 to C-6 in Figure 2, as Carrie made her move in the master. However, the primary object of camera position C-15 is to obtain an over-the-shoulder shot of Slade at S-3.

Slade, in his movements throughout this scene, will sometimes be facing the forge and sometimes be facing Carrie, probably using the diagonal between the extremes of these two positions quite a deal. You will see how important it was for the actor (in the master of Figure 2) to define and set his movements, so that he has them quite clearly in mind, and can duplicate them during the coverage of the scene with minor adjustments as necessary. C-16 is a closer shot of Slade at S-3 and, in this position, Carrie, at CA-5, would be on camera left and standing alongside the viewfinder while this portion of the scene was covered. Moving across Figure 4, the next shot would be C-18, which is complimentary to C-15, an over-the-shoulder shot of Carrie at CA-5 and Slade at S-3. Carrie's problem in this particular scene is somewhat simpler, in many ways, than Slade's, but also, she, too, has the opportunity in her movements of presenting herself full to the camera in this shot, of playing away from the camera, and so therefore, presenting herself, at certain times, in profile or of playing on the diagonal between the extremes of those two positions. Once again, this particular series of movements will have been determined and set during the rehearsal and the shooting of the second part of the master scene.

Camera position C-19, which is the complimentary of camera position C-16, is a single of Carrie at CA-4, and Slade at S-3 would position himself on camera right or alongside the gearbox of the camera. Keep in mind not to overlap during the close singles. At all times, when a performer is on camera by himself or herself, it is *most* important that this performer and the performer off-stage do *not* overlap their lines in any way. C-20 would again be a single, a rather loose single, of Slade at S-3, for his final line in the scene, "I'll be there," and, as I have said, the scene itself could dissolve out on this particular shot. The cutter, however, has an option here, as has been previously noted and he can either use the shot taken from camera position C-20 or even, if it suited him better, the final position of the camera at C-6, as in Figure 2, to dissolve out on this scene. C-17 is a single of Carrie just before she makes her exit from the stable and her looks, in this position, would be directed camera left, i.e., above the viewfinder. I would also like to point out that for camera position C-20, Slade's look to Carrie at CA-6 would be camera right—over the gearbox. C-17 would be shot after C-16 because the lighting of the set is in that direction. It could, of course, be picked up immediately after the end of the master, or after C-7, depending upon the decision of the Director and/or the cameraman. Personally speaking, if I was performing the part, I would prefer to pick it up at C-17 almost immediately following the over-the-shoulder shot in C-15 where Carrie could easily move to CA-6 during the shot.

In these four diagrams, Figures 1 through 4, you will clearly see the movements of the characters throughout the scene and the various positions of the camera for coverage. You will notice that, overall, there have been six camera moves and 14 set-ups needed to cover this particular scene. If you will refer to the written text of the scene itself, you will see quite clearly that each one of the moves of the two characters has been indicated. Apart from the necessity to assimilate the text first and to study closely the diagrams, it is now important for the player to work through the text himself and discover how the whole scene sets up. I would suggest that the two players concerned in this scene should institute a form of set for themselves, in the merest details, a table substituting for a forge, etc. There is no other equipment necessary, the personal business itself can be panto-mimed, but I would suggest that a third person be involved in the scene and act as camera. The two players concerned, playing Slade and Carrie, should block out the scene as I have indi-cated. Once having it firmly in mind, so that they can per-form it without hesitation, the third person should act as a cam-era and make his moves on the camera pattern, or assume those po-sitions of the camera as indicated in Figures 3 and 4 for the shots which are nailed down, i.e., the over-the-shoulders and the singles. Thus, at any point in the scene, the players should be able to stop and see if they are in the correct positions, checking at the same time with the person who is acting as the camera for the scene as to correct framing.

I would suggest that if there is a group of players together interested in pursuing this method of scene analysis further in a professional manner, without the benefit of being able to attend a school on film acting, that they might try to purchase or hire a viewfinder. If the person taking the part of the camera uses this, he can generally tell the players if they are in the right positions during the course of the scene. Then, too, he can step into the scene for either one of them, have that person step out of the scene, take the viewfinder, and view the scene from the particular position of the camera at that moment. In this way, each player will readily be able to see what he looks like on the screen at any given moment in the scene, and so be able to adjust his performance, which he must ultimately learn to do "mentally" as a performer, so that it is absolutely correct and photographable. In this way, working slowly and carefully through this scene, from the first camera set-up to the last camera set-up, the players, in any one of the positions which they may assume during the course of the scene, can see how they look and be a better judge of what is "happening" to them, cinematically and photographically, during the scene.

If two players work through the scene in this way, they will find that any number of problems arise, and must each, one by one, be solved in the course of the blocking-out, the rehearsing, and the subsequent playing of the scene itself. For instance, when Slade begins the scene at the forge, he must so arrange his business that in making his turn toward the camera, he can *push it back*, and activate its move from C-1 to C-2; at the same time, he must make his move in an exact relationship to the camera, arriving at his position of S-2 as the camera arrives at its position of C-2. From there, he must be sure, with the business of shaping the horseshoe to the horse's foot, that as much of his face as the director may require be seen in the shot during the course of this scene until the camera squares off at C-3 (when he is in his position of S-2 and Carrie is in her position of CA-4). From camera position C-2, the next problem, which is clearly indicated, is that of Carrie's entrance into the scene. She will have to come from the far background in this shot, and be sure to stay within the frame of the set-up itself. There should be no problems in the approach to the entranceway to the stable, except that she will be given a line of approach for composition purposes, and will have to adhere to that line, from her start in the far background, through to the midground of the shot, and finally to her position of CA-2, within the stable itself. It is important, as she progresses from CA-2 to CA-3, that she does not swing either too deeply to her right or too much away to her left, out of the frame of the shot. She must proceed from CA-2 to CA-3 to bring this resultant composition of S-2 and CA-3 into its correct proportions, and then, in that position, her next move from CA-3 to CA-4, which is virtually a move from right to left diagonally across the screen, will be in conjunction with the counter of the camera from C-2 to C-3. Here in this final position for the first part of the master, Slade at S-2 and Carrie at CA-4, the shot is covered by camera position C-3, where both players form a basic 50-50 shot.

In this particular position, a problem arises for the player playing Slade, in that, working away at the horse's hoof with several implements in his hand, all these movements must be neatly timed with his dialogue. It is very important also that he does not address *all* his remarks to the horse's hoof but sees that the most cogent parts of the dialogue itself, are addressed to Carrie herself, looking her over, looking up into her face, so that his expressions can clearly be registered during this part of the scene, in this and any other shot. Carrie's problem in this particular set-up is much simpler, and yet she herself, along with Slade when he straightens up from his work and reaches out to touch her, must indicate, with only the slightest amount of movement, that she does not wish him, at this particular moment, to make any gesture of love-making toward her. If, for instance, in the master shot, Carrie was to move a step or more away from Slade at this particular moment, the shot would have to be carried, i.e., used for cutting purposes, assuming it *could* be, in this looser shot, from camera position C-3. It simply wouldn't play as well, in this way, with the camera at C-12, which is the over-the-shoulder of Carrie at CA-4 with Slade at S-2. *It would be quite impossible* to cover this reaction of Carrie's at C-9 because clearly Carrie's step away from Slade would alter the composition set for the shot at C-9. In all probability, any such movement of Carrie would completely block a view of Slade in the shot. However, there is no big motion or reaction indicated in the script itself. The player should confine herself to conveying this rejection in the subtlest way possible, and not moving drastically out of the position that she has attained at CA-4.

The movement that Slade makes after his line, "It must have been," his movement from S-2 to S-3, must be done in such a way as to give the camera crew, at C-4 (the beginning of the second part of the master), every chance of knowing when he is about to make his move. In the first part of the master, with the camera at C-3, it is quite simple for him to move from left to right out of the scene. In picking up the master at C-4, although such footage would never be used, in order that the players can work into the proper mood for the second part of the master, the director might suggest that the scene itself begin prior to that point, possibly back at the time that Slade makes his movement toward Carrie, and then the lines run from there, "Don't" down through "It must have been," at which point Slade will make his move. However, after the delivery of the line, "It must have been," Slade will undoubtedly take a look at Carrie, and then squaring off away from her, begin his move. In this way, with those small movements, the line delivered, the beat or the look taken, the squaring away from Carrie preparatory to making the move, the camera operator and the crew are prepared for Slade's move. As he makes it, they can be pulling away in front of him, so moving from camera position C-4 to C-5, while he is moving from S-2 to S-3. Carrie, after Slade's exit from this particular set-up, will then turn to watch him, and it is at this point, after she has "settled in" to her slightly adjusted CA-4 position and is watching him, that Slade delivers his line, "I hear you're going to marry Charley." It would be, at this particular point, that the coverage of her at C-11 would be attempted, and since we would be shooting in a certain direction for C-9, C-10, and C-11, it is very clear that C-11 would be picked-up after C-9 and C-10, in order to avoid jumping backwards and forwards from one set-up of lighting to another. C-11 is a simple reaction shot of Carrie, a single, and must be quite full in relation emotionally to the line delivered by Slade, in position S-3. If I was directing the scene, I would have Carrie *turn into* the position, watching Slade as he moved to S-3, *in imagination,* and I would have him deliver his line camera right; she, of course, in the position CA-4, would be looking camera right to him, and I would have her begin to move out of the scene, camera right, duplicating the move that she makes from CA-4 to CA-5. With the camera at C-12, the director might instruct the player playing Slade McKee at S-2 to reveal a little bit more of his profile than might normally be the case in a shot such as this played almost vis-a-vis. In this instance, the horse would be angled around, if a portion of the horse or its head was in the shot, and the actor's right profile, in this instance, would be revealed a deal more to the camera.

Now, in the coverage in Figure 4, the problems involved here are more complicated. First of all, we have the position of Slade at S-3, covered in a single from camera position C-14. As I have said previously, this could be a single on Slade, eliminating Carrie in the background at CA-4, or, on the other hand, it could be a looser type of "single," a kind of two-shot, incorporating her in the left background of the shot. In covering this scene, I would certainly shoot C-14 in any case, although it is quite possible, with the camera at C-5, that this shot—C-5—could be effective. On the other hand, if I wanted to use the single, C-11 of Carrie at CA-4, I would need a single—C-14—of Slade at S-3 to complement it, rather than use the shot of the two of them that would be seen from camera position C-5 or a closer shot at C-14.

That portion of the second part of the master, with the camera at position C-5, would be used to bring Carrie down from CA-4 to CA-5. Her problem here is that as she comes down into the foreground of the scene, she *must not arc out* to left or right but make her move in a way that keeps the composition of the shot *firm* as she travels to and arrives at CA-5. From the first line of Carrie at CA-5 to Slade which is "How did you know that?" through the body of the scene, until she says, "See you at supper," the two players are in a close relationship *from which they should endeavor not to stray*. However, this does not mean that their movements should be restricted as far as their movements toward and away from the other player in *gesture* are concerned. Slade will be occupied, first, with the heating and shaping of the horseshoe, and toward the end of the scene, using it as a kind of a barrier between himself and Carrie to, in other words, *cool her off*, even to put her down in a certain way, and he must have these movements so integrated into the body of the scene itself that they can be repeated time and time again. Similarly, with Carrie, she need not be locked into playing directly to Slade, in a 50-50, but she must stay within the general periphery of the forge and him; she must, in other words, play within that 90° angle and match her movements from shot to shot.

I do not mean to infer in any way that when players are *nailed* onto marks, that they must stand like automatons and merely say their lines to each other, but it *is* most necessary for them to modify their movements in tight coverage. When I speak of tight coverage, I mean to imply the orthodox coverage of a scene which is the general practice in American film-mak-

ing. Other filmmakers in other countries do not always follow
this method. However, in America and usually in Europe, in
this type of scene, the filmmaker strives for matched coverage.
Tight coverage is more often practiced in television than it is
in the feature film, but a player should always impose that discipline upon himself and force himself to perform from a position
rather than to move about in undisciplined fashion during the
scene, unless called upon by the text itself. In television filming,
it is often necessary for the players to be *nailed* on these marks
so that the closer shots can be gained more easily without waste
of time, money, or effort on the part of all concerned.

If you will examine the text itself, from the beginning of the
dialogue at the forge between Carrie and Slade, you will see
clearly indicated in the text the primary pieces of personal business that the players must carry out during the course of the
scene—the reshaping of the horseshoe, the gesture of Carrie toward Slade, wanting to be more intimate with him, and his
movement of preventing her from doing so by the red-hot horseshoe held by the pincers in his hand. The primary coverage of
the scene, from C-15, C-16, C-17, and C-18, can be accomplished
in these four set-ups. The shot which will carry Carrie from
CA-5 to CA-6 can either be covered in the counter-move of the
camera from C-5 to C-6, or, as a second choice, and not a good
one, obtained in the camera position C-15 again with a small
camera counter. Carrie's problem in this particular move is that
she should not arc out too far to her left in the scene from either
position of the camera, C-5 through C-6 or C-15, although especially when the camera is in position C-15. In both set-ups, Slade,
in his position of S-3, can help by pivoting slightly to his left, so
enabling her to pass closer to him than perhaps she normally
would. When she has passed him, he can pivot back to his right,
even a little beyond, i.e., upstage, of his original position of S-3,
so that Carrie will be revealed quickly and quite clearly in the
right background of the shot as she moves to CA-6. Carrie's particular problem in coming in to CA-6 is to turn into the scene. I
would direct her so that she should, in moving to this position,
make her movement from left to right, i.e., in assuming her position, she should turn back over her right shoulder to Slade, rather
than over her left shoulder. I say this for a particular reason:
if we should examine the subsequent set-up of C-19 and visualize
it for ourselves, Carrie would enter the shot camera left, and if
when she was on her mark of CA-6, she turned to Slade over her

left shoulder, a deal of her back would be presented to us for a portion of the shot before she settled in facing the camera and looking camera left to Slade; whereas if she moved into the shot from camera left and turned back over her *right* shoulder, we would immediately see more of her face in this position. She is traveling a diagonal from left to right, and should continue into a *gentle hook* to the right at the end of that diagonal which brings her to CA-6, (instead of reversing the hook as she would if she turned back the other way over her left shoulder). I would recommend the actress moving into position CA-6, to come to her mark, take a slight beat, turn over her right shoulder to Slade. For a moment she finds his eyes, then delivers her lines, holds the look for a moment after his final line, then exits.

In the camera position C-20, Slade would be looking left to right, that is, he would be looking camera right, and Carrie would be placed in a relative position beside and behind the camera for the delivery of her lines in this particular shot. When he has delivered the line, and held the look on her as she is making her exit, he would then return to his work at the forge and continue that to give us a dissolve-out on the scene.

I think that if the performers have analyzed this scene thoroughly, from the players' point of view, they will have decided upon a definite line of interpretation in order to delineate the character with which they are involved. To *capsule* the scene generally: Slade himself has been very happy to run across Carrie again, although he has mixed feelings, about her impending marriage to Charley Dunham. Now, when she comes into the stable, he is again in close contact with the girl that he has been in love with. He endeavors, at the beginning of the scene, to make a physical contact with her, and is rebuffed by her lack of a response. He then attempts to discuss various matters with her socially and when she makes a move to be intimate with him, later on in the scene, he is able to, in his own way, by the using of the red-hot horseshoe and the fact that they are not alone in the stables, other troopers being there, attending to their horses, to make her aware, without putting her down too much, that it is too public a place to take up their affair again. We must have a feeling throughout the scene that these two people are *fencing* with each other, testing out how each feels about the other; perhaps wanting to commit to each other again, but, with so much that has happened in the time between, not being utterly sure whether or no they *should* commit once again. It is a scene

which recounts a certain amount of what they meant to each
other, of what the situation at the present moment is, of what
each feels about it; Carrie, about her supposed engagement to
Dunham, Slade's reaction to that engagement. This is the kind
of scene that is not played glibly, line after line. There is the
opportunity for the players, throughout this scene, to carefully
think about what has been said by the other, to react to that, to
look at the other player, to take those pauses which can fill out
so many thoughts between lines. It is not a slow scene, yet the
pace should be casual, deceptively so. The intensity of the relationship, of the emotions which are running between the two
characters, is considerably high. It is lightened, to a degree,
towards the end, by Slade's "humorous" attitude to Carrie's ad-
vances; and the scene itself concludes with a portent of what may
happen when they get together again. It is this *thrashing-out*,
this delineation of the characterization by the players concerned,
of their knowing what has gone before regarding both characters,
their relationships prior to this moment of meeting, how they
have felt and could feel about each other, that can make these
characters come alive. This is a kind of scene which is a very
personal scene, with certain sexual overtones, and must be played
utterly (and intimately) to the other player to give it full value.
It is not a declamatory scene; it is not a scene of evident conflict,
necessarily; it is not a highly dramatic scene. It is the kind of a
scene that we encounter many times in the development and
exposition of the story in the screenplay, and the more richly
played, the better the characters will emerge, and so start weav-
ing the tapestry of their progression throughout the rest of the
script.

To gain the greatest benefit from this section of the book,
I urge you to learn the text of the scene word-perfect; to block
out for yourselves, and mark out on the floor, the various positions that the characters assume during the course of the scene;
to move through these positions in the playing of the scene,
having a third person check you off from a camera's point of view
throughout both the first and the second master, and then
through the coverage of the scene; from time to time, taking
the opportunity to step out of the scene, assume the position of
the camera, while the other person steps into the scene in your
place, so that you can clearly see what is happening *on the
screen*, during that part of the scene. In this way, you can relate
the text and what the performer should be doing to the ultimate

cinematic image on the screen. By this method of study, by gaining experience in dry-runs of this nature, on the set the performer will, at all times, have a clear idea of what he should look like on the screen and work continuously with this in mind.

In the course of actual shooting, a scene like our example scene from *Slade McKee* may take a matter of 3-4 hours to shoot. If a feature film, it may take a little more; if television, a little less. Whatever the form of the film, the player must make a thorough preparation before he reports for work in the scene(s) in which he is involved. He must be sure that he is able to react quickly to suggestions made to him by the director, and apply them on the floor, so that results are gained as smoothly and as quickly as possible, and to the satisfaction of all concerned. If you apply yourself in this way to any scene, most times you will feel that you have satisfactorily performed your character and can then confidently go on to the next scene scheduled for the day's work. It is always possible that you will feel that you have not accomplished everything that you would have liked to in the scene(s), but as long as you have professionally managed to complete the scene to the director's satisfaction, then you are entitled to feel that a great deal has been accomplished. Put that scene out of your mind and move onto the next scene scheduled for shooting that day, or the next. It is now up to you to use our example scene from *Slade McKee* as a basis for analyzing all future scenes in which you might be engaged.

SLADE MC KEE: SCRIPT AND DIRECTION

CHARACTERS:
Slade
Carrie

Int. Stable and Blacksmith's Forge—Camp Courage—Day
Slade is heating and shaping a shoe at the forge. S-1 In the b.g. several other Troopers are tending to their horses and gear. Slade puts the shoe in the water bucket, goes to his horse, S-2 picks up a forefoot and starts preparing it for the shoe, with a paring knife and file. As he drops the foot and straightens up, he sees Carrie standing in the open doorway of the forge. She has put on a fresh dress and looks very lovely. CA-1—CA-2

Carrie
Hello, Slade.

She comes forward to him; CA-3 he looks her over appraisingly and grins.

Slade

Pretty dress.

Carrie

Thank you.

He starts work again on his horse's hoof. Carrie stands watching him. There is a lot of animal about Carrie—it shows through her "nice girl" veneer. Slade works carefully on the hoof. Carrie moves around him until she is facing him. CA-4 After a moment he looks up at her.

Carrie

What are you doing here? In a Union fort? I heard you were a prisoner at Andersonville. I didn't expect to meet you here.

Slade

Didn't expect to meet you here either. You never cared much for Yankees—far as I can remember. What made you change *your* mind?

Carrie

I still feel the same way about the North. Do you?

Slade

Spent the last four years fightin' against it. Saw a lot of men die in that time—Yanks and Rebs. Still think the South's right —no matter how the war goes. I was born a Reb. Guess I'll die one.

As he straightens up from shoeing the horse, Carrie is close to him. They hold a look between them.

Carrie

Remember the last time—we were together?

Slade

Surely do.

He starts to reach out for her but she avoids him, without really backing off.

Carrie

Don't.

Slade

Can't remember you ever objectin' before.

Carrie

That was a long time ago.

Slade

It must have been.

Slade moves back to the forge. S-3

Slade
I hear you're going to marry Charley.
Carrie is surprised that he knows about her and Charley Dunham; moves down to him. CA-5
Carrie
How did you know that?
Slade is working on the horseshoe at the forge.
Slade
I thought everybody knew—except me. And Charley didn't waste any time bringing me up-to-date minute I arrived here at the fort.
Carrie
He didn't have the right to tell you anything—yet.
Slade
That didn't appear to be the way he figured it.
Slade has gone to work on the horseshoe as Carrie comes over to him.

Carrie
That's not the only reason I came out here.
Slade
I know you're going to stay with your father-in-law—but you really came out here to marry Charley—didn't you?
Carrie
I don't know. I haven't—made up my mind about Charley.
Slade
He's made up his. Far as he's concerned—your answer's "yes."
Carrie
He shouldn't be so sure of himself.
Slade
Don't know about *that*. He seemed pretty sure of *you*.
Carrie
Then he shouldn't be. A woman has the right to make up her own mind—especially regards the man she wants to marry.
Carrie has moved in on Slade—close enough to be kissed—and it's clear that's what she would like him to do now. He gives her a wry look, after glancing around at the other Troopers working behind them in the stable.
Slade
Kinda public.
Carrie
I don't think so.

Slade brings up a red-hot horseshoe from the fire, holds it between them.

Slade

Gettin' kinda warm in here.

Carrie acknowledges her temporary defeat with a smile—the kind of smile that contains both a warning and a promise.

Carrie

See you at supper.

She moves to door of forge, turns back to Slade. CA-6

Carrie

(continued)

You *are* coming—aren't you? Charley said he asked you.

Slade

I'll be there.

Carrie leaves and Slade pushes the horseshoe back into the fire again, a grin on his face as he looks after her retreating figure.

3　　　　　　　　EXERCISES

The exercises contained in this section of the book were devised for use at Screen Actors' Studio in Hollywood. They were performed by the young professionals there and rearranged during the course of those sessions, until they resolved into the form that they are in now. The exercises became a major part of the curriculum at the Studio. It will be evident to you that these are exercises created essentially by working professionals. Each one of the exercises—and some of the exercises are broken up into many parts—were specifically chosen and constituted so that the young, beginning player could, in practicing all the moves contained in these exercises, discover, in due course, that these are precisely the moves that will be demanded of him or her when they begin working in films.

The exercises start very simply, and then become increasingly more complex, but, as with all *exercises, as with all scenes,* it is important to take them step by step, and then to meld each step into the following step, so that the complete exercise can be achieved without hesitation, and to the great satisfaction of the performers concerned. Before commencing work on the exercises in this section of the book, I would advise the young actor to construct for himself the gadget which is illustrated on page 193. It is the outline of the camera, the gearbox at camera right, the lens and matte-box in the center, and the viewfinder camera left. In this way, he will have those points of reference to use during the exercises themselves. This diagram can be constructed on a piece of thick cardboard or on a piece of plywood, and can be either hung on a wall or propped-up on a table, or perhaps attached to some kind of support, in order to simulate a camera at various heights.

The movements of a performer in any scene are basic and fall into two categories: firstly, the actor will be in movement from one position to another, and secondly, he will give, in certain

ILLUSTRATION FOR CAMERA OUTLINE

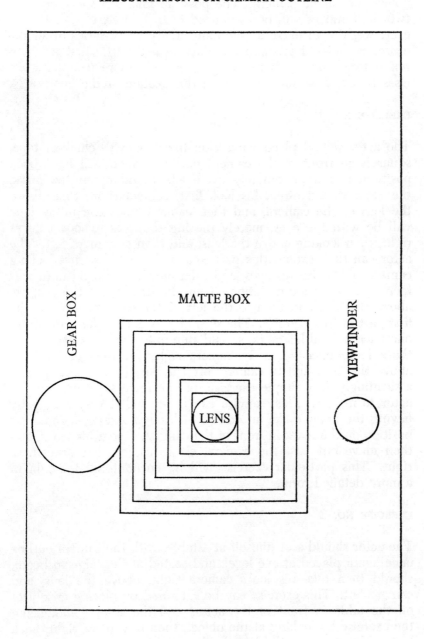

situations during the scene, a series of looks either to players or objects on- or off-camera. The possible infinite variety of these two basic moves will be evidenced in the course of doing these exercises, but to make a beginning, there are a series of simple exercises which I recommend that the actor tries first for himself before moving on to the progressively more complex exercises that will be encountered in this section of the book.

EXERCISE NO. 1

The actor should place a mark on the floor with chalk or tape, squarely in front of the camera outline, which will have been positioned at approximately eye-level. Standing on the mark, the actor should direct his look first, camera right, then above the lens of the camera, and then camera left. The initial look will be with the eyes, merely placing the eyes to look camera right, then looking above the lens, and then to camera left. The actor can then extend this particular movement by first looking camera right with his eyes, and then moving his head until it is facing in that same direction. Then, he can repeat the gesture, above the lens and then to the left of the camera. That is the first part of this exercise. The second part is that the actor, from one pace behind his mark, should step onto the mark and repeat those looks once again, to camera right (at the gearbox), to above the lens, and to camera left (at the viewfinder). This is a seemingly very simple exercise, but is a necessary one for the actor to master. This exercise can be extended very simply by having the actor make an entrance through a door, assume his position on the mark in front of the camera, repeat his looks, and then move out past the camera, either camera left or camera right. This particular exercise will be encountered later on in a more detailed form.

EXERCISE NO. 2

The actor should seat himself at a table, with the camera outline once again placed at eye level, and seated at the table to begin, should then take his looks camera right, above the lens, and camera left. This exercise can be extended by placing an object on the table in front of the actor, and the actor commencing the exercise by looking at the object, then to camera right, back to the object, above the lens, back to the object again, and then

camera left, and so, once again, going from camera left across
the camera to camera right, looking at the object between each
look. This exercise can be extended further by the actor sitting
into the shot and going, once again, through the process of
looking at the object, and then from camera right across to
camera left, and back again. The student performer, once he
has mastered the above two exercises, and can secure his looks
into each one of the places indicated, can, through the application of his own imagination, extend it into many forms. The
performer can jump his look from camera right to camera left,
and back again. He can take a look at a distance beyond either
camera right or camera left, and then bring his look closer to
the lens itself, as if a person had walked from the background
of the shot to the foreground of the shot. Take this basic exercise and work at it until your looks are direct and secure. Work
at this exercise until the exact object of your looks are able to
be called for, at any time, by another actor standing off-camera,
and that the look is a spontaneous one every time.

EXERCISE NO. 3

Now that you have attempted several basic moves—standing,
stepping into a mark, sitting in a chair, sitting down into a chair,
and then taking a series of looks directed camera right, above
the lens, and camera left—let us now move on to an exercise
which is designed, basically, to give the performer a chance to
stimulate his imagination and engage in pure reactions for the
benefit of the camera. I have broken this exercise up into a
number of parts.
A——The setting is a restaurant. You are arriving late to join
some friends for dinner. You begin the exercise by stepping on
to a mark in front of the camera. You search camera left, then
above the lens, then camera right, for your friends. You see
them, they see you, you acknowledge them and move out past
camera right.
B——You arrive home in a very happy mood, come to your mark
in front of the camera, and suddenly, at camera left, see that a
relative of yours—your mother, your father—has collapsed into
a chair. You take in the situation for a moment, and then move
out quickly, camera left.
C——Standing on your mark, squarely in front of the camera, you
listen intently while the foreman of the jury announces his ver-

dict. You are guilty of murder. You are sentenced to the gas
chamber. You are innocent. Stand there, react, look camera
right, camera left, once again camera right, asking people to
believe that you are innocent.

(In this form of exercise, and throughout the various parts
of this exercise, lines are not important. If you feel impelled to
say something, talk. Otherwise, try to do the exercise silently.)
D——You step into your mark in front of the camera, see something camera right, you look away, you look back again camera
right. Whatever you saw is what you thought you had seen before. You look at it again and then move out slowly towards what
you have seen camera right.
E——Stand on your mark with your back to the camera. Hear
something suspicious behind you. Turn slowly to your left into
profile, then more towards the camera, so that you can investigate
the sound or the movement that you believe you heard at camera
left. Search for the source of the sound or the movement. Find
it, play its full meaning to you, and then move out slowly past
camera, camera left.
F——You make an entrance to a mark in front of the camera. The
setting is a night club. You stand on your mark and look around
the night club. After a moment, at camera left, you see a very
attractive person of the opposite sex, obviously interested in
you. You return the interest, and move out, camera left, towards
that person.
G——Standing in front of the camera on your mark, looking
square into the lens, you are suddenly shot and killed. Take the
shot and die in front of the camera with your eyes open, then
sink slowly below "*frame.*"
H——Standing on your mark in front of the camera, at camera
right, you see a dear friend approaching you at a run. Halfway
towards you, he slips and falls, rather comically. You suppress
a desire to laugh, see that he is getting to his feet with an effort,
and move quickly out to him past camera, camera right.

EXERCISE NO. 4

This is an exercise, once again, in reactions. The setting is: a
jetliner—firstly, upon the ground as the passengers are coming
aboard, and secondly, in the interior of the jetliner itself, with
each one of the characters seated prior to take-off, and during
flight. Each one of the separate characters listed in this particu-

lar exercise, and you may do them one by one, according to whether the performer is an actor or an actress, will be photographed, that is, *come on camera* for a reaction in five situations: one—as the character enters the jetliner, two—as the character "*sits into*" a seat, three—as the plane is flying through bad weather and after the announcement has been made, by the pilot, that there is some danger of the plane crashing, four—as the plane starts into a dive and appears to be crashing, and five —when the plane is pulled out of its dive by the pilot and resumes its normal flight. In each one of those five situations, according to the character that you select to play in this exercise, a reaction is demanded of the person as they enter the jet, take their seat or are directed off-camera by another actor during flight (in this way the off-camera actor can provide the instigation for the various reactions demanded of the character at each particular moment in the exercise). Reaction #1 should be obtained when each character, one by one, steps on to a mark in front of the camera, moving out after the reaction camera right or left. Reaction #2 should be gained after the character *sits into* a seat. Reactions #3, 4, and 5 will be given while seated. All reactions should be played to a designated spot—camera right, above lens, or camera left. Here is the list of characters:

1. Man—returning from Mayo Clinic where he has been told that he has terminal cancer.
2. Man—a Syndicate contract-killer type.
3. Man—the person who has squealed on the mob and whom the Syndicate contract-killer is after.
4. Man—a big-time embezzler, who is trying to get out of the country before the FBI nails him.
5. Man—heroin addict who is flying to a clinic to try the cure.
6. Man—a police department undercover man who is tailing the Syndicate contract-killer.
7. Man—an alcoholic who has caused the death of his wife and family in a car accident, and is now returning from that holiday trip to his home city.
8. Woman—in her middle 40's, desperately afraid of growing old.
9. Woman—a young girl, rich, spoiled, running away from home.
10. Woman—a movie star who is trying to travel incognito.
11. Woman—a sedate, quiet type who has, that same day,

shot and killed her husband and his mistress, and is making her escape to another city.

12. Woman—an athletic, sportswoman type who really hates men, and prefers hunting in Africa to cosmetics or romance.

13. and 14. Newlyweds.

For the actor and the actress preparing for this exercise, it is permissible that they use some props, if necessary, to delineate their character, but these should be kept to the very minimum. Similarly, all the reactions should be silent, and words or lines not used, unless absolutely necessary.

In this exercise, it is important that each one of the players, in taking whatever part they select, should try to fill out in their expressions as much as possible about the characters that they are portraying. It is an exercise in intense concentration, and in an ability to react within the character that you have selected for a small, minimal amount of time *on camera*, in order to delineate as fully as possible, the character that you have chosen to portray.

EXERCISE NO. 5

This exercise is another example of the *reaction* exercise, and falls into two parts. The setting is a chapel in which a coffin is displayed. In the coffin is the local Mr. Big, who has died under quite mysterious circumstances. Each of the characters listed below will step into a mark, looking down into Mr. Big's bier, and for a short space of time, look at him, show a reaction to the deceased, and then move off the mark again. That is the first part of the exercise. The second part takes place outside of the chapel, where, one by one, the people inside the chapel as they leave are interviewed by a newspaper man, who, in the list of characters, will be Number 16. Here is the list of characters:

1. Woman—Mr. Big's mistress.
2. Woman—Mr. Big's wife.
3. Woman—someone he has used and destroyed during his climb to power and fame.
4. Woman—his secretary, a woman who has been in love with him all her life, even though their relationship was strictly business.
5. Woman—wife of a former law partner of Mr. Big, who

was sent to prison for his participation and apparent guilt
in a stock swindle. This man died in prison. Some feel
that Mr. Big was responsible for his implication in the
crime, and that Mr. Big himself was the main perpetrator
of the stock swindle, although he went scot-free.

6. Woman—Mr. Big's daughter, in her early 20's, who is just
   now understanding what kind of a man her father really
   was.
7. Woman—any age, dressed in black, a woman who appears
   at the funerals of all celebrities.
8. Man—the local Syndicate man, whose pay-offs to Mr. Big
   kept the various rackets in Bigtown healthy.
9. Man—an FBI man. He has only one question to ask:
   Was Mr. Big's death from natural causes?
10. Man—Mr. Big's heir apparent.
11. Man—Mr. Big's son, in his early 20's, a spoiled, self-indul-
    gent, self-centered young man.
12. Man—Mr. Big's hatchet man, who knows more than he
    is ever likely to say.
13. Man—Mr. Big's political opponent, who stands for every-
    thing that Mr. Big didn't.
14. Man—whose daughter was mis-used and discarded by
    Mr. Big.
15. Man—Mr. Big's man Friday, a close friend and servant,
    who has compromised himself once too often, to serve
    his master.
16. Man—a newspaper man, sent by his paper to observe the
    funeral, and who will later question the participants at
    the funeral one by one, as they emerge from the chapel.

It is important in doing this exercise to prepare your character thoroughly, and to endeavor, within the time limit given you
when you come into the mark and look down on Mr. Big, to
convey exactly what your character is thinking. The actor "directing" the exercise could place a strict time limit on each performer. At first, ask each performer to remain no longer than
fifteen seconds on the first mark. Reduce it to ten, and then reduce it to five, and so, consequently, compound the amount of
effort needed to gain an instant reaction, the moment that the
character comes to the mark and looks down at the bier.

For the second part of the exercise, where the people partici-
pating at the funeral are leaving the chapel, and are questioned
by the newspaperman, the newspaperman should be stationed

off camera at camera right or camera left. One by one, each one
of the characters who have been inside the funeral chapel should
come forward, stand on their mark, and, in an ad-lib fashion,
replying or not replying, as the actors have decided for their
characters, each character should respond to the newspaperman's
questions, allowing or disallowing the interview. Each performer
should simply step into the mark and then move out past camera, talking to or avoiding the newspaperman, according to your
decision regarding the character you are playing.

EXERCISE NO. 6

For the purpose of this exercise, it would be best to add an
additional mark on the floor, to supplement the mark that you
have in close proximity to the camera itself. In other words, the
close-up mark to the camera should be some three feet removed,
and what we may call the medium-shot mark will be some ten
feet removed, directly away from the camera. This exercise is
another reaction exercise, with further extensions of movements
and looks required from each of the characters as outlined in
various parts of this exercise.
1. Begin on your medium-shot mark. You are watching
   someone dear to you being executed by a firing squad.
   You move from the medium-shot mark to the close-up
   mark, and looking camera left, give as full a reaction as
   you can to the command to the execution squad to aim
   and fire, the volley itself, and your loved one crumbled
   on the ground.
2. Position yourself on the medium-shot mark, with your
   back to the camera. Hear a squeal of brakes. Turn and
   look camera right. Move forward to the close-up mark,
   and see that a very dear, close friend of yours has just
   been knocked down by a huge truck.
3. Start a clean entrance out of frame, camera left. Come
   into frame and settle on the medium-shot mark. Something stops you as you come onto your mark, you turn
   and direct your look camera left. You come downstage
   to the critical close-up mark, playing the look to camera
   left all the time, and once there, having examined what
   it is that has attracted your attention, change your mood
   completely.
4. You are an undercover policewoman posing as a waitress.

You are on your medium-shot mark to start. Someone at a table behind camera, camera left, calls to you, and you come into your close-up mark with pad and pencil poised to take an order. There you recognize the customer. He is the wanted man you are after. You must signal, in some way, to a fellow officer, stationed camera right, that the man you are both seeking is sitting at the table camera left.

5. Man and Woman dancing. They begin on the medium-shot marks, dance down to the close-up marks, and take a position that is an *over-the-shoulder* shot, favoring the man. They hold the position, then dance around until the over-the-shoulder shot favors the woman. Hold there for three beats, and then dance away back to the medium-shot mark again.

6. Making a clean entrance from camera left, you assume your position on the medium-shot mark, facing camera. There, you let us see that you have an envelope in your hand. You move down to the close-up mark, open the envelope, above or below frame, and completely change your mood. (In this particular exercise, begin in one mood and make the change when you come down to the close-up mark, *after having read the contents of the letter.*)

7. Clean entrance from camera right to the medium-shot mark, there something attracts your attention camera left. You are struck by a bullet, you stagger forward to the close-up mark. There you determine who your assailant is, someone who is known to you, and that you have trusted deeply, and then you sink below the frame.

8. This is an exercise for actresses. You are fixing your face at a ladies' powder room mirror. Use the close-up mark for this exercise. You must assume that the mirror into which you are looking is behind the camera and above the lens. In the mirror, you see a little old lady enter the powder room. She looks around the room, and then comes forward to your left. As she becomes larger and larger in the mirror in front of you, you realize that the little old lady is really a man dressed in woman's clothing.

9. This is an exercise primarily for actors. Taking one step into the close-up mark, you are staggered by a powerful blow. Determine the effects of the blow, and then decide

what you are going to do about it. Play your assailant in
the viewfinder, i.e., camera left. When you have determined what you are going to do about him, either move
out camera left or retreat back to your medium-shot mark.

10. Make a clean entrance, camera left, come to your medium-shot mark, come slowly down to your close-up
mark, and there search camera left and camera right, as
if you had heard something or someone in the room with
you. Turn your back to camera. Hold that position for
a moment. Hear the sound or the movement again. Turn
to your right, so that you are looking camera right. Once
again, let your eyes go across the camera, until you are
looking camera left. Locate and identify with the sound
or the movement or the person. Play the full meaning
of it to you. Then make a decision—either move forward,
out, camera left, or retreat back to your medium-shot
mark. There, once again, consider the sound, the movement, or the person that has attracted you, make another
decision, and exit out of frame camera right.

11. This exercise is designed to have the actor practice looking below and above the lens, from left to right or from
right to left. It must be remembered at all times, with
rare exceptions, that the performer must *never* look directly into the lens itself. In other words, his look, as it
passes across the lens, must not hesitate, except for a very
specific reason which might be contained in the context
of the scene, or unless the actor has been instructed by
the director to look directly into the lens.

The "setting" for this exercise can be the top of a tall
building, a high window, a cliff, somewhere that will enable the performer to imagine in his mind that he is looking down under the camera. In this particular exercise,
the performer should start out of frame, make a clean
entrance into his medium-shot mark, and then proceed
forward to the close-up mark. On the close-up mark, he
should find the object that he is seeking—if he is looking
down, it could be a person or a car approaching down the
street at camera right—and fastening his look upon the
object, travel the look across the lens from camera right
to camera left, hold the thought, his reaction to that particular person, car, etc., and then turn away from the
camera, and move out of the frame, camera left. Simi-

larly, for the exercise looking above the camera, once again, enter the scene to the medium-shot mark, come down to the close-up mark, find the object in the sky, whether it is an airplane or a rider moving along a ridge high above you, follow that particular passage of movement of the plane or of the rider from camera right to camera left, and hold the thought for a moment before you make your exit. This exercise can be repeated in an infinite number of ways, either back across the lens from camera left to camera right, both below and above, or on both diagonals, taking the look from the top of the right diagonal down to the left, or from the top of the left diagonal down to the right, following, let's say, the passage of someone coming down a hillside or down a flight of stairs or proceeding out of a building and across camera, right to left or vice-versa. There is an infinite variety of ways that this exercise can be adapted. First, set up the situation in your own mind as to what you are looking at, and then proceed to carry your looks across camera.

12. The setting of this scene is an exclusive gambling casino in Monaco, London, Vegas—choose a locale and start creating a character. You are a gambler, male or female. You make your entrance to your medium-shot mark, and then move to your close-up mark, where, directly below the camera, is the gaming table. Decide what game is being played—roulette, craps, chemin de fer, baccarat, whatever. In the close-up, you observe the play on the table below you. You try to make a decision as to whether or no you will take your seat and play. As you are about to make that decision, your attention is attracted camera right. Seated on the far side of the table is a very pleasant person of the opposite sex, who obviously finds you equally appealing. You acknowledge her, or his, response to you, and then finally decide whether or no to take your seat at the table. If you do sit into the chair, the camera will pan down with you, and you must continue your look camera right. If you decide against taking your place at the table, take your reaction to the obvious disappointment of the person who found you attractive, and make your exit camera left.

EXERCISE NO. 7

In this exercise, you will notice that, for the first time, two performers are employed, rather than just the single performer.
Only in the first section of this exercise is any property required,
and that is a single chair, placed squarely facing the camera.

1. The actor seated on the chair, in a close shot, will rise out
   of the shot camera right and make his exit in that same
   direction. The actress who has been standing out of frame,
   to camera left of the chair, will now settle into the shot from
   camera left, keeping her look on the actor who has made
   his exit camera right. After a short pause, the actress will
   rise out of the shot camera left, the actor will make his
   entrance, camera right, and settle into the shot, that is,
   take his place in the chair, hold his look towards the actress who has exited camera left, then bring his look
   around more toward the viewfinder and hold it there for
   a moment or two.

   The very simplicity of these movements in this exercise
   would seem to indicate that it is an extremely easy one to
   perform. You will find that if you can accomplish this
   small exercise expertly, then there will be no situation that
   you may encounter in the playing of any scene that you
   will not be able to handle, under similar circumstances.
   The important thing in this exercise is to settle into the
   shot first and then take the look at the player exiting, finally looking at a different "mark" for reaction purposes,
   if you should be the last one remaining in the scene.

   The order of this exercise can, of course, be reversed,
   both from the actor's and actress' point of view. The *set-
   tling-ins* and exits may be made from any side of the camera. They may be begun by the actor or the actress, it
   does not matter which, as long as a certain sequence of
   movement is maintained, and as long as these movements
   retain to a greater degree, the original form of the exercise
   as you see it above.

2. Actor (downstage) and Actress (upstage) will make a
   clean entrance into the frame and, without covering each
   other, come to the medium-shot marks, and there assume
   a fifty-fifty, actor camera left, actress camera right. They
   will then break from these positions by a movement of the
   actor downstage, so that he creates an over-the-shoulder

shot favoring the actress, the actress being on the right-hand side of the frame, and the actor's back being on the left-hand side of the frame. Hold this position for a moment, and then the actress should lead the actor in an exit, camera right, out of frame.

You should repeat this exercise, so that when the players have assumed the fifty-fifty shot, they break into an over-the-shoulder shot favoring the actor, who then leads the actress off camera left in the same manner as before. This exercise can be varied with actor making entrance upstage of actress and she first assuming an over-the-shoulder shot favoring actor. Similarly, in making the entrance from camera right of frame and exiting either camera left or right of frame, both players can rehearse and rerehearse this particular exercise, and the manner of doing it, favoring one or the other, according to how they want to do it.

3. The actor and actress will enter the set (or enter into the frame) from camera left, and come to their medium-shot marks, and there assume what could be termed a two-shot, with the actor in the background of the shot and both performers facing the camera. For the second part of this particular exercise, it is important that the person who is assuming the position of the camera, should then proceed to come forward, as though the camera was dollying forward on a crab dolly, so that a *close-up* of the actor is attained. In such a movement of the camera, it would be necessary for the actress to *bleed* out of the shot.

You can see, if you analyze this particular exercise, with the actor and actress entering the set from camera left, that it is important that the actress should be downstage, so that when she comes to the medium-shot marks, she can swing into the foreground of the shot without making an unnecessary movement. This exercise should be repeated with the actor making his entrance downstage, and so, therefore, enabling the actress to be singled out for a close shot. The action of entering the set should then be reversed with actor and actress making their entrance from camera right of frame, and once again alternating upstage or downstage.

4. The actor and actress will enter the set, coming into frame from camera left. The actor will walk to the medium-shot mark, the actress will blend with him in this shot, upstage

to a window, look out and then come downstage to a medium, over-the-shoulder shot, favoring her, as the actor
turns to her.

You will see in this particular exercise that once again
it is necessary for the actor to enter from camera left,
downstage of the actress, and so, therefore, in the final,
over-the-shoulder shot, his back will be on the left-hand
side of the frame and the actress will occupy the right-
hand side of the frame.

Once again, this exercise can be attempted with the
actress downstage, and with the actor going up to the window, coming back downstage to her, and being favored in
the over-the-shoulder shot as she turns to him. Further,
making the entrance from camera right, the positions are
merely reversed once again, and so, there are four ways
in which this exercise can be attempted by the performer.

5. Here is another exercise for two players. In the first version of it, the actress makes her entrance from camera left
of frame, coming to the medium-shot mark, and then proceeding very carefully until she is on her close-up mark.
This she must do by pre-measuring the amount of steps
that she will take between the medium shot mark and the
close-up mark, because it is important that when the actress settles on to her close-up mark that she is able to let
us know, to *show the camera,* that she is *blind.* Now, the
actor will enter the frame camera left and come on the
diagonal to the actress on her close-up mark, turning her
into a fifty-fifty shot. He will then pass his hand, either
upstage or downstage, past her eyes to see if she is really
blind. Convinced, he will take her by the arm and lead
her ahead of him camera right, that is, he will make an
exit with her camera right. The actor and actress can alternate in the *blind* part in this particular exercise, and further extend the exercise by making their entrance from
camera right and going out camera left.

The use of the actor's hand in this particular shot is
an important one, and I would like you all to try out the
use of both hands to see which might be considered best
from the camera's point of view. Both can be used, but
I do believe that to show the most part of the *blind* actress' or actor's features, whenever the other performer is
passing a hand in front of the *blind* person's eyes, that you

will find that it is much better to use the downstage hand.
6. This is another exercise where the actor and the actress
   can exchange parts. Here it is: the actress enters frame
   camera left, comes to the medium shot mark, there hears
   a noise camera right, comes forward into the close-up mark
   to investigate the noise, decides to investigate, and exits
   camera right. There is a beat before the actor enters the
   scene camera right and assumes the close-up mark, looking back over his shoulder in the direction from which he
   has made his entrance, his face exposing the fact to us
   that he has just murdered the actress. He holds the look
   for a moment, decides to leave, and exits camera left.

   The performers can change parts and go through the
   exercise from the same directions, and then, once again,
   repeat it with those camera directions reversed. In every
   way with this particular set of exercises, the actor and the
   actress can reverse the roles, and reverse the directions of
   their entrances into and their exits from the scene itself,
   thus making every exercise in this particular section possible to be performed in at least four different patterns. Go
   over these exercises time and time again until you have
   developed an ability to enter out of frame to whichever
   of the marks is designated and to exit out past the camera.
   It is important, too, throughout the exercises to have created some form of character for yourself to play; not just
   to mechanically walk through the movements and to take
   the looks, and then make the exits from the scene. Make
   the exercises work for you by establishing, in your mind,
   the character that you intend to play; then exercise your
   way through these little set-ups until you have developed
   the ability to perform these simple exercises without hesitation.

EXERCISE NO. 8

This exercise is one which is broken up into some twelve separate parts, but primarily, the exercise concerns itself with the
actor or the actress, making entrances into a room and leaving
a room through a door. There will be few properties required
for any one of the sections of this exercise—a small table and two
chairs should be sufficient. Once again, you will notice in these
small exercises the necessity for the actor to move fluidly, reach

a certain mark, take a certain posture, a certain look, and then, sometimes, to leave the scene once again.

Here are the sections of this exercise:

1. Actor enters door camera right, closes it behind him, says, "Hello, anybody home?" He then crosses down to the back of a table placed in front of the camera, sees on the table a note addressed to him, picks it up, opens the envelope, reads its contents, reacts, replaces the sheet of notepaper in the envelope, and then exits by the same door that he entered, leaving the door open.

2. Actress enters door camera left, turns in doorway and looks back over her left shoulder, holding that look for a long four-beat, and then very slowly, thoughtfully, comes into the room, closing the door behind her, and leaning back against the closed door.

3. Actor enters door camera left, closing door behind him. After a beat, he crosses to a table in front of the camera, comes to the downstage side of the table, and sits there on the corner, camera left, looking out camera right just above the gearbox.

4. Actress enters camera right and leaves the door open behind her, walks to door, camera left, favoring camera during walk across set, letting her look travel from camera right to camera left and then to the door camera left. She stops at door camera left, and looks back at the camera just above the gear box, camera right.

5. Actor enters open door camera left, making a clean entrance. He then crosses the set diagonally to a close-up mark in front of the camera and plays a reaction to camera left just above the viewfinder.

6. Actress enters door camera right, closing it quietly behind her. She opens door again to peer back into the room that she has just come from. Satisfied that all is well, she closes the door again, and then crosses the stage to the door at camera left, stopping square in front of the door, relating to the closed door and what could lie beyond it. She then turns back toward the camera, directing her look camera left and holding her position for a close-up.

7. Actor enters door at camera right, crosses down to the close-up mark in front of the camera, comes to attention in a smart, military manner, and holds the look above the gear box, that is, camera right for a long beat, and then

turns in a military manner and makes his exit through
the door camera right, closing it behind him once again.

8. Actress makes a clean entrance through door camera left,
crosses down to the back of a table in front of the camera, dials the phone which is on the table, and listens for
six beats as it rings. She then hangs up the phone, plays
a reaction directly into the viewfinder, turns and makes
her exit, through the door at camera left, closing the
door behind her.

9. Actor enters door at camera left, leaving it open, crosses
to a mark behind the table, picks up a note which is lying there, reads it, and then puts the note down on the
table, comes down around table camera right to a close-up
mark directly in front of the camera and says, directing
his look above the gear box camera right, "Have you
read that?"

10. Actor and actress enter door camera right, actress on
downstage side. They stay together in frame as they cross
up to window backstage, where they form a two-shot at
the window, favoring the actor. In this position, the actress would be looking out the window itself, as she
positions herself at the left hand side of the window, and
the actor, camera right, turning into the shot, now would
have his back to the window and be looking at the actress.

11. The actress first and then the actor enter camera left,
making a clean entrance through the door, the actress
waiting downstage while the actor closes the door behind
him. They then cross to table, which is center stage, the
actor leading. The actor pulls out a chair, camera right
of the table, for the actress to sit in. She does so. He
then takes the other chair from behind the table, places
it on camera left of table, so that when he sits, with the
table between them, the actor and actress are in a perfect fifty-fifty shot.

12. Actor and actress make clean entrance into room from
camera right, the actor closing door behind them. They
move forward to the camera into close-up marks, where
the actor then turns the actress into a fifty-fifty. He looks
at her for a three-beat, releases her, and moves one step
upstage, so as to form an over-the-shoulder shot, favoring
him.

You will see that these simple exercises demand of the actor a precise and fluid form of movement in making an entrance and moving to marks, and subsequently, in most instances, making an exit. The business within each part of the exercise itself brings out some points that we have mentioned in the Terminology before—the making of a two-shot; of an over-the-shoulder shot, the direction of looks to certain positions off-camera, etcetera. In working at Screen Actors' Studio, after a certain amount of participation in exercises of this kind, it became second-nature for the student to devise similar exercises to these we have attempted above, and, having set them down, to practice them. Any number of the exercises that we did at Screen Actors' Studio were "sketched out" as problems by the student performers themselves, and subsequently displayed in class for criticism. I urge you now to create some exercises for yourselves. Write them down exactly how you feel that they should be done. Try them out for yourselves, demonstrate them to other students who may have gathered together in a study group with you. In this way, you can offer them problems which they can try to solve. They can ask you to participate in and criticize exercises which they have written. In a group activity of this kind, everyone gains, both from the effort to construct the exercises, by participation in them, and by the subsequent criticism by fellow students of every performer while doing these exercises.

EXERCISE NO. 9

This particular set of small exercises extends the form of exercise that we have been doing up-to-date, and progresses into a more complicated form of movement and gesture. You will require a certain amount of furniture and hand properties in order to be able to do the following sets of exercises fully, although in lieu of hand properties, the business, of course, can be pantomimed. The set is basic: doors camera right and camera left, a window center in the upstage wall.

    1. Actor and actress will enter room through door camera left. The actress will cross to the downstage center of a table placed close to the camera. The actor will blend with her as she makes her move, staying upstage of her, and coming to the back of the table, favoring camera left of the window, and look out, totally and completely intrigued and held by what he sees. He will then call or

beckon the actress to the window. She will go to the actor by crossing around the table camera right, and the actor, now on the left-hand side of the frame, at the window, will accommodate the actress, at the window camera right of the frame, so that she is, to a degree, in front of him. They will look out the window, she will turn to him. They will look at each other, awestruck and wondering at what they have seen, and hold the look until the director calls "Cut!"

2. Actor will enter door camera left. He will cross down to the close-up mark in front of the table, and dial the phone, referring to his wrist watch while waiting for an answer to his call. When the answer does not come, he will hang up the phone angrily, and go camera right to a small bar, and there, favoring camera and relating to the phone, which he has just used, he will pour himself a drink, drink it, and then come back to the phone again. There, at the table, he will dial once more, listening to the phone as it rings unanswered, begin to chuckle to himself as if at some private joke that he has just thought of, hang up the phone with a rueful smile, and then make his exit, once again through the door at camera left.

3. Actress will enter door camera right. She will close the door behind her, and then come quickly and happily to the back of the table, placed in front of the camera. There, she will see on the table a note. Still in a happy frame of mind, she will pick it up, and as she opens it, move around the table camera right, come down to a close mark directly in front of the camera, read the note, take her reaction, which will be in a directly opposite mood to the one she conveyed when she entered the room.

Conversely, in this exercise, the performer may enter the room in a dejected mood, read the note, and react happily to it. This exercise, from an interpretative point of view, is designed purely to give the performer a chance to make a complete change of mood. It is important, in the close-up mark, in reading the note, that the change of mood is clearly evident on the performer's face. This change of mood need not be hurried. The performer can take whatever time he feels is necessary to make the complete change from one mood to another. At the conclusion of this exercise, the performer may stay on his mark, or they may elect to make an exit, sustaining the mood to which they have changed.

4. Actor and actress will enter through door camera right and cross to table center, making sure they clear each other. There, at the back of the table, the actor will light a small stub of candle, after taking out his lighter or finding some matches on the table itself. The actor and actress will now look around the room to see what kind of a room they are in, making sure that their reactions to their surroundings are clearly evident to the camera. The actress will then notice a note lying on the table. She will pick it up and, positioning herself so that the actor can illuminate the note with the candle held high, they both begin to read the note. As they read the note, they relate to each other, and begin to laugh, building the laugh until they are ordered to "Cut!"

5. Actor enters from off-stage, back of camera, camera left, close by the viewfinder, into close-up marks in front of the camera, and there, with his back to the camera, stops, looks back over his shoulder, gestures with his head to actress standing off-stage by viewfinder, the gesture to mean "Come on!" He then goes to the back of the table, which is situated in the middle ground of the scene, and, favoring the camera, begins to light a candle, camera right-end of the table. The actress makes her entrance, camera left, stopping on the close-up marks with her back to the camera. She, too, then takes a look back at the viewfinder to see if anyone is following them, then joins the actor in a fifty-fifty shot at the table, actress being framed camera left. The actor gestures with his head towards camera right, the gesture to mean, "Check the bedroom!" (Here, once again, in this type of exercise, either the gesture can be used or the line itself. Preferably start with the gesture first, and then, later, in repeating this exercise, use appropriate ad-lib lines.) The actress, taking up the candle, crosses in front of actor who eases back, goes to the bedroom door at camera right, the camera panning with her, leaving the actor off-camera. As actress crosses actor and clears him, he can begin his move, up to a window in the background of the set, and there, assume a position camera left of the window. The actress will go to the bedroom

door, open it, check to see that there is no one in there, close the door once again behind her, and then move upstage to a position on the camera right side of the window, joining the actor. As the actress arrives at her position camera right of the window, the actor is completing his business of checking the situation outside the window, and now gestures the actress towards the door camera left. First, she will move downstage to the table, blowing the candle out and placing it on the table, and then crossing to the door camera left, the actor blending with her from the window during this movement, so that they both arrive at the door camera left at the same time, form a fifty-fifty there, take a beat as they look at each other, the actress downstage, the actor upstage. The actor then opens the door for the actress, she makes her exit, he follows her, closing the door behind him.

Watching this exercise through the viewfinder could be illuminating to the student performer, but in lieu of being able to use that piece of camera equipment, might I suggest that, in all of these exercises, the actor who is serving

ILLUSTRATION FOR HAND HELD 'VIEWFINDER'

CARDBOARD, THREE-PLY, STEEL, ETC.

CUT-OUT

PAINT THIS AREA BLACK

as the camera, standing behind the outline of the camera, that I've suggested you make for these exercises, also equips himself with another small piece of "equipment" which will enable him to see whether or not the players are staying together and blending within the frame as they make these series of moves. He should take a small piece of cardboard or three-ply, some three by two inches in measurement, and in the direct center of that rectangular piece of cardboard or plywood, cut a small rectangle, some inch-and-a-half by one inch. In this way, this small opening, held an inch or two in front of his eye, will, in its way, simulate the dimensions of wide-screen framing, the kind of framing which is used predominantly in theatrical films today. (Refer to illustration on page 213.)

6. Actor will enter door camera left. He will hear the phone begin to ring on the table set in front of the camera. He will close the door quickly behind him, come down to a chair camera left of the table, sit and answer the phone. As he picks up the phone, he will hear a click, as if someone has just hung up. The actor must show the camera that he realizes that this was the person who has sworn to kill him, now checking to see if he is home. The actor hangs up the phone, moves quickly from the chair upstage to the window, there being sure not to expose himself to anyone outside the window. He carefully checks through the curtains to see if his possible flight from the house is blocked. He realizes that it is. He now returns downstage, slowly, to the chair, sits, and plays the full impact of his predicament into the viewfinder, camera left.

7. Actor will make a hurried entrance through door camera right to table and chair, downstage in front of camera. He will come to back of table, pick up briefcase from the floor behind table, and put three objects which are lying on the table into the briefcase, exposing each of them to the lens of the camera, so that we can clearly identify them. After having done this and closed the briefcase, the actor will take an overcoat from the back of the chair, camera right of table, and put it on. The actor must then react to a sound off-stage camera left without turning to the source, still facing camera right. In other words, the actor must make us aware that there is possibly someone else in another room, off-stage camera left, or else give us to believe

that someone is approaching the room from off-stage camera left. The actor will then make his exit through door upstage camera left, favoring his look to camera left at all times, until he has made his exit from the room.

8. Actor and actress will begin dancing upstage, and the actor will dance the actress downstage to the close-up marks, so that they come into an over-the-shoulder shot, favoring the actor, the actor being on the right-hand side of the frame, the actress on the left-hand side of the frame. In this position, the actor will say, "Think it over." He will then dance his partner into an over-the-shoulder shot favoring her. She will say, after a beat, "I have." The actress will then slap the actor across the face, take in his reaction to this, and then make her exit camera right, close to the gearbox. The actor will turn to camera over his right shoulder, move a pace forward into his close-up, and follow with his eyes the line of the actress' departure out of the scene.

9. Actress will enter door camera right, just awakening from a deep sleep. She will cross set, to camera left and open the door camera left. Actor enters door downstage of actress, crosses to back center of table, actress blending with him accordingly to front of table, staying left side of frame while actor stays right side of frame. Actor shows actress his credentials, saying, "LAPD" or "NYPD," (Los Angeles or New York Police Department.) Actor will then cross to door camera right. Actress will blend with him and so get ahead of him in her movement that she bars his entrance into room camera right, and in the position there of an open-two, actor upstage, actress downstage, say to him, "No one's in there!" Actor and actress will look at each other for a beat, actor will push actress away upstage, enter room. Actress moves into open doorway, looks into the room that actor has entered, turns to camera and registers her reaction to the siutation for a beat, then follows actor into room camera right.

EXERCISE NO. 10

The following exercise extends the basic form which you have encountered to date from the previous simple form into a full dialogue exchange between two performers involved in a series

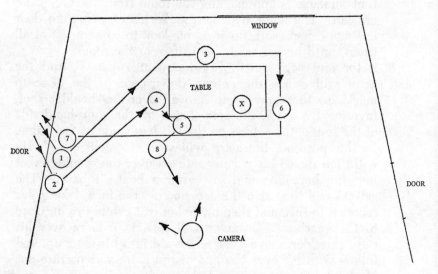

of moves. You will find the moves of both players clearly illustrated in the accompanying diagram of the *blocking-out* of this
exercise.

Here is the text of the exercise:
The actor preceding the actress, actor (upstage mark 1) and
actress (downstage mark 2) enter door camera left, the actor
closing door after actress enters. Actor and actress cross to mark
3 (actor) and mark 4 (actress), staying in frame as they do so,
actor leading and actress making sure to clear actor on the cross
from door to marks 3 and 4. Actor will settle into mark 3 at
back of table and actress into mark 4. Actress will take money
from her purse and throw it onto downstage corner of table,
marked "x." After she does this, she will move to a new mark,
5, saying as she does so:

Actress

There is the money. Now let's get this over with in a hurry,
    shall we?
Actor moves to mark 6 and picks up the money.

Actor

As of now—it's over. Thank you.
Actor crosses downstage of actress and moves to door, settling
on mark 7. As he crosses to door, actress will step into mark 8,
making an over-the-shoulder shot as the actor reaches the door,
saying:

Actress
Wait—please, I didn't mean it. I want to talk.
Actor
(turning back over left shoulder to actress)
I don't. Goodbye, Baby!
The actor exits out of door camera left, closing it behind him.
Actress turns back into close-up, taking center of frame, and
camera holds on her.

During this exercise, it will be necessary, of course, for the
camera to pan from time to time, at the beginning of the exercise and at the conclusion of the exercise. It is important that the
performers in this exercise hit their marks accurately, and take
care in making movements together, so that they blend, and stay
perfectly framed at all times. This should be checked for them
by the person who has assumed the position of the camera.

EXERCISE NO. 11

This exercise for actor and actress contains more dialogue than
Exercise No. 10, and the problems posed to the performers are
more numerous. They will be required first of all to do certain
small pieces of business, using hand properties; to blend with
each other, staying in frame, and clearing each other from mark
to mark. In subsequent moves, they will have to form other shot-
compositions—50/50s, over-the-shoulders, and so on. The camera in this exercise would pan the performers from camera left
to camera right, and the players will have to be sure, in making
their moves, that they are properly framed at all times.

Here is the text of the exercise:
Actress enters door camera left, comes to mark 1, leaving door
open. She must position herself close enough to small table,
downstage of door, so that she can light the lamp on table. As
she turns on lamp, actor makes clean entrance from upstage of
the outside of door camera left, to mark 2. He closes door behind him. As he turns to actress, she turns to him, so that they
are in a *fifty-fifty*.
Actress
I could have danced all night.
Actor
So I noticed.
Actor crosses upstage to mark 3 in front of bar, actress moving

ILLUSTRATION FOR EXERCISE No. 11

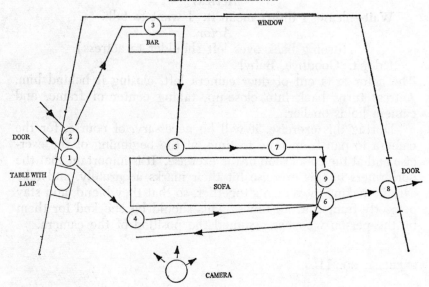

across stage with him, blending and keeping in frame, to mark 4, downstage of corner of sofa, camera left.

Actress

Jealous?

Actor

That'll be the day.

Actor comes down to mark 5 at back of sofa, hands actress her drink.

Actor

(continuing)

Do you mind drinking alone?

Actress shrugs, crosses to end of camera right sofa to mark 6, actor blending with her, settling at back corner of sofa, on mark 7.

Actress

I'm sleepy. I think I'll have this for a nightcap.

Actor

Sweet dreams!

Actress crosses to door camera right to mark 8, actor moving downstage to mark 9, which closely approximates mark 6, a previous mark for the actress.

Actress

Aren't you coming to bed?

Actor

Later. Don't wait up for me!

Actor exits out of shot camera left. Actress reacts to his departure, then goes into bedroom, shutting door behind her.

At the conclusion of this exercise, the actress must hold her
look to the actor exiting camera left, until either she "sees" him
go out the door, or "hears" the door close off-stage. In filming
this scene, we would naturally come around on a reverse and
shoot the actor's exit, but with the camera holding on the actress
at the conclusion of this exercise, it is most important that she,
in her mind, "sees" the actor exit, takes her reaction, then goes
into the bedroom, closing the door behind her, staying off-stage
until she hears the director call "Cut!"

EXERCISE NO. 12

This is a comparatively simple exercise, as you will see from the
accompanying illustration of the camera position and movements. It is designed, primarily, to place the burden on the
actor of creating certain set-ups for the camera. You will see,
in the first position of both players, that the woman is found
at the window W1, and that the man joins her M1 from the
camera left, making a raked two-shot, or a variation of an over-
the-shoulder shot. The man moving to the bar camera right

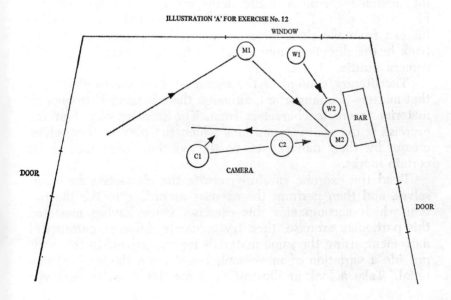

ILLUSTRATION 'A' FOR EXERCISE No. 12

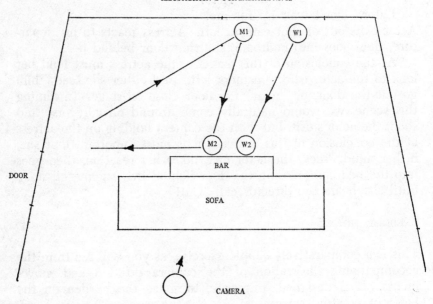

M2, creates another composition, which is a two-shot. When the woman moves down to the bar to join him W2, instead of a loose two-shot, in depth we have a much tighter two-shot into which the camera could dolly and further tighten at the bar for the part of the scene which is played there. In making his exit from the shot, the man will make his exit camera left, back in the direction from which he first made his entrance in camera position 1, C1.

The literary content of the exercise—of all the exercises, for that matter—is unimportant, although there is more than enough material to create characters from. The primary object of the exercise is the shot-compositions which the players themselves, create, by their movements, or the positions they assume on certain marks.

Read the exercise carefully, create the characters for yourselves, and then perform the exercise according to the illustration which accompanies this exercise. Once having mastered this particular exercise, then try to create different patterns of movement, using the same materials for yourselves. In this way, provide a variation of movement, based upon the original material. Take a look at illustration B for this exercise, and you will have a completely different set-up, or blocking out, of this scene, indicating how you can create a variation of the movements of the exercise.

Here is the text of the exercise:

Woman is at camera right of window, downstage, looking out W1. Man into shot from camera left, joins her in a two-shot M1.

Man

When do you expect him?

Woman

He didn't say exactly—just this afternoon.

Man

(Walking to bar)

Then come away from the window. He'll get here sooner or later. M2.

Woman moves down to bar, joins man W2, upstage and camera left.

Woman

You really have no idea how I feel about meeting him again, have you?

Man

(Making a drink)

Feel anyway you want to! Makes no difference to me!

Woman

Nothing gets to you, does it?

Man

Not a thing!

Woman

Do me a favor. Finish that drink and get out.

Man

Afraid I'll make your ex-husband nervous?

Woman

Just get out. I don't want to see you anymore.

Man shrugs, finishes drink, puts down glass, and leaves, exiting camera left.

EXERCISE NO. 13

Camera framing doorway. Man makes entrance camera right, rings door buzzer, M1, camera left of door, then assumes mark favoring camera right of door, M2. After a four beat, woman opens door, swinging it wide, W1.

Man
(Confidently)
Hello, Baby! Look who's here!
Woman
I thought you were out of town.
Man
I'm back to stay—if you're interested.
Woman
I'm not. Not now or any other time.
Man
Can I come in for a while and talk it over? Or would you
like to come out and we'll . . .
Woman
No—you can't come in. You can't call me and you can't see
me—here or anywhere else.
Man
Now wait a minute, Baby.
Woman
Goodbye.
Woman starts to swing door shut, but man holds it open with
his hand.
Man
Oh no you don't! I know when I'm not wanted— but no one
slams a door in my face. Think it over. I'll be around.
Man closes door quietly but firmly, turns to camera, thinks back
to closed door behind him for a beat, then exits camera right.

You will see, in the accompanying illustration for this exercise, that the exercise is an extremely simple one. The camera
is close and square to the door, and makes no attempt to open
up the shot more than a tight two-shot. This, in itself, places a
burden upon the players to accurately hit the marks that have
been placed for them on the floor, and to maintain them during
the playing of the scene, without, in any way, inhibiting their
particular performances. In such a tight two-shot, the framing
of the shot being critical, the players must make sure that they
maintain their positions so that the framing of the shot is con-
sistent.

In this exercise, the man makes his entrance from camera
right, positioning himself center of the door, as he rings the
buzzer. After having done so, he should take a casual look
left and right of camera, then ease back, as he hears the door
being opened, into his second mark for the scene, which is M2.

ILLUSTRATIONS A, B, AND C FOR EXERCISE No. 13

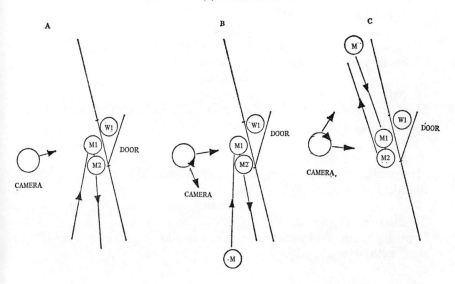

When the woman opens the door and makes her entrance into the scene, she should come forward to the mark that has been placed for her at W1 and maintain her position on this mark so that she is framed camera left in the shot.

It is possible to create slight variations in this particular exercise, by having the camera pan the actor in from camera right until he assumes his first mark in front of the doorway. As another variation, the camera can pan him in from camera left. He will assume the two marks—first M1 in front of the door and the caseback into M2, when the camera is square to the doorway. (See illustrations B and C.)

EXERCISE NO. 14

Woman comes through door, camera left, carrying groceries. As she closes door behind her, W1, man steps into fifty-fifty, M1, from off-camera left.

Man

(Showing ID)

Wallace . . . L.A.P.D., ma'am.
Man walks to window upstage center, M2. Woman blends to sofa, W2.

Woman

What do you want?

Man

(Looking out window)
Seen your husband lately, Mrs. Davis?

Woman

No.

Man walks down to back of sofa M3, indicates grocery bag which Mrs. Davis still carries.

Man

Eating for two?

Man walks to bedroom door, camera right, M4. Woman blends to middle of sofa, W3.

Woman

There's no one in there.

Man looks in bedroom door, then walks back into fifty-fifty shot with woman, M5.

ILLUSTRATION FOR EXERCISE No. 14

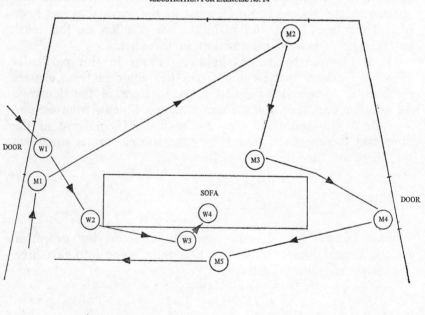

Man

The police officer your husband killed had a wife about your age . . . *and* two kids.

Man exits camera left. Woman sits on sofa, W4, and starts to cry, gradually breaks down and collapses onto sofa, sobbing broken-heartedly.

You will see from the illustration of the movements of the players and the camera positions for this exercise that the demands upon the two players are greater than in previous exercises. The first few movements of the players are blends primarily, as the man moves from M1 to M2, the woman moves from W1 to W2. She holds the second position, W2, as the man comes from M2 to M3. As the man makes his movement to M4, the woman moves her position W3, holding that as he rejoins her in his position M5. After his exit camera left, she takes her position W4, seated on the sofa. The timing of the movements of the two players is of utmost importance. It is ensemble playing. They must stay correctly framed during the course of the movements from one mark to another, thus enabling the camera, if desired and possible, to photograph this particular exercise from one set position, merely panning from left to right and holding on certain positions during the course of the action of the scene. Of course, each time that the players assume new positions and are not in motion, they could be covered in those positions, according to the director's desire.

As you can see, this is a more complicated exercise than the ones you have attempted before, but, once again, after you have attempted the original exercise, I urge you to set-up the exercise in other ways for yourself, attempting variations from the illustration that is included with this exercise, and try to create other block-outs of the exercise.

EXERCISE NO. 15

Man enters from street door, camera left, M1. He has been eluding his pursuers by running and dodging in doorways for several blocks. He is exhausted, out of breath, desperate. He crosses to camera right side of window, backstage, M2, camera panning with him, to include bedroom door, extreme camera right. Taking care not to be seen, man peeks out through curtain window.

ILLUSTRATION FOR EXERCISE No. 15

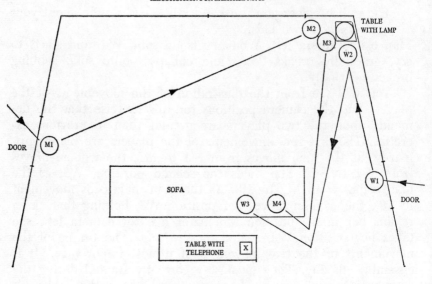

Man
(At window)
Connie? . . . Connie!
Woman appears in bedroom doorway, W1. She has awakened
from a deep sleep.
Woman
Joe? . . . Joe, honey?
Woman crosses to lamp and lights it, W2. Man jumps to lamp,
puts it out, M3.
Man
Call the police!
Woman
What? . . . Why? . . . what are you . . . ?
Man
(shoving her toward phone)
I said call the police! ! !
Woman comes downstage to sofa and coffee table, sits, W3;
picks up phone, listens. There is no dial-tone.

Woman

Joe, the line's dead! ! !

Man comes to sofa, sits, M4, takes phone from woman, listens, hangs up. They look at each other and hold look.

You will see in this exercise that, once again, the camera does not indulge in any movements, merely panning from left to right after the entrance of the man into the scene, and holding there until the scene concludes, with the two players seated on the sofa, in a close two-shot. The demands upon the players are few and simple, but must be carried out fluidly, in order to achieve the desired shot-composition and the right action-tempo in the scene. The movements themselves are combined with certain small pieces of personal business, the closing of the door by the man when he enters the scene, the peeking out of the window, the woman's quiet entrance into the room, her turning on of the lamp, the man's turning off of the lamp, her business at the sofa with the phone, his business with the phone when he joins her at the sofa, and the final look between the players should tell the audience of the strain and tension that they are experiencing in the situation. You will notice in the background of this scene, at the beginning, that the players are in a *loose* two-shot after the woman makes her entrance. Next, they come together in a *tight* two-shot. When the woman has come down to the sofa and is listening for the dial-tone, it is an open over-the-shoulder, a basic *open two-shot*. When the man joins her, it is once again a *tight* two-shot. In other words, throughout this type of exercise, the players moving in concert with the camera are creating, by their movements, a variety of shots. It is quite possible, in scenes like this, with a little more movement from the camera, that there would be no necessity at all to shoot other "coverage" shots. This type of blocking-out of the scene can enable the scene to play very effectively in a master shot.

EXERCISE NO. 16

Man and Woman are playing gin rummy at the bar. Man is behind bar, M1. Woman is seated on bar-stool, W1. Woman picks up one card from the deck, puts it into her hand, studies it. Man waits, woman lays down hand.

Woman

Gin!

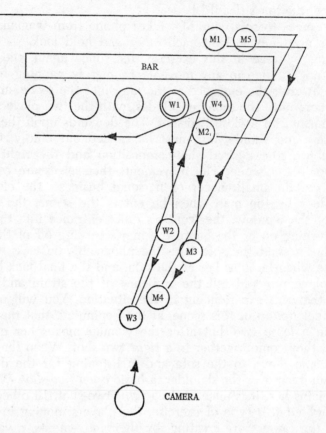

Woman writes score on pad, man turns on radio and starts his following speech as he comes around the bar into a fifty-fifty with the woman, M2.

Man
You're too good for me! Dance, lady?

Man dances woman downstage into an over-the-shoulder shot favoring the woman, W2 and M3.

Woman
Thanks for the "lady", anyhow, Charlie!

Man dances woman around until the fifty-fifty shot favors the man, W3 and M4.

Man
Why not? That I can afford!

Woman slaps man and returns to a seat at the bar, W4. Man

first reacts to slap to camera, returns to a position behind the bar, M5, turns off radio, picks up the cards and starts shuffling them.

Woman
(shaking her head)

That's all for tonight!
She studies score card.

Woman
(continued)

You owe me a dollar-seventy-five!
Man takes out money, counts it onto bar. Woman picks it up, drops it into her purse, and exits camera left.

If you will look at the illustration showing the block-out for this particular scene, you will see that it is primarily an exercise in *moving in depth,* toward and away from the camera. It is possible that this exercise could be extended, camera-wise, by having the camera close on the players at the bar, at the commencement of the scene, and moving away from them as they dance towards the camera, then having the camera follow after the man when he rejoins the woman at the bar toward the conclusion of the scene. You could attempt this variation of the exercise after havin done it with the camera in a fixed position, as illustrated in the diagram.

Another possible variation of this exercise is to make the movements not downstage and upstage, but on the diagonal, that is, from right to left, with the camera placed left of scene, or from left to right, on that diagonal, with the camera, of course, placed on the right hand side of the scene. Fundamentally, the movements of the players, irrespective, in any of these four variations of this particular exercise, are the same. Marks should be placed on the floor for each one of the positions, and the players will be expected to hit these marks accurately, so that their framing at any point during the scene can be checked by the person acting as the camera.

EXERCISE NO. 17

Man is standing near the window, camera right, looking out, M1. He moves nervously, obviously under a certain strain. He looks at the woman, who sits downstage of the window, her back to the wall, W1. Their exchange of looks is sympathetic. The man turns and looks out the window again.

ILLUSTRATION FOR EXERCISE No. 17

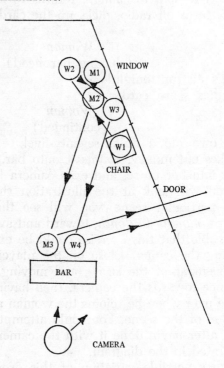

Man
If only I could do something. Just standing here, waiting . . .
not able to do anything. It's driving me out of my mind!
The woman goes to him, stands close behind him, W2.
Woman
There's nothing you can do. We just have to wait.
The man turns to her; she smiles up at him. He puts an arm
around her, comfortingly.
Man
I don't know what I'd do wthout you.
They cling together. After a moment he kisses her very gently,
before he breaks away and turns to the window again.
Man
Where are they? What are they doing out there? I can't
see them now.
The woman joins him at the window, downstage of man, W3.
Man comes close behind her, M2.

Woman

There they are. They're coming up to the house.

Man

Good. Now we'll find out what it's all about.

Woman

You'd better let them in.

Man

There's one thing I need first.

Man comes down to bar, M3, sets up glass and bottle, pours himself a drink. Woman comes down to him, W4.

Woman

Do you really want that drink?

Man puts down glass.

Man

No, not really.

Woman

Then let's go down and meet them together.

Man nods, puts his arm about the woman and they exit through door, camera right, the man opening the door, the woman preceding the man out of the room.

This exercise provides the players with more dialogue than they have previously encountered, and imposes upon them the necessity, at certain points throughout the scene, to communicate with looks that must be clearly revealed to the camera. In other words, in their positions at the beginning of the scene, it is important that the players, whether they are facing each other or not, relate to the other player, in such a way that this will be evident to the camera. The scene itself is not complicated in movements, but you will notice, at the beginning of the scene, that there is an interchange of positions at the window, that when the man moves down to his M2 mark, it is important for the woman, on her W3 mark, to be clear to the camera, and that when she joins him on her W4 mark, there to play an open-two, so that what the players are thinking at this moment, is clearly revealed to the camera.

The camera, at the conclusion of this scene, would pan the two players for their exit through the door camera right, the man undoubtedly opening the door for the woman, allowing her to pass through, and then closing it after they have exited the scene, both players making sure to *clear themselves* to camera.

In all of these exercises, I would like to emphasize, once

again, that the dialogue in these scenes is not important in itself. It merely provides some form of literary framework for the scene, and enables the players to communicate with each other, rather than just making a series of movements. Do not be concerned with the literary quality of these particular scenes; try, as best you can, to create a character for yourself, and then concentrate on completing the necessary movements in the scene as fluidly and as fully as possible.

In all of these exercises, it is very important that the person who is acting as camera should check to see that the framing on the players is correct, and if it is not, he should stop the scene and correct the players in their positions, stepping in himself for one of them, so that they may view the particular framing of the shot at that particular moment, and so, when they attempt the exercise again, achieve a correct framing, at that particular point and others, during the course of the exercise.

In all the exercises, the handling of personal properties— in this exercise, the liquor bottle and the glass, for instance— is very important. It is absolutely necessary that the player does these particular little pieces of business so that they do not *overlap in sound* on the lines of the scene itself. If the player finds that there is a certain awkwardness in performing such a simple action as pouring a drink for himself, then he should spend some time practicing it. It would seem that to pour a drink would be a very simple matter, but when called upon to do so in a scene, it sometimes assumes proportions that causes the player to be unnaturally awkward in doing such a piece of business. I repeat: the player, if necessary, should rehearse this particular piece of business for himself, so that he can unstopper the bottle, pour the liquor into the glass, put the bottle down again, stopper it, pick up the glass, and take a sip of the drink, as he would normally in life. Most importantly, the player must make the decision as to when he will do this, and be sure that the sound of the pouring of the drink, the setting down of the bottle, the setting down of the glass, will come cleanly between the lines or the words that he is playing in the scene, and/or those of the other players.

ILLUSTRATION FOR EXERCISE No. 18

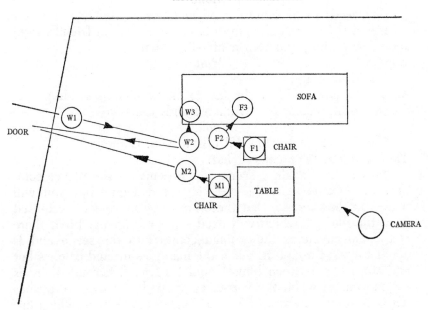

EXERCISE NO. 18

Woman enters W1 and crosses stage to her first mark, W1, and man, M1, and friend, F1, are seated at a table. As woman arrives at her first mark, W2, man rises and stops her, M2.

Man

Wait a minute, baby—I want to talk to you.

Woman

I don't want to talk to you. Get out of my way!

Man

I will when I'm ready.
Woman slaps man.

Woman

Are you ready now?
Friend rises from chair, moves to woman, F2, and pushes her onto corner of sofa, W2.

Friend

You know who you just slapped?

Man

Shut up, Max—I don't need your help.

Friend

She needs to be taught some manners . . .

As friend says "taught," man puts his left hand on friend's right shoulder, pulling him into a fifty-fifty shot.

Man

I said shut up!

Man now crosses his right fist to friend's chin; sending him sprawling onto sofa, F3. Woman stands up.

Woman

Thank you, Jack. Now I'll talk to you. Come on!

They exit out door camera left.

This is once again a scene which demands the player combine movements with the speaking of dialogue, but you will notice, in the exercise, that there are three movements required from the players, which will need some rehearsing. First, there is the movement as the woman comes into the scene and is about to pass through it, when the man gets up and catches her and stops her between himself and his friend. Second, there is the movement when the friend, angry with the woman, pushes her back onto the arm of the sofa. This is a movement which has to be accomplished smoothly and safely for the woman concerned. She must rehearse this piece of action with the person who is playing the Friend, so that it goes quite smoothly. Third, the action when the Man strikes his Friend and causes him to fall onto the sofa. This, in itself, is a minor stunt, but if you will refer to the Teminology, you will see, under *Stunt Doubles*, that it is often required of the actor that he throw a punch. Of course, the punch does not strike the Friend, but merely passes his face in such a way that it looks to the camera as if he has been struck. It is important, then, that the Friend takes the blow and falls onto the sofa, still staying on the right hand side of the frame, so that he can be seen. When he rises again, as he might during the end of the scene, it is important that he stays within the frame as the man and woman are talking, prior to their exits. In the course of the exit, it is natural that the camera might pan the man and woman out of the door camera left.

When blocking out this scene, those three movements should be rehearsed *separately*, a number of times, and then rehearsed in the normal flow of the exercise itself. If any one of these three pieces of action is not quite perfect, it should be rehearsed until it becomes smooth and easy, and able to be executed comfortably and without danger to any one of the players involved.

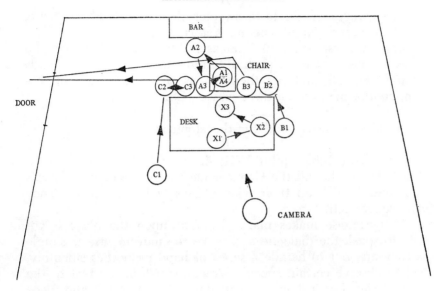

EXERCISE NO. 19

Scene opens with A seated upstage at the center of the back
of the desk A1. B is standing with back to camera at middle
of desk camera right B1. C is offstage camera left C1.

Scene starts with C putting briefcase on the desk, at X1.
B pulls case to him, X2, without exposing face to camera, places
briefcase, lock facing A, in front of A, X3.

A takes out three books from the briefcase, identifying them
as he does so, in this way "exposing" them to the camera. He
places the three books on desk, camera right of briefcase.

A

You've brought them! Good! The Gutenberg Bible . . . Shakespeare First Quarto . . . the Chaucer. A million dollars in
first editions . . . Excellent!

A hands money envelope, which he takes from desk drawer, to
B. He then goes to bar upstage center, A2, and returns with
wine bottle, and three glasses, A3.

C comes on camera, camera left, C2. She is holding a gun pointed
at A. A sees the gun.

A

What does this mean?!

B moves to corner of table, B2, picks up the Shakespeare.

B

"The wages of sin taste sweeter than wine!" Shakespeare,
Midsummer's Night Dream, Act II, scene 4!

B drops Shakespeare into briefcase. From his coat pocket, he
takes out piece of rope, pushes A into chair, A4, puts his hands
behind him, B3, and ties them. C, as B is completing his action, pours wine into the three glasses, C3.

C

"A little wine is good for the stomach's sake!"

B

Gutenberg Bible, John VIII, 4.

B puts the Bible and the Chaucer back into briefcase and locks
it. B and C pick up their wine glasses and drain them. They
exit camera left.

This exercise makes many demands upon the players; not
only to speak the dialogue and make the movements, as simple
as they are, but to handle a series of hand properties smoothly,
and to observe certain specific directions within the text of the
scene it self. For instance, C will start off camera left and place
the briefcase into the forepart of the desk, X1, without coming
on camera. B, placed camera right of desk, is asked not to expose
his face to the camera, but to merely pull the briefcase to him,
X2, and then push it across in front of A, with the lock facing A
so that he can easily open it as it stands, without having to turn
it around, X3. A small condition, to impose upon a player, but
one that will make the movement of the briefcase, the opening
of it, a great deal easier for player A. You will notice, too, that
A must look at the books, and "expose" them to camera, in a
way that the audience can gain the impression that these are
actually the three books that he has mentioned. He must then
take out the money envelope and hand it to B, who would surely
check the money to see that it is right, and put it away in an
inside pocket while A goes to the bar and brings the wine bottle and the three glasses back to the desk.

Next, you will notice that C must make an entrance camera
left, C2, after A has returned to his position at the back of the
desk A3. The gun which she holds in that position would, I
suggest, be best held in her right hand(the majority of people
being right-handed), and the pouring of the wine be done with
her left hand. If this proves too awkward, the business as far as
the hands is concerned, could be reversed, but *it is most important*

that the player C is able, in these positions, C2 and C3 to reveal a great deal of herself to the camera in this three-shot. Next in the scene, you will notice that B takes a piece of rope from his pocket, pushes A down into his chair, puts his hands behind him, and proceeds to tie them. It is important here that B should clear himself to camera right of A, so that the two players can be clearly seen, and the *simulation of the action* of tying-up A observed by the camera. C, having poured the three glasses of wine, would have placed one wine-glass in such a position that B can pick it up easily. They drain their glasses, place them back down on the table. B crosses camera left to C, and then both exit out camera left, the camera panning them out of the room, if that is the director's desire, or centering upon A at the back of the desk as B and C make their exit.

Once again, in this scene it is very important that all marks be placed on the floor or positions given to the players on the desk at which they can *dress off* so that perfect framing by the camera can be achieved at all times. In the course of the exercise itself, it is very important that the players assume all these marks very accurately, so that throughout the exercise the framing can be checked by the person acting as camera. In a scene like this, it is essential, too, that players B and C do not play more than is necessary with their backs to the camera. For the most part of the scene, they are almost virtually playing an open fifty-fifty to each other with A between them.

EXERCISE NO. 20

Woman sits at desk shuffling through a bunch of canceled checks, W1. Man is pacing up and down, M1, M2, M3. Finally, he stops and leans on end of desk M4.

Man

Look, Carol. I asked you to come because I thought you could help. If you'd rather not, just say the word.

Woman

(with checks in hand, rises)

Okay, okay, old friend, I'm saying it. Frankly, there are lots of things I'd rather be doing than going through these. You're a big boy now, Tim . . . .

What else she might be about to say is interrupted by the sudden entrance of Fiancée, F1.

ILLUSTRATION FOR EXERCISE No. 20

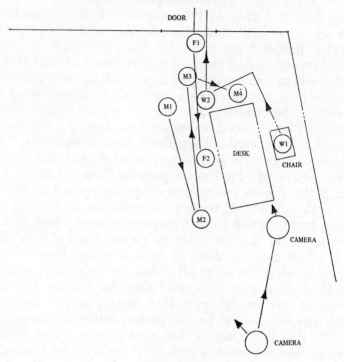

Fiancée
(at door)
Oh . . . excuse me. Am I breaking in on something?
She closes door behind her and comes down to desk, F2.
Fiancée
(continued)
Why, Tim, you're not even ready to go! We're supposed to
meet my parents at six o'clock. It's five-to now.
Man
Didn't realize it was so late! Sorry!
Woman
(To man)
Is this the next Mrs. North?
Man
Oh, Lisa, this is my ex-wife, Carol. Carol, I'd like you to
meet Lisa Ramsey.
Fiancée
I'm Tim's fiancée. We're getting married in two weeks.

Woman

Congratulations! And good luck! You're going to need it!

Man

(To fiancée)

Honey, Carol's helping me go through some old checks. The boys at Internal Revenue want me to explain some of last year's write-offs. It'll only take a few minutes.

Woman

I can't help you, Tim. It would take too long.

(Crossing around to Fiancée, W2, and giving her the checks)

Woman

(continued)

Here, you should be interested in these. They're Tim's life story. Sensational reading!

She exits from room, leaving man and fiancée looking after her.

This scene is similar in many ways to the average, run-of-the mill scene that a performer might encounter in television today. The literary content of the dialogue is not likely to make too many demands upon the players. At the beginning of the scene, the woman is seated at the desk, sorting out the checks while the man paces up and down, to and away from camera, finally coming to the upstage end of the desk and beginning the scene there. It is quite possible that the camera might open on this scene in a wide shot. As the man moves from M2 to M3 and then to M4, according to what the director decides, the camera could dolly in on the two performers, framing the door in the background of the shot toward the left hand side of the frame. Through this particualr door, the fiancée then makes her entrance, holding at the door, closing it behind her, and then coming down to her position at F2. Here, for the first of two occasions in the scene, we have a three-shot. The scene proceeds until the woman moves around to between the fiancée and the man, changing the composition of the previous three-shot. As she makes her move from right to left, it may be necessary for the camera to counter from left to right to adjust to this particular grouping, centering the woman with the door just off-center behind her. At the conclusion of the scene, when the woman makes her exit, it is quite logical, that, for a moment, the two players would look after her, until she has exited through the doorway, and then turn to each other, and hold a look between them.

In carrying out the movements of this scene the players,

without any major change of camera position, create the shot-compositions of the scene, particularly in the instance of the move of the woman from her first mark to her second mark, moving, as she does, out of the first three-shot and into the second three-shot. All of the marks should be placed carefully on the floor, and the players must assume them accurately to enable the camera to frame them correctly at various points throughout the scene.

Here, then, you have twenty exercises, some of them containing a number of short, related exercises. I suggest that you begin to set up the exercises for yourself and rehearse them one by one, starting at the beginning of this section and proceeding slowly through it, until you have mastered all of the moves in each particular exercise.

I further suggest, as I have before, that, at various stages during the rehearsing of these exercises, you attempt to create for yourselves variations of the exercises. Try to put together completely new ones, writing the scenes, finding pieces of dialogue, and business that would be suitable as an exercise. In attempting these exercises, you will be practicing many of the movements which will be demanded of you when you go to work as a professional player. The more time you devote to these exercises, the more confident you will feel when you face these similar problems on the floor, and the better you will be able to do your work when you arrive on a soundstage or location to begin a day's shooting.

It is important, in approaching any scene which is to be filmed, that, in your prior preparation of the scene, you concern yourself, primarily, with what the story is, what your character is, and the relationship of that character to the other characters in the story. I would warn you that, because of the way the scenes in the film are blocked out on the floor, the player would be wise not to set too definitely in his mind certain movements that he might make from one position to another. It is all very well to concentrate and to rehearse small pieces of business—the handling of hand properties, etc.—but to so completely *visualize* the scene and rehearse it at home so that you are *locked—into* what you have decided upon there, often can cause the player, when he goes on a set, a deal of trouble, *because what he has set in his mind may not be what the director has in mind.* The player will possibly have to undo, in rehearsals, a great deal that he has set his mind on. *It is best to know the story, to investigate your character, to see its relationship to the others, and then to stay loose as the rehearsals begin on the soundstage or on location, so that you can readily take direction and move in concert with the other players and the camera to achieve what the director has in mind.*

I hope that you have found the book readable; it is not easy, as you will undoubtedly find yourselves, to write about or teach the art of acting, whether for the stage or for films. I have attempted to tell you what I know about the business from a personal point of view. I suggest that, at every opportunity, you should discuss what knowledge you have gathered from this book with other players, and so develop this introduction to cinematic knowledge into a storehouse of technical know-how that can be drawn upon by you every day that you work in the future.

INDEX